STRATEGIC ALLIANCES

STRATEGIC ALLIANCES

An Entrepreneurial Approach to Globalization

Michael Y. Yoshino
U. Srinivasa Rangan

HARVARD BUSINESS SCHOOL PRESS
Boston, Massachusetts

99 98 97 96 95   5 4 3 2 1

Library of Congress Cataloging-in Publication Data

Yoshino, M. Y. (Michael Y.)
    Strategic alliances : an entrepreneurial approach to globalization /
Michael Y. Yoshino, U. Srinivasa Rangan.
        p.   cm.
    Includes index.
    ISBN 0-87584-584-3
    1. Strategic alliances (Business)   2. Competition, International.
I. Rangan, U. Srinivasa.   II. Title.
HD69.S8Y67   1995
658—dc20   94-39669
                                                                CIP

The paper used in this publication meets the requirements of the American
National Standard for Permanence of Paper for Printed Library Materials
Z39.49-1984.

To Chiyoko Yoshino
    M. Y. Yoshino

To my parents U. Vijayaraghavan and
Alamelu Vijayaraghavan
    U. Srinivasa Rangan

Contents

Preface

In recent years, we have witnessed a surge of alliances among major corporations throughout the world; hardly a day goes by without announcements in the business press of new linkages, partnerships, or alliances. Whatever they are called, these interfirm relationships involve partners from varied parts of the world and cover a range of functions and activities. Often, they tend to be "strategic," formed in direct response to major strategic challenges facing the partner firms.

This emerging phenomenon captured our curiosity, leading to several years of research. As business academics, we were intrigued by questions such as, Why do firms enter into alliances? How do they go about forming an alliance? and How can the partners manage the alliance to achieve their common goals? Not surprisingly, these questions are also of paramount interest to practicing managers.

The primary driver of strategic alliances is the emergence of intense global competition, which has rendered simple but time-tested strategies, a staple of major corporations, less effective. Firms must constantly innovate to forge ahead of equally innovative rivals throughout the world. They must develop new capabilities—often simultaneously—in a number of areas, ranging from technology development to manufacturing processes, from plant economics to marketing and distribution, and do so quickly. In our view, imaginatively developing such competitive capabilities with limited resources is at the very core of entrepreneurship. Our central argument is that alliances allow firms to recast entrepreneurially their competitive strategies in response to globalization.

Having examined the major forces leading to alliances, we have developed a roadmap that we believe will lead to successful alliance formation. Throughout our research, we observed that firms often entered into alliances on an ad hoc basis driven largely by immediate or tactical concerns, and that such moves often have disastrous results. Our roadmap reflects best practices in firms that have furthered their strategic goals through carefully considered and effectively executed alliances.

We also examined the difficult and often perplexing issues of alliance management. We heard many war stories, ranging from rather comical mishaps to the unintended consequences of apparently well-thought-out actions taken by one of the partners. The complexity and difficulty of alliance management stem from its very nature. That is, an alliance brings into a collaborative relationship two or more independent companies, each with its own agenda, strategy, and culture. Moreover, the alliances that yield the greatest value are often those forged by competitors. Thus, maintaining a balance between competition and cooperation is a major challenge in alliance management.

Successful management of alliances, we argue, requires systematic attention and commitment from both those directly responsible for the alliance and senior-level management. Various groups at multiple levels of the business unit, if not the entire company, must commit to deep involvement. Traditional measurement systems and mind-sets run counter to successful alliance management.

The bulk of *Strategic Alliances* examines strategic alliances in a single-business firm, the arena in which the competitive struggle is fought and strategic alliances are forged as part of the effort to win. Our research, however, suggests that alliances should be examined from the perspective of corporate as well as strategic-business-unit management. This distinction, we feel, is not clearly made in the current academic or managerial literature. Thus we devote a chapter to examining roles alliances can perform in diversified companies.

We conclude the book by looking ahead. We see the emergence of a new type of corporation, which we call the "global network corporation." We see a trend toward reliance on strategic alliances to create "networks" of intricate business relationships among major corporations worldwide. To manage such a corporation effectively will most certainly call for innovative managerial systems and skills.

Acknowledgments

Throughout our research, we interacted with hundreds of managers in dozens of corporations throughout the world. These managers have forged and managed strategic alliances of every kind, in the process developing a great many practical insights, which they so graciously shared with us. Our contact with these people has renewed our abiding respect for managers who, even as we record their problems and solutions, are searching for pragmatic responses to new and vexing organizational questions at the frontier of international management. Without their help and generosity, this book could not have been written.

A number of other individuals also contributed to our effort. We are especially grateful to Rosabeth Moss Kanter, Warren McFarlan, Peter Williamson, Jean-Pierre Jeannet, and Stephen Allen for their thoughtful and incisive comments about the manuscript. We also thank Professor Raymond Vernon, who has shared his wisdom and insights with us over the past two decades, and Dean John McArthur of the Harvard Business School and Allan Cohen, academic vice-president of Babson College, both of whom have not only created a climate conducive to field-based empirical research, but have also provided constant encouragement.

We are indebted to the Division of Research at the Harvard Business School for its generous financial support. We thank Warren McFarlan, senior associate dean and director of research at the Harvard Business School, and Walter Burnett and John Trapani, associate deans at the A.B. Freeman School of Business, Tulane University, New Orleans, for their unflagging support for the project. We appreciate the encouragement and assistance provided by Ann Walter, the administrative director of the Division of Research. We would also like to thank Sarah Eriksen, business research analyst at the Baker Library, for her excellent assistance. Throughout the project, she met our often complicated and difficult requests in a most competent and professional manner.

Many people helped us prepare the manuscript. We extend special thanks to John Simon, who provided invaluable editorial advice. The book has benefited a great deal from his thorough, rigorous, and thoughtful comments. We appreciate Aimee Hamel's professionalism and commitment as she prepared many versions of the manuscript, and Cynthia Mutti's editing assistance in the final stage of publication.

We extend sincere appreciation to the editorial staff of the Harvard Business School Press. Carol Franco, executive editor, kept a watchful eye on the book virtually from its inception. Her gentle reminders from time to time motivated us to keep the project on track. Nicholas Philipson, editor, was a joy to work with. We found his timely, thoughtful advice extremely valuable. Nindy LeRoy, manuscript coordinator, helped greatly in the preparation of the final manuscript.

Finally, we would like to acknowledge our profound gratitude to our families. Throughout the research, writing, and production of this book, they maintained their good humor and offered exceptional support.

Winter 1994
Boston, Massachusetts

PART **I**

ALLIANCES OLD AND NEW

CHAPTER 1

The World of Alliances

Alliances are a big part of this game [of global competition] . . . They are critical to win on a global basis. . . . The least attractive way to try to win on a global basis is to think you can take on the world all by yourself.

> Jack Welch, CEO, General Electric
> (Speech at Harvard Business School, October 28, 1987)

The growing integration of the global marketplace over the past decade has been termed "globalization" of industries by some, although globalization of competition seems a better description.[1] Others have termed the integration of world markets "triadization," reflecting the advanced degree of integration in the three developed regions of the world—North America, Western Europe, and Japan.[2]

By whatever name, the global marketplace has spawned new strategic approaches in many industries. The forging of what have become known as strategic alliances has been noted by senior management of firms in all regions of the "triad." Akio Morita, chairman of Sony, observed, "No company is an island. In an interdependent world, every company has to think in terms of working with others if it wants to compete in the global marketplace."[3]

Alliances—*Merriam-Webster's Collegiate Dictionary,* tenth edition, defines them as "association[s] to further the common interests of the members"—or intercorporate agreements cover a wide gamut of functions, ranging from component sourcing through research and development to production and marketing. Examples include

3

- IBM, Siemens, and Toshiba's cooperating to develop a new generation of memory chips
- DuPont and Sony's working jointly to develop optical memory storage products (which they will market separately)
- Leading semiconductor manufacturers Motorola and Toshiba's allying to exchange vital technologies and information on manufacturing processes and planning a joint venture to produce memory chips and microprocessors (which both will sell)
- General Motors (GM) and Hitachi's working together to develop electronic components for automobiles

A list of companies involved in alliances would read like a *Who's Who* of the global corporate world. General Electric (GE), IBM, AT&T, Ford, Kodak, Philips, Olivetti, NEC, Toshiba, Daewoo, and Samsung are all actively involved in alliances of one form or another. Their variety and number make them a relevant management topic, particularly since the way they are forged and managed has a bearing on whether they contribute to or detract from corporate strategies.

We ask three questions of alliances on behalf of managers. Why establish an alliance? How is one best forged? What constitutes successful management of one? We ground our analysis and the answers it suggests in an understanding of the growth and impact of alliances in recent years. What is new about companies situated in different countries initiating joint projects? Have firms not collaborated previously to achieve a common set of strategic objectives? Are close relationships with suppliers and distributors not alliances, and have firms not pursued such relationships in the past?

Such questions point to a major weakness in what academics and other observers have been saying about alliances. The remark of a consultant—"Strategic alliance is just a buzzword used by corporate hipsters for what used to be called joint ventures"—is indicative. Writers who treat alliances as glorified joint ventures shed little light on the subject. The notion of strategic alliances, like entropy, is much talked about but little understood.[4]

WHAT IS A STRATEGIC ALLIANCE?

A strategic alliance links specific facets of the businesses of two or more firms. At its core, this link is a trading partnership that enhances the effectiveness of the competitive strategies of the participating firms by providing for the mutually beneficial trade of technologies, skills, or products based upon them. An alliance can take a variety of forms, ranging from an arm's-length contract to a joint venture. Because varied interpretations of the term exist, we define a strategic alliance as possessing simultaneously the following three *necessary* and *sufficient* characteristics:[5]

- The two or more firms that unite to pursue a set of agreed upon goals remain independent subsequent to the formation of the alliance.
- The partner firms share the benefits of the alliance and control over the performance of assigned tasks—perhaps the most distinctive characteristic of alliances and the one that makes them so difficult to manage.
- The partner firms contribute on a continuing basis in one or more key strategic areas, e.g., technology, products, and so forth.

One writer referred to the merger of the global power systems industry firms ASEA and Brown Boveri as a strategic alliance. Another used the term to describe the Fuji-Xerox joint venture in Japan. Other observers have termed licensing and cross-licensing agreements and franchising deals "strategic alliances." None of these arrangements constitute a strategic alliance by our definition.

Mergers, takeovers, and acquisitions in which one firm assumes control of a new entity are not alliances. The ASEA union with Brown Boveri Corporation that spawned Asea Brown Boveri (ABB) occasioned the exit of one of the firms from the global power systems industry. It was a move toward rationalization in an industry beset by excess capacity. ASEA and Brown Boveri have put their entire power systems business in Asea Brown Boveri, but neither shares control in nor makes any continuing contribution to the new company.[6] The parent firms merely maintain portfolio-style investments in the new entity, which performs the necessary business functions.

Similarly by our definition, overseas subsidiaries of multinational corporations, even if they are joint ventures, are not alliances. Country-specific ventures undertaken for the purpose of entering new geographic markets are well known and have existed for many decades. Such ventures between multinational corporations (MNCs), which typically supply technology, marketing know-how, and sometimes financing, and local firms, which provide local legitimacy, market knowledge, contacts, and often management, have been the subject of considerable research.[7] They are often tactical or reactive responses by multinationals to host-nation government pressures or ingrained cultural barriers. The jointness of a venture is frequently a compromise rather than a goal; even when the local partner is an established firm, strategic control over the joint venture, more often than not, rests with the MNC.[8]

That joint ventures of MNCs are often a response to government pressures is best illustrated by what happened in India in the past two decades. In the 1970s, the Indian government decreed that MNCs could not have a majority equity stake in local subsidiaries. Accordingly, most MNCs reduced their equity to less than 50%; a few, like IBM and Coca-Cola, exited the country rather than lose control. New entrants, such as Pepsi-Cola, formed joint ventures with local partners and investors' holding majority stakes. In the early 1990s, the Indian government reversed its policy. Promptly, almost all the MNCs operating in India, among them Unilever, Colgate Palmolive, ABB, Suzuki, Pepsi-Cola, and DuPont, forced their local partners to give them majority stakes.[9] Coca-Cola reentered the country with majority ownership, IBM through a fifty-fifty joint venture with a local industrial group (though strategic control is believed to rest with the multinational).

Many multinationals have come to appreciate the useful role subsidiaries might play in global strategy.[10] Once regarded largely as detached revenue generators, subsidiaries are increasingly being integrated into the corporate system. In general, parent firms and subsidiaries exhibit a high degree of congruence, with tensions tending to revolve around the balance between local autonomy and global integration concerns. Subsidiary relationships do not constitute strategic alliances because they do not involve independent firms with separate goals.

Japan's Fuji-Xerox, for example, is a fifty-fifty joint venture between Fuji Photo Film Company and Xerox, for which Xerox has generally set policy.[11] At the same time, Fuji-Xerox has enjoyed much autonomy for historical reasons. Reports suggest that Xerox is trying to integrate the joint venture ever more tightly into its global strategy, even as it has agreed to permit the Japanese subsidiary considerable autonomy in a wide range of areas such as product design, manufacturing, and marketing.[12] Fuji has brought little to the venture beyond its initial capital contribution.[13] Given a new strategic mandate, Fuji-Xerox may play a significant role in Xerox's global product design and development activities, but it will still be merely a subsidiary of Xerox.[14] It is certainly not a strategic alliance.

Licensing and franchising agreements, because they do not call for continuous transfer of technology, products, or skills between partners, are not strategic alliances, nor are cross-licensing arrangements that involve continuing exchange of technology but not shared control over technology-related tasks.[15]

Consider, for example, the California-based designer and developer of semiconductor chips and systems Mips Computer Systems, which between 1987 and 1992 entered into more than a score of licensing and cross-licensing agreements with such companies as LSI Logic, Sony, Siemens, NEC, Philips, Toshiba, and Daewoo. Some observers have hailed the firm as having executed an alliance-based strategy. But entering into licensing agreements to make products based on one's technology is hardly a new arrangement.[16] Firms often must choose between exploiting a new technology or product directly or through licensees. "I think we are getting a bit too schmaltzy in American business in using words like partners and alliances," said the president of Mips. "What we do is provide our semiconductor partners with the design [of a chip] in return for a royalty and leave it to them to do the manufacturing and marketing."[17] So much for the alliance-based strategy at Mips.

Like simple buy-sell agreements for commodities or raw materials, these sorts of arrangements involve no long-term mutual dependence, shared managerial control, or continuing contributions of technology or products. Hence, they do not constitute strategic alliances.[18]

Figure 1.1 illustrates the range of possible interfirm links and the subset encompassed by our definition of a strategic alliance. The linkages reviewed at the opening of this chapter, because the allied firms—IBM, DuPont, Siemens, Sony, GM, Hitachi, Toshiba, and Motorola—which continue to exist as independent companies, share control over the performance of their joint projects, and make continuing contributions of technology and products, fall into this subset. Given that firms have for years worked with other firms without so naming the arrangements, why the considerable interest in strategic alliances? The answer, in part, is that in recent years interfirm links have grown in both number and importance.

THE "NEW" ALLIANCES

As early as the 1970s, Professor G.B. Richardson's research in the area of industrial economics suggested that a network of relationships with other firms is a *sine qua non* for success in the competitive market. Firms need suppliers of raw materials, components, services, and equipment, as well as distributors and retailers, to get products to market. Moreover, firms often work with independent contractors to achieve specific objectives. Richardson wrote:

> We must not imagine that reality exhibits a sharp line of distinction. What confronts us is a continuum passing through transactions, such as those on organized commodity markets, where the cooperative element is minimal, through intermediate areas in which there are linkages of traditional connection and good will, and finally to those complex and interlocking clusters, groups, and alliances which . . . represent cooperation fully and formally developed.[19]

Although interfirm linkages are clearly not unusual, the "new" strategic alliances are different, perhaps most strikingly in the seeming readiness of firms that have long shunned joint ventures or close collaboration with other firms in their core business areas to enter into such arrangements. General Motors, for example, traditionally avoided joint ventures in which it did not have majority control; a 1966 policy statement on the issue of control of foreign operations declared that "unified ownership for coordinated policy control of all operations throughout the world is essential for [GM's] effective performance as a worldwide corporation."[20] When it sought to gain control over Japanese carmaker Isuzu in 1969, GM accepted a minority shareholding only after Japanese investment laws thwarted its efforts to secure a greater share.

Figure 1.1
Range of Interfirm Links

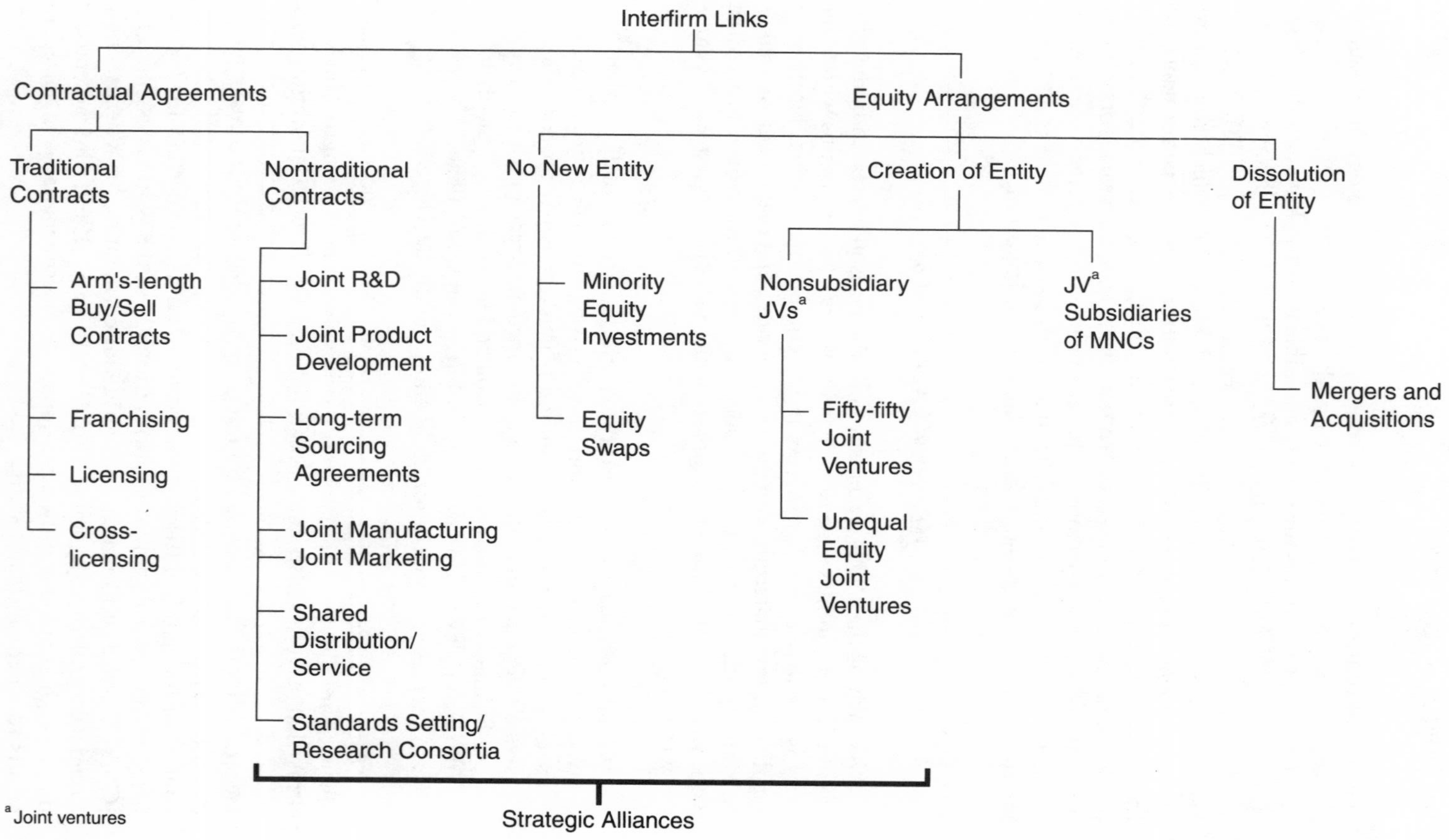

Interfirm Links

Contractual Agreements

Traditional Contracts
- Arm's-length Buy/Sell Contracts
- Franchising
- Licensing
- Cross-licensing

Nontraditional Contracts
- Joint R&D
- Joint Product Development
- Long-term Sourcing Agreements
- Joint Manufacturing Joint Marketing
- Shared Distribution/ Service
- Standards Setting/ Research Consortia

Equity Arrangements

No New Entity
- Minority Equity Investments
- Equity Swaps

Creation of Entity
- Nonsubsidiary JVs[a]
  - Fifty-fifty Joint Ventures
  - Unequal Equity Joint Ventures
- JV[a] Subsidiaries of MNCs

Dissolution of Entity
- Mergers and Acquisitions

Strategic Alliances

[a] Joint ventures

GM subsequently relaxed its insistence on majority control of interfirm links. In 1978 it accepted a minority stake in Suzuki of Japan, and since 1983 has formed fifty-fifty joint ventures with Daewoo of Korea, Toyota (in the United States), and Suzuki (in Canada), entered into a joint-venture agreement with Japan's Fanuc (a leader in factory automation), and begun cooperative research and development with Hitachi in the field of automotive electronics.

IBM was equally reluctant to concede a voice to outsiders in its ventures, even through equity participation by minority shareholders, notably in its 1970s exit from India.[21] Throughout the late 1970s, IBM steadfastly refrained from collaborating with other firms in core areas of research and development, manufacturing, marketing, and services. Then, in the early 1980s, it seems to have concluded that even a giant needs allies in an era of global competition. In response to ferocious competitive pressure and explosive technology developments, IBM breached its traditional strategy and began to form alliances, cautiously at first, then with quickening pace. By 1992 the company was engaged in more than 20,000 alliance-style relationships worldwide, including 400 equity investments.[22]

IBM's entry into the personal computer market was greatly facilitated by its willingness to rely on outsiders for development and production: Intel for chips, Microsoft for operating systems software, Epson for peripherals, and a number of Asian vendors for other components. In 1988, IBM concluded an original equipment manufacturer (OEM) agreement with Ricoh of Japan to supply personal computers to be sold in Japan under Ricoh's name, the first time IBM had ever permitted one of its products to be sold under another company's name.[23]

The foregoing examples illustrate the three characteristics that make the new strategic alliances at once interesting and managerially important. First, interfirm linkages between firms and their domestic suppliers and distributors are increasingly giving way to relationships that often cross national boundaries. General Motors' partners include Isuzu, Suzuki, and Toyota; Ford is allied with Mazda, Nissan, and Kia; and Chrysler with Mitsubishi. (Figure 1.2 illustrates the complexity of interfirm relationships in the auto industry.) A similar picture of cross-relationships is evident in the semiconductor and computer industries.

The auto industry examples also illustrate the second characteristic of the new alliances—they are often between rival firms. Many of these alliances would have been unthinkable just a few years back. A decade ago, who would have predicted working relationships between Toyota and General Motors or Ford and Nissan? Similar associations between rival firms exist in consumer electronics, semiconductors, computers, office equipment, telecommunications, and biotechnology.

Third, not only rival firms and firms in different countries, but firms in industries thought to be entirely unrelated, are joined by the new alliances.

Figure 1.2
Interrelationships among the World's Major Automakers (as of September 1988)

Company	Equity Arrangement	Joint Venture	Supplies or Buys Major Components	Marketing/ Distribution Arrangement	Technology Arrangement	Manufacturing/ Assembly Arrangement
General Motors (USA) (Includes Opel, Vauxhall, Holden's, Saturn)	Isuzu Mercedes-Benz Suzuki	Chrysler Daewoo Ford FSO Isuzu Nissan Saab Suzuki Toyota Volvo	Fiat Fuji Heavy Honda Isuzu Mitsubishi Nissan Renault Rover Saab Suzuki Toyota VAZ	CAC Isuzu Renault Saab Toyota	Chrysler Ford Honda Isuzu Suzuki Toyota	Bertone CAC Daewoo Isuzu Suzuki
Ford (USA) (Includes Jaguar)	Aston-Martin Kia Mazda	Fiat GM Mazda Nissan Toyota Volkswagen Volvo	AZLK Fiat Fuji Heavy Mazda Nissan Renault Volkswagen	Fiat Kia Mazda Suzuki	Chrysler GM Kia Mazda Nissan	BMW Kia Mazda Nissan Rover Suzuki
Toyota (Japan)	Daihatsu	Daihatsu Ford GM Nissan Renault	Daihatsu GM	Daihatsu GM Volkswagen	Daihatsu GM Nissan Volkswagen	CNAIC Daihatsu Volkswagen

Company						
Volkswagen (Germany)	BAZ Skoda	CNAIC First Auto Works Ford Mercedes-Benz	BAZ CNAIC First Auto Works Ford Nissan Rover Skoda Volvo	Skoda Toyota	First Auto Works Porsche Skoda Toyota	BAZ First Auto Works Porsche Skoda Toyota
Fiat (Italy) (Includes Alfa Romeo, Autobianchi, Ferrari, Iveco, Lancia)	FSM Zastava	Ford Peugeot	FSM Ford Fuji Heavy GM Peugeot Renault Steyr	Ford Mazda	FSM Fuji Heavy Nissan	Bertone FSM Mazda Pininfarina
Nissan (Japan)	Fuji Heavy Siam Motors Yulon	Ford Fuji Heavy GM Toyota	Daewoo Ford Fuji Heavy GM Peugeot Second Auto Works Volkswagen Yulon	Fuji Heavy Mazda	Daewoo Fiat Ford Fuji Heavy Mazda Second Auto Works Toyota	Ford Fuji Heavy Siam Motors Yulon
Peugeot (France) (Includes Citroen)		Daihatsu Fiat Renault Rover Suzuki	Fiat Nissan Renault Rover Steyr	CAC Mazda	Daihatsu Renault	CAC Chrysler Honda Isuzu Pininfarina Renault

Figure 1.2 *(Continued)*

Company	Equity Arrangement	Joint Venture	Supplies or Buys Major Components	Marketing/ Distribution Arrangement	Technology Arrangement	Manufacturing/ Assembly Arrangement
Renault (France)	Volvo	Peugeot Toyota Volvo	Fiat Ford GM Mitsubishi Peugeot Volvo	GM	Peugeot Volvo	Peugeot
Honda (Japan)	Rover	Mitsubishi Rover	Daewoo GM Mitsubishi Rover	Chrysler Daewoo Rover	Daewoo GM Rover	Daewoo Isuzu Mercedes-Benz Mitsubishi Peugeot
Chrysler (USA)		Beijing Auto De Tomaso GM Mitsubishi Steyr-Daimler-Puch	Beijing Auto Mitsubishi Rover Steyr-Daimler-Puch	Honda VAZ	Beijing Auto Ford GM Mitsubishi Steyr-Daimler-Puch	Mitsubishi Peugeot Steyr-Daimler-Puch
Mazda (Japan)	Ford Kia	Ford Isuzu	Ford Isuzu Kia Mitsubishi Suzuki	Cycle & Carriage Bintang Fiat Ford Isuzu Kia Nissan Peugeot	Ford Kia Mercedes-Benz Nissan Porsche	Cycle & Carriage Bintang Fiat Ford Kia Suzuki

Mitsubishi (Japan)	China Motors Hyundai Proton	Chrysler Honda Mercedes-Benz Suzuki Volvo	Chrysler GM Honda Hyundai Mazda Mercedes-Benz Proton Renault Volvo	Hyundai Mercedes-Benz	Chrysler Hyundai Proton Volvo	China Motors Chrysler Honda Isuzu
Hyundai (South Korea)	Mitsubishi		Mitsubishi	Mitsubishi	Mitsubishi	
Mercedes-Benz (Germany)	GM Ssangyong	Mitsubishi Volkswagen	Mitsubishi Porsche Ssangyong	Cycle & Carriage Bintang Mitsubishi Ssangyong	Mazda Porsche Ssangyong	Cycle & Carriage Bintang Honda Porsche Ssangyong
Rover (U.K.)	Honda	Honda Peugeot	Chrysler FSO GM Honda Peugeot Volkswagen	Honda	Honda	Ford
BMW (Germany)			Bertone Daihatsu			Ford
Suzuki (Japan)	GM	GM Mitsubishi Peugeot	Daewoo GM Mazda	Ford	Daewoo GM	First Auto Works Ford GM Mazda
Volvo (Sweden)	Renault	Ford GM Mitsubishi Renault	Fuji Heavy Mitsubishi Renault Volkswagen	Daewoo Fuji Heavy Izuzu	Izuzu Mitsubishi Porsche Renault	Fuji Heavy

Figure 1.2 *(Continued)*

Company	Equity Arrangement	Joint Venture	Supplies or Buys Major Components	Marketing/ Distribution Arrangement	Technology Arrangement	Manufacturing/ Assembly Arrangement
Fuji Heavy (Subaru) (Japan)	Nissan	Isuzu Nissan Siam Motors	Fiat Ford GM Nissan Volvo	Nissan Volvo	Fiat Nissan	Nissan Volvo
FSM (Poland)	Fiat		Fiat		Fiat	Fiat
FSO (Poland)		GM	Rover			
Zastava (Yugoslavia)	Fiat					
Daihatsu (Japan)	Toyota	Peugeot Toyota	BMW Kia Toyota	Toyota	Kia Peugeot Toyota	Bertone Toyota
Isuzu (Japan)	GM	Fuji Heavy GM Mazda	Daewoo GM Mazda	GM Mazda Volvo	Daewoo GM Volvo	GM Honda Mitsubishi Peugeot
SKODA (Czechoslovakia)	Volkswagen		BAZ Volkswagen	Volkswagen	Volkswagen	BAZ Volkswagen
Daewoo Group (South Korea)		GM	Honda Isuzu Nissan Suzuki	Honda Volvo	Bertone Honda Isuzu Nissan Suzuki	GM Honda
Kia (South Korea) (Includes Asia Motors)	Ford Mazda		Daihatsu Mazda	Ford Mazda	Daihatsu Ford Mazda	Ford Mazda

Company	Alliance partners
Ssangyong (South Korea)	Mercedes-Benz
SAAB-Scania (Sweden)	GM
Proton (Malaysia)	Mitsubishi
Yulon (Taiwan)	Nissan
Porsche (Germany)	Mercedes-Benz; Mazda; Mercedes-Benz; Volkswagen; Volvo
Bertone (Italy)	BMW; Daewoo; Daihatsu; Fiat; GM
Pininfarina (Italy)	Fiat; Peugeot
Steyr-Daimler-Puch (Austria)	Chrysler; Fiat; Peugeot
China Motors (Taiwan)	Mitsubishi; Lotus/Bugatti
Cycle & Carriage Bintang (Malaysia)	Mazda; Mercedes-Benz
Beijing Auto Works (China)	Chrysler
First Auto Works (China)	Volkswagen; Suzuki
Second Auto Works (China)	Nissan
Siam Motors Co. Ltd. (Thailand)	Nissan; Fuji Heavy

Source: Reprinted by permission, © 1994 Ward's *Automotive International.*

Examples include Sony and Apple Computer, General Motors and Hitachi, Ford and a number of software firms.

These characteristics have important implications for managers, not least of which is a need for new management skills. It is to stress this need that we devoted much discussion to defining what a strategic alliance is and what it is not. Designating overseas joint-venture (JV) subsidiaries or licenses as alliances tells managers that they are on familiar ground. So when they are involved in a truly strategic alliance as we define it, managers believe they know how to manage it. After all, haven't they dealt with JV subsidiaries and licenses all their lives?

Presumed familiarity breeds a false sense of security. Nothing could be more dangerous. In a JV subsidiary there may be managerial conflicts but no marketplace competition. Firms may quarrel over contractual details in a license. Rarely do such quarrels affect a firm's long-term ability to compete. JV subsidiaries and licenses do not involve ongoing shared control by two independent firms either. Alliances are different. The new alliances often combine both competitive and cooperative elements in an environment of shared control. Hence the need to master new management skills.

Management Implications

Interfirm relationships are, as noted earlier, neither new nor novel. Interfirm links with suppliers and distributors, with firms having related technology, and even with rivals have received in-depth analysis in the management literature. For example, Japanese automobile firms' close links with suppliers, Matsushita's success with its VHS videocassette recorder format over Sony's Betamax format through extensive licensing, and the Japanese consortium approach to research have all been separately studied to explain the importance of such interfirm links in global competition.[24]

What is lacking in the management literature is an integrated perspective on alliances. Current enthusiasm notwithstanding, there is considerable conceptual ambiguity about what alliances really mean for managers and even, among some writers, confusion about what an alliance is. Moreover, observers of alliances between rivals have tended to treat these associations as a new phenomenon, unrelated to other types of interfirm links.[25] Is it any wonder that prescriptions for managing alliances have varied widely and often even contradicted one another?

For Howard Perlmutter and David Heenan, who have argued that cooperative strategies are the wave of the future,[26] the essence of the alliances' managerial task is to work toward harmonious relationships and thereby enhance the value of a cooperative activity. They have little to say about the rivalrous aspect of such relationships. Kenichi Ohmae, too, deems strategic alliances essential to effective global strategy, particularly in Japan;[27] he dwells not at all on the notion of competition, seeing harmony as a by-product rather than an end in itself.

Gary Hamel, C.K. Prahalad, and Yves Doz, in prescribing a Machiavellian approach to alliance management, contradict Perlmutter more sharply.[28] They view management's key task to be to learn—openly if possible, surreptitiously if necessary—from alliance partners and to use that learning to win in the marketplace, presumably at the expense of erstwhile allies. R.D. Reich and E. Mankin's alliance manager is alert to the Trojan horses endorsed by Hamel et al. They view alliances as "giving away the future" of the firm (usually American) to foreigners (usually the perfidious Japanese or Koreans). Their implied prescription? Avoid alliances like the plague.[29]

These are but a few of the many recommendations the literature proffers for managing strategic alliances. All have been derived from rich and insightful analyses of real-life situations, and all are reasonable and intuitively appealing, but their managerial implications are not easily reconciled. Are alliances, for example, always benign? Should managers always strive for harmony? When should a firm seek an "understanding" of partners' objectives as opposed to "pursuing" its own interests? Is "learning" relevant only when working with competitors or also when working with suppliers or distributors? Is not learning per se a good thing? Are alliances always Trojan horses? Should managers avoid alliances because they are likely to be Trojan horses?

An Integrated Framework

Practitioners dealing with the small but rich literature on global strategic alliances have lacked an organizing framework for assimilating the different perspectives. Corporate strategic objectives, like said literature, are multidimensional and often contradictory. Actions dictated by one strategic objective frequently impede another, equally important objective, requiring managers to prioritize, often with limited success. Managers rely on a framework to identify trade-offs among strategic objectives and thereby assess their relative benefits and potential costs. They also need a framework to help them sort out the advice for managing global strategic alliances.

A framework for organizing strategic alliances literature should satisfy three criteria. One, it should encompass all types of alliances (supplier relationships, interindustry cooperation, alliances between nonrivals within the same industry, and links with direct competitors). Two, it should take as a point of departure the definition of alliance—set forth earlier in this chapter—as cooperation between two or more independent firms involving shared control and continuing contributions by all partners. Three, it should facilitate identification and recognizing the urgency of key management issues in each type of alliance.

The premise behind our framework is simple. An alliance-seeking firm must take into account two managerial dimensions—cooperation and competition or, more generally, cooperation and conflict. The task of managing alliances is to optimize along these two dimensions. Stress on the dimensions varies with the nature of the partner firms and extent of organizational interaction needed for the cooperative effort to bear fruit. Successful alliance management turns on managing the interactions between cooperation and competition by prioritizing the firm's key strategic objectives.

What are those objectives? The strategic goals of partner firms fall into four broad categories. Two are positive and relate to enhancing firm effectiveness, two defensive, aimed at preventing loss of effectiveness. A firm must derive more value from a cooperative activity than from going it alone; otherwise, there would be no point to the alliance. The first strategic goal, then, is to add value to an activity. The second goal of a partner is to augment its strategic competencies through learning from its opposite. Learning is an implicit, if not explicit, strategic objective of every firm that strives to maintain its competitive position.[30] Willingness to learn leads to product and process innovation.

On the defensive side, a partnering firm must maintain strategic flexibility. An alliance should not render the operation of a firm overly reliant on one interfirm link or another. Managers are well acquainted with the need to manage diverse strategic risks—political, competitive, and technological, to name a few—by keeping their options open and creating new options when feasible. Maintaining flexibility is particularly critical in the case of interorganizational efforts. Alliances, as ties that bind in a world of rapid change and obsolescence, can restrict managers' strategic options. Explicit consideration of flexibility as a strategic objective reduces the possibility of a firm's becoming unthinkingly entangled.

Finally, a firm must guard against its core competencies or strategic advantages' being appropriated by a partner.[31] It can be argued, with some justification, that a firm's competitive edge derives from proprietary knowledge. This is obvious in the case of patents; often it is not. Firms rely heavily on accumulated knowledge in R&D, manufacturing, marketing, and other areas for competitive success. Such knowledge often is not codified, and its confidentiality is critical to firms' strategic plans. To prevent interfirm links from leading to uncontrolled disclosure of such information, protection of core competencies must be treated as an explicit strategic objective.[32]

How these strategic objectives fit the agendas of managers in different types of alliances is illustrated by our conceptual framework (Figure 1.3). The framework is new, but has benefited from existing research on interfirm relationships. Most writers on strategic alliances have concentrated on the nature of the partner firms or the cooperative activity. Our framework considers both. The nature of the partner firms largely determines the competitive aspect, the nature of the joint activity, and the cooperative aspect

Figure 1.3
Typology of Alliance

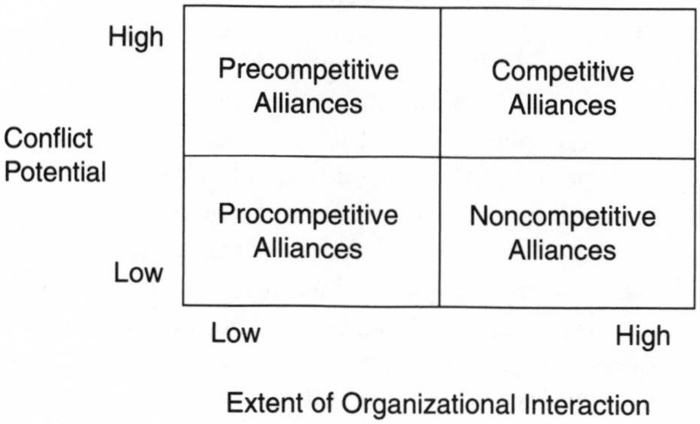

	Low	High
High	Precompetitive Alliances	Competitive Alliances
Low	Procompetitive Alliances	Noncompetitive Alliances

Conflict Potential (vertical axis: High to Low)

Low   High

Extent of Organizational Interaction

of the relationship. By considering cooperation and competition simultaneously, our framework captures the essence of the dilemma in managing alliances.

The intensity of potential conflict between partner firms constitutes what we term "conflict potential." In any joint work, firms are likely to be concerned with sharing the pie, but another, more serious aspect to conflict is that firms may be, or anticipate being, rivals in the marketplace. Our analysis considers both the tactical and the strategic conflict potentials inherent in collaboration.

The "extent of organizational interaction" required to succeed in the cooperative approach to a joint activity is not merely the frequency of interaction between partners but a proxy for a number of related issues.[33] It subsumes, among other things, the intensity of interaction, the number of functional areas in each firm that are involved in the interaction, the organizational levels to which the interaction is largely confined, the extent to which interaction is routinized, and the kinds of information (routine or noncritical versus nonroutine or critical) that have to be exchanged. In other words, it is the overall scope of interaction between the collaborating firms.

Taking the extreme values, high and low, of conflict potential and cooperative interaction yields four possible types of strategic alliance,[34] which we term "procompetitive," "noncompetitive," "precompetitive," and "competitive."

Procompetitive alliances are generally interindustry, vertical value-chain relationships, as between manufacturers and their suppliers or distributors. Once managed at arm's-length, they are now accorded much more attention as the strategic nature of these links is widely recognized.[35] Of the examples cited earlier, General Motors' link with Hitachi is representative of procompetitive alliances. In such links, although firms work closely to develop or improve products and processes, this type of cooperation requires low levels of organizational interaction.[36] Moreover, the firms tend not to be rivals. Indeed, some firms, such as Toyota, rely on a federation of procompetitive alliances to compete against their market rivals, adding further dimensions to the arena of competition. The potential for conflict in such alliances is low. With both interaction and rivalry at low levels, the strategic objectives of protecting core competencies and learning take a back seat to those of maintaining strategic flexibility and adding value. Hence firms like General Motors tend to maintain more than one link for the same activity.

Noncompetitive alliances tend to be intraindustry links among noncompeting firms, for example, General Motors and Isuzu, which are jointly developing a small car that both will sell. The level of interaction in this cooperative effort is high; joint development of a new car calls for close contacts at different levels and in multiple functions (e.g., design, engineering, manufacturing, and marketing, to name a few). The firms' competitive universes meet, but only occasionally, and neither views the other as a major rival. Given the partners' significant commitments of time and effort, neither is likely to seek to duplicate its efforts in another alliance. The firms are therefore unlikely to rank flexibility maintenance and protecting core competencies as high priorities. Learning, on the other hand, is likely to be very high on the agendas of the partner firms' managers. Although in the same industry, the partners are sufficiently dissimilar to render an alliance worth considering.[37]

Competitive alliances are similar to noncompetitive alliances in terms of the joint activity (and hence in the level of organizational interaction) but differ in that the partners are apt to be direct competitors in the final product market. Examples include the ties between General Motors and Toyota, which are jointly manufacturing cars in Fremont, California, between Siemens and Philips, which are jointly developing a one-megabyte chip, between Motorola and Toshiba, which jointly plan to manufacture microprocessors in Japan, and between Ford and Nissan, which are jointly to manufacture vans in the United States. Such cooperation calls for intense interaction between the paired firms, even though they are direct rivals, with an implicit high potential for conflict. Here, as in the case of noncompetitive alliances, maintaining strategic flexibility is unlikely to be uppermost in the minds of managers. Adding value is likely to be important, but not the highest strategic priority. In the face of competitive rivalry, leakage of information is apt to be detrimental; hence, protection of core strategic competencies is critical. Learning, given the opportunity for it, is also apt to be ranked high by managers.

Precompetitive alliances typically bring together firms from different, often unrelated industries to work on well-defined activities such as new technology development. DuPont and Sony's cooperative development of optical memory-storage products is an example. Working together, the two firms, neither of which possesses the technological or market know-how to succeed alone, expect to develop a product they will subsequently manufacture and market independently. The joint activity is well defined, involving only limited interaction between the firms, largely confined to researchers from the respective companies.

But being potential rivals in the memory-storage market adds another dimension to the relationship. Because a technology explored by partners in a precompetitive alliance is liable to be just one of many possibilities, the cooperating firms tend to maintain strategic flexibility by not confining themselves to one relationship. That is, flexibility is a key management concern. Moreover, as product development proceeds and commercialization nears, the competitive element may begin to color the relationship, with each firm's trying to gain insight into the core competencies of the other, rendering protection of core strengths another critical strategic management objective in precompetitive alliances.

An important characteristic of these types of alliances is their capacity to transform; an interfirm relationship initiated in one box in Figure 1.3 may, after a time, migrate to another. IBM's precompetitive alliances with Intel and Microsoft are examples of such a transformation. The alliance that brought together IBM on the one hand and the world's dominant chip maker and largest software company on the other helped popularize and standardize the personal computer industry. But with success came mounting conflict. The erstwhile partners began to compete, each trying to cast itself in the role of standard setter. IBM's loss was its former partners' gain. A *Wall Street Journal* story called the IBM-Intel relationship one of "high technology's most tangled relationships.[38] As one of IBM's own senior executives put it, "Our relationships include customer, supplier, partner, and competitor."

In sum, managers involved in strategic alliances must attend to all four objectives—maintaining flexibility, protecting core competencies, enhancing learning, and maximizing value—recognizing that their relative priority or order of importance tends to vary among the different types of alliances, as illustrated in Table 1.1. In addition, as the IBM-Intel and IBM-Microsoft alliances demonstrate, firms need to be alert in managing these relationships.[39]

Strategic Trade-offs

Alliance management presents supervisors with a complex and multidimensional reality. Pronouncements such as "Learn through alliances with competitors," "Alliances are Trojan horses and should be avoided," and "Cooperate to create harmony" are at best partial and at worst simplistic. The manager's task is to discover how broad insights, arising from their authors' individual vantage points, might be combined to guide the

Table 1.1

Relative Importance of Strategic Objectives in Alliances

	Strategic Objectives[a]			
Alliance Type	Flexibility	Core Protection	Learning	Value Adding
Precompetitive	****	***	**	*
Competitive	*	****	***	**
Noncompetitive	**	*	****	***
Procompetitive	***	**	*	****

[a]Number of asterisks indicates relative importance in each alliance type.

building and management of a flexible, multidimensional, alliance-based strategy. This task is fraught with complications owing to inherent contradictions among the different strategic objectives managers seek in alliances.

Consider, for example, the potentially contradictory objectives of learning from one's partner and protecting one's own information. It seems fair to say that learning, particularly the acquisition of not readily codifiable knowledge, is best facilitated by wide-ranging, continuous, intense contacts between two organizations, a strategy that increases the risk of uncontrolled information disclosure. As contact points between firms proliferate, it becomes increasingly difficult to monitor, let alone control, the flow of information from one's own organization to the other.

Similarly, intense interaction aimed at adding value to a joint activity may occasion increasing dependence on an alliance. Massive efforts to make the alliance successful may leave managers reluctant to develop alternatives in the name of maintaining flexibility. On the other hand, developing multiple alliances for the same activity to ensure flexibility may compromise the fundamental learning objective. As the number of alliances multiplies, managers spend more time fighting operational brush-fires and less time trying to learn and internalize new ideas, concepts, and technologies.

These sorts of contradictions between strategic objectives and alliance types necessitate trade-offs, sometimes explicit, but more often implicit in management decisions. In a given set of circumstances, one strategic objective may dominate others and play a more important role in alliance management. Indeed, the complexity of managing strategic alliances arises from the need to understand these situational contingencies and evaluate the implied trade-offs before adopting a specific approach to alliance management.

OUR AGENDA

The focus of this book is on forging and managing strategic alliances. Hence, its main audience is managers. Interviews with managers involved in alliances and an extensive review of secondary data pertaining to these alliances, together with an examination of other alliances to the extent that relevant data were available in the public domain, are the basis for the insights and observations presented here.[40]

The alliances we analyze are largely international, that is, between U.S. and foreign firms, primarily in the automobile, consumer electronics, mobile communications, medical systems, power generation and transmission equipment, personal computer, semiconductor, factory automation, biotechnology, and office equipment industries. A few alliances involving domestic firms in different and unrelated industries are also included.[41]

The book is partly descriptive, some of the alliances' being examined in detail, and partly positive in that some of the findings it reports confirm our hypotheses regarding the management of such relationships. It is also partly normative in implicitly assuming that certain best practices abstracted from successful alliance management approaches might find wider applications.

We emphasize developing and illustrating the use of a framework that can help managers to formulate, review, analyze, and implement alliance-based competitive strategies. The result is not ready-made, standardized solutions, but a schema of steps to guide management thinking and actions. Indeed, the animating spirit behind the entire book is that in forging and managing alliances, as in every other area of managerial action, there are no one-size-fits-all solutions. What is feasible is to identify systematic ways of thinking about issues. It is in such a spirit that this book was written.

Of the four types of alliances, we stress the competitive alliance in our discussion because it is the most complex to forge and manage. Managers who become familiar and comfortable with the principles that relate to competitive alliances should have little difficulty dealing with other types of alliances. As Isaac Newton's friend is reported to have told the famous scientist, "It is unnecessary to provide for a separate entry each for the cat and the kittens. A large one for the former should serve the latter, too."

We contend that managers who forge and manage alliances effectively and thus to competitive advantage view them as creative responses to the pressures of global competition. They understand the strategic logic of such links and recognize that alliances which confer optimum benefits are not short-term palliatives but part of long-term strategic plans.

Building on the strategic logic of alliances, we propose specific analytical steps, in effect a road map, to alliance formation. We suggest that it must begin with a thorough examination of a business's strategy and offer specific suggestions for crafting an alliance strategy and choosing an appropriate structure. We conclude with a discussion of the importance of continuing attention to alliances once they are formed.

Alliance management must begin with a clear recognition of the challenges and tasks involved. These include information-flow management, organizational learning, and cultural change. Implementation problems implicit in all alliance structures have to be addressed within the context of each organization. We review the significant impact of alliances on internal processes and procedures, attending particularly to the role of the alliance manager, an organizational innovation adopted by many firms.

Too often alliances are viewed as the domain of middle management. Because top management involvement is essential, not only in forging alliances but also at various stages of implementation, we examine the variety of challenges and tasks that have to be tackled at the top management level. The task of corporate managers in multibusiness companies is complicated by the existence of alliances at different business units. Indeed, in the course of our research we came to recognize two levels of strategic alliances—those intended to further business-unit-level strategy, and those intended to further corporate-level strategy. The formation of different types of alliances at different business units calls for management along additional dimensions.

As alliances proliferate, firms that can effectively manage networks of alliances will fare best in global competition. We conclude with consideration of the challenges of managing external networks of alliances, even as firms struggle to control internal networks of domestic plants and overseas subsidiaries.

CHAPTER 2

A Tale of Two Alliance Companies

In Chapter 1 we cited a number of examples of well-known firms that have turned to alliances for help in competing in the emerging global environment. We now attempt to present a more comprehensive overview of the role alliances play in such companies, including how they can be incorporated into the overall strategic framework of partner firms. Specifically, we examine how two major U.S. companies in quite different industries have made excellent "strategic" use of alliances.

One, Ford Motor Company, (eighty-year-old) is in a mature industry, comprising mainly North American, European, and Japanese fiercely competitive firms.[1] Internationalized only since the 1960s, the industry has not had a new global entrant in recent years.[2] The other, Motorola Inc., is in the rapidly developing semiconductor industry, which though dominated by American and Japanese firms was thrust into the global competitive arena early in its development. Even today it sees, in the memorable phrase of an industry observer, new entrants coming "out of the woodwork." In their quest for sustainable competitive positions, both have found it necessary to tread similar paths in their vastly different industries toward alliance-based strategies. What is more, the two firms have followed rather similar approaches to forging and managing alliances.

Both Ford and Motorola came under considerable competitive pressure in the late 1970s and early 1980s. Facing severe resource constraints as they sought to counter competitive threats from domestic and foreign rivals, both firms chose to pursue global strategies even as they struggled with what was widely perceived as flagging competitiveness. Both resorted to innovative use of alliances, in the process learning the art of forging and effectively managing advantageous ones. Today they are on the way to building a well-integrated external network of alliances to complement their internal network of international subsidiaries.

THE STRATEGIC ALLIANCES OF FORD MOTOR COMPANY

Ford's use of strategic alliances is best understood in the context of a number of interrelated sets of issues that confronted the company in the late 1970s and early 1980s: the energy crisis and the demands it imposed in terms of technology and product-development needs, intensified global competition in the automobile industry and the demands it imposed in terms of investments in process technology development, and the severe resource constraints the firm faced as it struggled to meet the foregoing demands. Singly, these challenges would have been formidable enough; combined, they presented an overwhelming challenge. Ford's use of alliances was a bold and risky but highly imaginative way out of the hole in which it found itself. To understand such an alliance-based strategy we need to understand how Ford's basic competitive strategy evolved over the years.

The Evolution of Ford's Global Strategy

Ford Motor Company's competitive strategy has come a long way from the early decades of the twentieth century when Henry Ford's introduction of the Model T positioned the firm as the low-cost producer of cars for the low-end segment. The strategy then revolved around the twin concepts of mass production and mass marketing. The central thrust was to lower prices as costs dropped, thereby making the standard model more accessible to ever larger numbers of people. This in turn increased volume, leading to another round of lower costs and lower prices.[3]

By the mid-1930s, Ford had made the transition to a more differentiated producer and marketer of cars. Its introduction of the Lincoln, Mercury, and Thunderbird nameplates over the next several decades signaled its discontent with competing only as a low-end producer and ceding a large part of the market to its more differentiated competitor, General Motors (GM), whose motto was "A car for every purse." By the time Ford adopted GM's strategy of segmenting the automobile market according to price points and producing cars to meet the needs of each segment, another facet of its strategy was also in place.

Even before World War II, Ford had begun to serve lucrative overseas markets. Postwar, the pace of internationalization quickened, with Ford's locating first assembly operations and later manufacturing plants in Europe and Latin America. By the early 1970s, its presence abroad was leading the company to talk in terms of a "global strategy" and advance the notion of a world car. That it was serious about competing worldwide with an integrated strategy and designing and manufacturing a car to be sold in many parts of the world is reflected in the extent to which the overseas market became a major contributor to Ford's sales and profits. By the late 1970s, 43% of Ford's sales originated abroad. In terms of profits, the proportion was even higher. But even as overseas sales and earnings grew, other developments were challenging the company's very existence.

Global competition. First and foremost among these developments was the globalization of competition in the automobile industry. European firms arrived first on the shores of the United States. The growing popularity of cars made by such firms as Volkswagen, Mercedes-Benz, and BMW was already hurting domestic producers when Japanese firms—Toyota, Nissan, and Honda—began to gain U.S. market share at the expense of the Big Three. Between 1975 and 1980, foreign automobile manufacturers' share of the U.S. auto market jumped from 14% to 26%, most of the increase going to the Japanese. Over the same period, Ford's own share of the U.S. auto market fell from 23% to 17%.

A major contributor to the growing success of Japanese automakers was the oil crisis of 1973, which took the U.S. automakers, including Ford, by surprise.[4] U.S. firms had traditionally concentrated on making their vehicles larger, more comfortable, and pleasing to look at, but hardly ever more fuel efficient. U.S. auto manufacturers responded to the fourfold increase in oil prices with consternation. U.S. producers, Ford among them, were unable to meet customers' demands for fuel efficiency. Japanese manufacturers, on the other hand, used to designing and manufacturing smaller, more fuel-efficient models, responded with vigor. U.S. firms, Ford included, were faced with the prospect of either investing heavily in product development or leaving the small-car segment to the Japanese.

Obsolescing investments. The shift in market demand from large to small cars hurt U.S. firms in other ways as well. Lower demand for large cars meant that U.S. automakers' huge fixed investments in plants and facilities had to be spread over a smaller volume. Labor, too—in the short run at least—was for many manufacturers a fixed cost to be allocated over a smaller sales volume. Resulting higher prices further drove buyers from domestic products to cost-competitive imports, triggering a vicious spiral. Were this shift in consumer preference to become permanent, as seemed probable to many, Ford's expensive, and in some cases new, plants might be rendered obsolescent by the coming competitive battle.[5]

The changing competitive balance. The entry of aggressive, opportunistic importers transformed the domestic U.S. auto market from a cozy oligopoly to a competitive battlefield. "It is no longer the Big Three running the industry in this country," remarked one of Ford's senior executives in 1980.

"It is now the Big Seven."[6] His count included Honda, Toyota, Nissan, and Volkswagen. This change in competitive dynamics exerted its own impact on the fortunes of Ford and other U.S. automakers.

The new entrants to the U.S. market scrambled the carefully crafted competitive strategies of firms like Ford and GM. The conventional wisdom of market segmentation had been that firms should choose between being a full-line or specialist producer—be a GM or Ford or a BMW, but nothing in between. Ford had been a full-line producer, competing with standard products and the presence of its badge across the entire automobile market. Japanese automakers' development of higher-performance but relatively inexpensive cars in different segments and introduction of new models of different sizes were evidence that there was considerable latitude for creative strategies.[7] This put pressure on Ford to develop products for specialized market segments even as it was facing the problem of investing in technology development for fuel efficiency.

At the same time, the new entrants began an end run around the domestic firms' core strategies. Ford, as a full-line producer, relied on its ability to spread its huge corporate overheads, administrative as well as research and development, over a large volume of cars. This strategy required the company to be cost competitive to do well in the marketplace. But Japanese automakers were threatening the cost leadership of U.S. firms as well. U.S. automakers improved fuel efficiency and styling only to find their Japanese rivals doing so at a lower cost.[8] A U.S. Department of Transportation study found that Japanese producers had a $1,000- to $1,500-per-unit cost advantage over U.S. producers, a consequence of lower wage rates, tax concessions, and less regulation. Japanese producers, in effect, set the ceiling on U.S. auto prices so low that Ford officials believed the company could not make profits.[9] Thus, at the very time it needed to make massive investments in product and process technology development, Ford was being deprived of necessary profit and cash generation.

Japanese competition did not stop at prices. Japanese cars, though priced comparably to or lower than Ford's, were also of better quality. By the late 1970s, Ford was plagued by a reputation for poor quality and safety. A string of highly publicized lawsuits related to exploding gas tanks, premature rusting, disintegrating engine fans, and problem transmissions had shaken consumer confidence in the company. Even as it lost more sales to competitors, particularly the Japanese, Ford was faced with the necessity to make massive investments in the process technology required to meet market demand for better quality and safer cars.

The Strategic Challenge

By the late 1970s, Ford management faced a daunting strategic challenge: how to regain competitiveness under severe and worsening resource constraint. Ford's cash flow was being adversely affected by the company's poor performance in the marketplace at a time when Ford needed to invest millions of dollars in product- and process-technology developing, scrap old plants and build new ones, and retrain its workforce in quality practices. Robust profits from its European operations masked a decade of decline in profitability in Ford's North American market. But the 1980 recession in Europe, coupled with significant gains by Japanese firms in Europe and North America, resulted in Ford's worst performance in decades; the company lost $1.5 billion on sales of $37 billion worldwide. Faced with this profound threat to the firm's financial health, top management had to rethink Ford's overall strategic thrust.

Analysis of the competitive realities of the marketplace led Ford to conclude that it had two choices. First, it could adjust its strategy to its existing resource base.[10] For example, it could choose to restructure as a North American car company with some useful and profitable appendages, but nothing more, in Europe and elsewhere. At about this time, Chrysler, facing similar competitive pressures, opted for this strategic response.[11] Alternatively, Ford might formulate a more entrepreneurial response. It might, for example, choose a strategy that fit its competitive traditions and held the promise of long-term viability, then search for ways to secure the needed resources.[12] Ford's choice of the latter approach was risky and called for imaginative implementation.

Top management decided that Ford should be a global manufacturer of automobiles offering a full line of cars in most, if not all, market segments. Ford managers reasoned, rightly it would appear, that becoming a regional player in an increasingly global industry was to invite long-term decline and demise.

Ford's first step was to undertake an aggressive rationalization program. The firm trimmed fat, lowered operating costs, and reduced excess capacity. In 1980 alone, it chopped $1.5 billion in fixed costs from its North American operations. Over two years—1979 and 1980—the company phased out 16,000 white-collar jobs, closed two major plants, and pared its parts inventories. In 1980, controller Allan Gilmour told a reporter, "The fat is gone. . . The only thing left is to do different kinds of restructuring of the business."[13] That restructuring, it turned out, was to rest on the extensive and imaginative use of alliances.

Ford decided to utilize a string of strategic "partnerships" or "linkages" with other manufacturers, key suppliers, and firms in related technology areas to bolster its competitive position. At the same time, it decided to take advantage of its worldwide expertise by linking its European subsidiaries with Detroit to promote cross-fertilization of ideas. With Detroit serving as clearinghouse and facilitator of innovations originated by its subsidiaries and alliance partners, Ford would avoid duplication of effort and expenditures and be in a position to leverage its partners' resources.

Evolution of Alliance Strategy

Ford's alliance-based strategy evolved with management's realization that the company needed partners to be a global player.[14] Partners would enable Ford to share its resource burdens, exit areas in which it lacked technical expertise by handing them off to specialist firms, and afford opportunities for learning.[15]

In the late 1960s, with the Japanese market undergoing rapid growth and Japanese automakers fast becoming a power to reckon with, Ford looked to Japan for a low-cost production base from which the U.S. market might be served. An alliance with a Japanese firm would also permit Ford to become familiar with Japanese management and operational practices.[16] In 1969, Ford selected Toyo Kogyo (later renamed Mazda) and Nissan as partners in a joint venture to manufacture automatic transmissions. The Japanese firms divided a 50% interest.[17] Ford owned the other half and provided patent rights for an automatic transmission to the joint venture.[18] Taking note of rapid growth in the domestic market, and stimulated by the earlier equity participation by GM in Isuzu and Chrysler in Mitsubishi,[19] Ford sought to expand its presence in Japan. Limited equity participation in an existing firm was the only feasible possibility, given government restrictions. Deeming Toyota and Nissan too strong and independent to be viable candidates, Ford focused on Mazda.

In the course of negotiations, Ford's North American operations decided to source a compact truck to be sold under its badge, enabling Ford to gain entry into an expanding market segment until its own Ranger model could be introduced in 1982. When the initial round of negotiations failed to secure it equity participation, Ford expanded its relationship by sourcing from Mazda small cars, to be sold in Australia, to meet rising Japanese competition in that market.

Ford's relationship with Mazda matured over a period of four years into a strong alliance. Even as it worked to tighten its links to Mazda through contractual relationships, Ford began to explore other prospects. It had already begun preliminary talks with Nissan and Toyota about possible cooperative deals and with Germany's BMW about joint production of diesel engines. Although nothing was to come of them immediately, these preliminary explorations were later to stand Ford in good stead.

Competitive pressures on Ford intensified in the late 1970s and early 1980s. Profitability lagged, constraining its ability to invest at a time when changing market requirements and competitive reality were demanding massive capital outlays. Rising global rivalry challenged Ford's strategy of competing with a full line and exploiting global scope and exposed Ford's Achilles' heel—weakness in process technology. With its rivals stressing automation and quality, Ford was forced to respond with heavy investments in process technology. Moreover, it was, in the words of one industry observer, chasing a moving target; its rivals, particularly the Japanese, were not standing still but constantly improving their own performance.

When Ford realized that strategic alliances could be more than a temporary palliative as part of an innovative, permanent long-term approach, alliance-based competitive strategy became even more attractive. In early 1979, Ford, perceiving a number of benefits in the deal, moved to strengthen its alliance with Mazda by seizing an opportunity to buy up to 25% of the company's equity. Mazda would continue as a reliable source of pickup trucks and could develop the next generation of small cars Ford needed to complete its product line. Ford could thereby secure the low end of the product range without expending development and manufacturing resources to produce a new car.

Three years later, Ford acquired a 15% interest in Kia Motors of Korea, in which Mazda already had a 15% stake. This time the motive was to provide an alternate base for sourcing inexpensive small cars in the expectation that the yen would appreciate in value against the U.S. dollar. The Kia link also presented an opportunity for Ford to break into the growing Korean market.

Through the 1980s and early 1990s, the Ford-Mazda relationship expanded considerably, to the partners' mutual benefit. The companies collaborated on a large number of joint projects involving the design of new models. The way the nature of the projects evolved over the years attests to the excellent working relationship they were able to build. Early collaboration involved Mazda's supplying to Ford key components such as engines or fully assembled cars. Subsequently, the relationship expanded to include joint development of new models and construction of a new Ford plant in Mexico, with Mazda's playing a major role in providing manufacturing expertise. In the late 1980s, the relationship took another major turn; lacking a utility car of its own to market in the United States, Mazda decided to source a version of the Explorer from its partner.

The companies coupled even more tightly in early 1992, when Ford acquired 50% ownership and management control of Mazda's U.S. plant. Ford also supplied a pickup truck to be sold in the United States under Mazda's badge. According to a 1992 *Business Week* article, Ford and Mazda had worked jointly on ten current models; one of every four Ford models sold in the United States in 1991 had some Mazda input, and two of every five Mazda cars sold had some Ford influence.[20]

When it turned its attention to another segment in which its product offering had to be upgraded—the minivan market—Ford's first choice seems to have been Toyota. But when differences in strategic objectives led the companies to break off talks, Ford drew a second arrow from its quiver. Following much negotiation, Ford and Nissan announced in 1988 that they would jointly make and sell a new minivan in the United States. Nissan would do most of the design and engineering, and Ford would expand its Avon Lake, Ohio, site to accommodate both firms' production needs.

Ford had meanwhile begun to work closely with a select group of suppliers on projects related to major components. Such working alliances enabled Ford to improve component quality and thereby the quality of the final product. Concurrently, Ford acquired a minority stake in a number of software companies, which it recruited to work on automation projects.

Ford did not omit frontier technologies from its areas of collaboration. Recognizing that the nascent field of microelectronics held immense potential for the automobile industry, Ford's top management concluded that it was essential that the firm's researchers, engineers, and product designers quickly become familiar with the capabilities of new technologies. To gain a foothold in emerging technologies, Ford again turned to alliances, often holding minority stakes in partner firms.

According to then Ford chairman, Donald Petersen, the company wanted not only access to frontier technology, but also to provide a nurturing environment for the often small entrepreneurial companies that developed it. Alliances were a way to ensure balance between stability and the autonomy needed to foster innovation. "We have tried to let our operations people know there are funds available for venture in small acquisitions or small investments if those operations decide that is the best way to acquire a new technology or the best way to apply a new technology to an integral part of the business," Petersen explained.[21] John Wallace, head of Ford's microelectronics operations, outlined Ford's view thus: "We have a number of excellent cooperative agreements with major semiconductor manufacturers, which we have found gives us access to a lot of different philosophies and technologies and a lot of manufacturing capacity without having to own [them]."[22]

Thus, Ford used a variety of affiliations. Compare Ford's alliances with the typology presented in Chapter 1. Ford forged procompetitive links (with key component suppliers), precompetitive ones (with software firms and in microelectronics), noncompetitive relationships (with Kia), and competitive alliances (with Nissan).

Moreover, Ford's alliance with Mazda illustrates several important points we made in the previous chapter. One, it is sometimes difficult to distinguish among the types of alliances. Unlike Nissan and Ford, Mazda is a niche player, so it is easy to think of the Ford-Mazda alliance as noncompetitive. On the other hand, Ford and Mazda do compete in some segments, and to that extent the alliance is competitive. Two, alliances can evolve and move from being one type to another. The Ford-Mazda link may have started as a noncompetitive alliance, but may now be viewed more as a competitive one. Three, part of the art of forging and managing alliances lies in the way they are structured to better manage their process of evolution. Ford's seeking a substantial chunk of Mazda's equity should be seen in that light. We will return to this topic of alliance structuring in a later chapter.

Alliances enabled Ford to leverage its resources, both human and physical, and thereby accomplish far more than it would have been able to do alone. Then vice chairman, Harold Poling, acknowledged the role of alliances in the resource-allocation process at Ford; announcing the Nissan deal, he remarked that Ford simply did not have sufficient numbers of engineers and technical personnel to develop a minivan without cutting into programs of higher potential. Indeed, according to one automobile industry analyst, the Nissan link alone would save Ford about a billion dollars in design and development costs.[23] Alliances freed up resources that could be committed elsewhere, as witnessed by Ford's highly successful entry into the aerodynamic cars segment.

Similar resource allocation and utilization considerations lay behind Ford's other alliances. Its network of strategic alliances enabled Ford not only to leverage its resources, but also to reduce its risk profile. By enticing Mazda and Nissan into product-development alliances and offering to take only minority stakes in high-technology companies, Ford was able to minimize its risk of losing heavily if a particular product or technology did not succeed. Hedging its bets in both technology and product development enabled Ford to keep its future options open.[24] As we shall see, Ford also gained access to its allies' process technologies and further reduced its risks through mechanisms for administrative control.[25]

THE STRATEGIC ALLIANCES OF MOTOROLA CORPORATION

Whereas Ford's pioneering use of alliances occurred in a mature industry, Motorola's alliance forging was accomplished in a much younger high-technology industry, specifically, semiconductors. Although semiconductor manufacturers are known for extensive use of second-sourcing and cross-licensing arrangements, alliances of the type we discuss here have not been tried by any firm in the industry. Nevertheless, Motorola's was a truly bold approach to alliances.

The Evolution of Motorola's Global Strategy

Motorola, like Ford, employed strategic alliances in the context of a number of largely competition-related challenges that confronted the company from the mid-1970s to the early 1980s. Motorola began in 1928 as a manufacturer of radios, branched out into two-way radios and other communication products in the mid-1960s, and by the early 1970s had become a major player in consumer electronics. Its conservative management ran a tight ship but lacked a cohesive strategy for growth. Flush with surpluses from its core businesses, Motorola, during the late 1960s and early 1970s, acquired and later divested itself of a host of businesses in industries as diverse as aircraft radios, hearing aids, chemicals, and recreation. This cozy world of corporate strategy by trial and error, backed by easy profits from maturing businesses, was brought to an abrupt halt in the mid-1970s.

Global competition. By that time Motorola had gotten into trouble. Aided by global volume and growing consumer recognition of Japanese quality, companies such as Matsushita and Sony aggressively assailed Motorola's radio and television businesses, leaving the company stalled in the number four spot in the U.S. market, while other Japanese rivals began to challenge its semiconductor business.[26] Motorola management confronted these challenges by undertaking a serious comprehensive reappraisal of the company's strategic approach. "Before, we were simply reacting to ideas that the operating guys had," said Kenneth Bane, then vice president and director of corporate strategy "[Then] we began strategizing. We began thinking about where we wanted the company to go."[27] Motorola decided to remake itself, leaving the businesses that had been its mainstay for decades. The company shifted its focus from consumer electronics to high-technology industrial electronics, including advanced telecommunications (e.g., cellular phones) and advanced semiconductors (e.g., microprocessors).

If its leap from consumer electronics to high technology was "unusual" and "proactive," as some described it,[28] Motorola's new competitive strategy was equally daring. The company had decided to pursue a global strategy in every business it competed in. Motorola chairman, Bob Galvin, asserted that he wanted the company to remain number one in two-way radio communications and become number one in semiconductors, both on a worldwide basis. Then executive vice president, Stephen Levy, recalling that, remarked, "We have learned our lesson from our experience in consumer electronics. Never again do we want to be caught with a strategy that relies only on the American market."

Levy described the strategy as global in another sense as well, specifically, that Motorola thought in terms of different applications in the businesses in which it competed, particularly semiconductors and communications. Motorola semiconductors, for example, were used in a variety of products ranging from mass-market video and audio receivers, cameras, and computers to industrial automation systems to automotive controls and defense equipment. According to Levy, Motorola did not want to cede any application to another firm.

> In semiconductors, it is just a matter of time before an application geared to a field becomes the useful starting point for another, hitherto totally unrelated, field. In this business, the artistry lies in constantly looking to extend the usefulness of your library. After

all, you have invested heavily in developing the technology. Why not get the maximum mileage out of it?[29]

Equally important was the competitive reason; an application ignored is a gateway for entry by a potential competitor.

A similar logic prevailed in Motorola's two-way-communication business. Motorola sold equipment and services to such public-sector users as utilities and law enforcement agencies as well as to such private-sector customers as taxicab operators and hospitals. Technical developments and innovations in one sector quickly found application in others.

Changing competitive balance. Motorola's adoption of a global strategy was prescient. In the mid-1970s, when the firm embarked on this course, its main competitors were largely domestic—General Electric and E. F. Johnson in communications, Texas Instruments, Intel, National Semiconductor, and Fairchild in semiconductors. Japanese and European firms were far behind. This quickly changed in the 1980s.

By the early 1980s Motorola could add to its list of major competitors NEC, Matsushita, and Fujitsu of Japan and L. M. Ericsson of Sweden in communications and Philips of Holland, Siemens of Germany, and NEC, Toshiba, and Hitachi of Japan in semiconductors. These firms, like Motorola, sold to users in diverse industries all over the world, ensuring Motorola of global competition in both senses of the term. Unlike Motorola, however, most of its new competitors were diversified firms.

Compounding its woes, the competitive balance in Motorola's industries, particularly in semiconductors, was shifting. According to a report prepared in 1986 by the Office of the Secretary of Defense of the United States, Motorola's Japanese competitors, none of which had been among the top ten in sales in 1975, were there by 1980, as were its new Japanese competitors in telecommunications, NEC, Hitachi, Fujitsu, and Mitsubishi.

Japanese firms differed from Motorola and its American rivals both in strategic approach and country-based advantages. Japanese semiconductor manufacturers tended to be large and diversified, with a substantial portion of sales going to other divisions. This helped the firms in two ways. Semiconductor division engineers were able to work closely with their consumer division counterparts to develop and improve chips for specific applications, then adapt and market them to other users. And in times of slump—a frequent occurrence in the industry—consumer divisions' purchase preference favored in-house production, ensuring a stable volume of business. With profitability largely a matter of yields, learning from experience, and forward pricing, stability of demand was a major advantage. Moreover, Japan's growing share of global semiconductor sales, up from 20% in 1975 to 30% in 1981, reflected heightened Japanese penetration in new, more powerful memory chips. This had ominous implications for U.S. manufacturers inasmuch as it threatened to make their key investments obsolete.[30]

Obsolescing investments. To understand the implications of rising Japanese market share in more powerful memory chips, it is necessary to understand the economics of semiconductor technology. In the semiconductor industry, learning from experience—the experience curve, in industry parlance—and yields are critical. Experience and yields are further linked by what, in the industry, are known as process drivers.

The notion of process drivers includes the standard experience curve effect—as a firm gains manufacturing expertise, it is able to increase the yield of fault-free memory chips. As most costs of manufacturing are fixed, the higher the yield, the higher the profits. Process drivers also exert a subtle impact on long-term competitiveness. The manufacture of basic memory chips drives technology not only in the memory area, but also in the microprocessor area (microprocessors incorporate hundreds of thousands, sometimes millions, of memory chips). As fault diagnosis is accomplished more readily at the chip than at the microprocessor unit (MPU) level, learning to increase yields at the memory level drives the technology of manufacturing at the MPU level. Thus, manufacturing expertise must be gained at the memory level to drive technology at the MPU level.

Developments in the global semiconductor market in the early 1980s threatened U.S. firms' ability to maintain access to technology drivers, thus jeopardizing major investments in fixed as well as human capital formation as through training of key personnel. U.S. firms first tried to retreat from Japanese firms' market share gains by concentrating on differentiated, special-feature chips with higher margins. Volumes, however, were small, limiting the potential of firms such as Motorola to gain the manufacturing expertise so crucial to long-term viability. Process technology engineers and specialists, for example, were afforded fewer and fewer opportunities to improve through learning by doing.[31]

A senior Motorola executive who had been heavily involved in mid-1980s discussions of process drivers recalled the situation.

> From the first quarter of 1985, the prices of 64K DRAMs [dynamic random access memories], the bread-and-butter part of our business, began to fall dramatically. We could not even cover variable costs. By the end of 1985, the industry as a whole had lost over a billion dollars . . .The situation was such, we had stopped working on the 256K RAMs (the next generation of chips). Soon we were faced with a major technological issue. Every three years or so a new generation [of chips] comes along. We began to worry about losing our technological leadership. . . By not gaining manufacturing expertise with 256K RAMs, we were faced with the

possibility of losing touch with the "process drivers," with serious implications for our growing microprocessor (MPU) business. Already, we could see the next generation—one megabyte DRAMs—over the horizon. At the same time, all our investments in fabrication and testing facilities and, of course, in top-notch process engineers were also threatened with obsolescence if we continued to retrench from chip manufacturing.

Motorola could have preserved access to process drivers by subsidizing the DRAM business with surpluses from the MPU and telecommunications businesses. Organizationally, this was not an attractive proposition. "The Japanese are quite willing to cross-subsidize their operations," added the senior executive. "Here in the United States, particularly in our company, we all operate as separate business units with profit-and-loss responsibility. It is not easy to convince the managers who run these businesses of the desirability of cross-subsidy in the long-term interest of the entire firm." Organizational resistance aside, there was no guarantee that cross-subsidization would pay off.

Motorola, of course, faced the more fundamental problem of a shifting market. With consumer electronics and other user industries becoming more concentrated in Far Eastern nations, it was imperative that U.S. semiconductor manufacturers gain market share in these countries, particularly Japan.

Motorola was one of the few American firms in any industry to recognize early on Japan's growing importance as a market for sophisticated products such as semiconductors and telecommunication products.[32] "We could see the writing on the wall," stated another Motorola senior executive. "We knew our survival would depend on how we confronted the Japanese challenge. Japan had the second largest market in the world for our products and some of the biggest and best competitors." Motorola established a semiconductor manufacturing facility in Japan in the late 1970s, but had difficulty gaining market share; by the mid-1980s, it had managed to gain barely a one percent market share.

Failure to establish a foothold in Japan also threatened Motorola's technological lead in the rapidly growing and highly lucrative microprocessor area. The company stood to lose links to users that would be valuable for developing future generations of microprocessors. One senior manager explained:

> Every time a major MPU user firm in the United States, be it an automobile manufacturer or a computer maker, loses market share, it means not only current sales forgone but also the loss of potential profits in the future. Indeed, if we are not able to work on the next generation of MPUs with users, it makes all our past investments in design and development obsolete.

By the mid-1980s, the upfront design and development investment requirements of successive generations of MPUs were increasing enormously. By
one design engineer's estimate, it took more than 300 labor-years to design
a microprocessor compared with three labor-years to design a memory.
Without close links to highly sophisticated users, such costs could rise further.

The strategic challenge. The situation Motorola faced in the mid-1980s was
in many ways similar to that faced by Ford in the late 1970s: relentless
global competition, particularly from the Japanese; shifting competitive bat-
tlegrounds; a need to invest heavily in process and product technologies;
and a need to regain access to process drivers. In short, the company had
to renew its competitive edge in the face of severe resource constraints.

In 1985 Motorola lost $44 million on semiconductor sales of $1.7
billion, its first loss in a decade, and saw return on equity fall to 3.2%
compared to an average of 14% in the previous decade. Yet R&D expenditures remained at the same level as in previous years. An executive said,
"We simply dared not cut our R&D for fear of losing our long-term competitiveness. At the same time, the losses were putting a serious constraint on
our ability to fund our R&D activities adequately."

Motorola, like Ford, had two options: (1) to confine itself to the North
American and European markets with the expectation of eventually
regaining its competitive edge, a defensive strategy and (2) to continue to
compete globally and press for greater access to the Japanese market, an
offensive, entrepreneurial strategy. Like Ford, Motorola chose to remain a
global player.[33] Motorola top management reasoned that it was futile, in a
global industry such as semiconductors, to try to be a regional player. As
Stephen Levy observed, "Global competition, with or without the Japanese,
is inescapable. You can run but you can't hide."

But a global strategy did not address Motorola's problem of resource
constraints and need to regain competitiveness quickly. Consequently, the
company decided to move on several fronts simultaneously. It filed a trade
complaint against Japanese semiconductor companies, alleging collusive
practices to keep its products out of the Japanese market and concurrently
increased investment in its subsidiary, Nippon Motorola, to make it a fully
integrated manufacturer engaged in everything from wafer fabrication to
assembly to testing. But the nub of Motorola's new strategy was alliances.

Motorola top management concluded after some soul-searching that
the firm had to focus its resources. There were several reasons for focusing
on microprocessors over memories. Motorola had established a competitive
edge in microprocessors, which were becoming the fastest growing and
most profitable segment of the semiconductor industry. It made sense to
concentrate the firm's resources in an area where it had distinctive competence.

Motorola acknowledged two critical requirements for continued success in the semiconductor market: (1) close working relationships with Japanese user firms and (2) access to process drivers. These needs, coupled with the need to optimize limited resources, led Motorola to begin to think in terms of an alliance-based strategy.

Evolution of Motorola's Alliance-based Strategy

There was nothing sudden about the emergence of Motorola's alliance-based strategy. It was the culmination of a succession of cooperative efforts Motorola embarked on, as circumstances demanded, in the 1970s and early 1980s. Licensing deals were followed by cross-licensing and sourcing arrangements and, ultimately, by collaborative R&D. Motorola's alliance-based strategy grew out of these experiences.

Like other U.S. semiconductor manufacturers, Motorola had entered into licensing deals with other producers, American and Japanese, to create second sources for its products. Motorola's second sources in semiconductors had been Toshiba in memories and Hitachi in microprocessors. Although second-sourcing was a business necessity, often insisted upon by customers to avoid dependence on a single producer, it also afforded opportunities to penetrate markets that might otherwise be inaccessible. Second-sourcing agreements also provided Motorola an unplanned opportunity for learning the risks and benefits of working with other firms.[34]

Motorola had become aware of the benefits of close working alliances with key users of its microprocessor units during the early 1980s. Subsequently, it moved beyond its traditional close ties with Apple Computer, for which it had developed its flagship 64K family of microprocessors, to embrace as user allies Hewlett-Packard, Unisys, and NCR, among other firms. Such user alliances were part of Motorola's strategy to increase the volume over which it might spread its base costs. Close research and development links with important users led Motorola to design and build more versatile MPUs than it might otherwise have.[35]

Motorola subsequently concluded sourcing arrangements with other firms. Facing huge losses in semiconductor memories in 1985, it had decided to exit the business. To preserve a marketing presence, it sought to source basic memories (dies or wafers) from other manufacturers and assemble, pack, and market the chips under its own name. There was nothing unusual about such an arrangement. National Semiconductor had been sourcing DRAMs from Japanese vendors, and Texas Instruments had been buying EPROM dies from Mitsubishi for more than ten years. In early 1986, Motorola selected Toshiba of Japan for its sourcing arrangement in 64K RAMs. Considered a tactical move at that time, this alliance afforded Motorola further experience in making such arrangements work.

The Toshiba link whetted Motorola's appetite for strategic use of alliances. A Motorola senior executive stated, "By mid-1986, our strategic thinking had begun to evolve differently. We began to see alliances in a broader context than mere tactical responses. We started asking ourselves, 'Why not use the alliance [with Toshiba] to gain access to the Japanese market as well as to process technology?' " Motorola executives, as we shall see, had come to view alliances as part and parcel of their overall competitive strategy.

As a more strategic view of alliances developed within Motorola's top echelons, events moved swiftly.[36] Toward the end of 1986, Motorola entered into a far-reaching cooperation agreement with Toshiba that called for the two firms to exchange technology, buy each other's products, and develop and make products in a jointly owned plant in Japan. But perhaps most important, the accord called for Toshiba to actively support Motorola's efforts to expand its access to the Japanese semiconductor market.[37]

Having learned from its ill-fated second-source licensing deal with Hitachi, Motorola recognized a number of risks associated with the Toshiba alliance. In particular, Motorola senior executives were keenly aware that, the alliance notwithstanding, Motorola and Toshiba were still rivals in the marketplace. Consequently, Motorola's negotiating team took great care to structure the deal so as to minimize the risks. "In such an arrangement," remarked a member of the negotiating team, "it is tempting to leave manufacturing to the Japanese and become overly dependent on them for product and process technology. The result is we become a shell corporation doing only marketing. This deal incorporated features to avert precisely that kind of situation's ever developing."

For instance, Toshiba was to transfer its manufacturing process technology and representative designs to Motorola's plants worldwide, but Motorola was to transfer its microprocessor technology only to the joint venture (fifty-fifty owned), with the proviso that Toshiba not use it in its other facilities. Moreover, the transfer of technology from Motorola was contingent on steady progress's being made in the company's efforts to gain share in the Japanese semiconductor market. In other words, Toshiba's access was dependent on how much help it provided to Motorola. Along similar lines, a number of provisions were meant to protect Toshiba's interests and technology.[38]

By the late 1980s, dictated partly by the evolution of the semiconductor industry, alliances had become part of strategic thinking at Motorola. Global competition and a technology base that permitted quick entry and exit by new companies geared toward specific applications had rendered the semiconductor industry an expensive game. New microprocessors and memories called for investments of hundreds of millions of dollars with no guarantee of success in the market. In light of these circumstances, any move that could spread costs, as alliances did, was welcomed.

Referring to customer demand for features that enhanced chip value, an observer described a semiconductor industry which found that "the value it was being increasingly required to add was service."[39] In the new semiconductor industry structure, service was not only a function of manufacturing a quality product at a competitive price, but also of closer identification with the customer's products and processes, and ultimately with the customer's customer.[40] In short, semiconductor manufacturers were expected to deliver both low cost and differentiation in the form of better service via better design and greater user orientation.

"Around 1985," said a semiconductor industry executive, "we began to realize that we had to serve two masters—designing and developing new products with an eye toward application and improving the process technology with an eye toward better yield management. The feedback effect from one to the other made it necessary that we do both well." Such a requirement for success in the industry translated into heavy investment demands on Motorola. By recognizing the need, Motorola went about implementing through alliances with other firms a complex strategy that combined low cost and differentiation.[41]

Motorola's alliance with Toshiba, for example, served several strategic purposes. It helped in the process technology area; it afforded greater access to the Japanese market, thereby improving economies of scale and enhancing Motorola's ability to design better products; it called for Toshiba to share investment costs for the new facility in Japan at a time of competing demands for Motorola's investment dollars; and by providing for future joint product-development work with Toshiba, it permitted Motorola to hedge its bets in the uncertain world of new microprocessors. Thus, Motorola achieved through its alliance with Toshiba the same strategic benefits that Ford enjoyed with its Japanese partners.

Like Ford, Motorola learned a generalized lesson from its Toshiba alliance, namely, how well alliances could serve its strategic goals. Motorola has since extended the concept to other firms and its other businesses. In 1988 Motorola and Data General formed an alliance (NND) to develop special microprocessors for mainframe computers. Motorola established alliances with IBM in the areas of X-ray lithography technology in 1989 and mobile data nets in 1990. In 1989 Motorola joined hands with Cable and Wireless of Great Britain for developing the next generation of cellular phones and Digital Equipment Corporation for developing new microchips. In 1991 came the alliance with IBM and Apple for the development of a new generation of microprocessors. Alliances are now a way of life at Motorola.

THE LESSONS OF FORD AND MOTOROLA

Some observers have suggested that alliances are appropriate only in particular industries or for weak or unsuccessful companies. The experiences of Ford and Motorola suggest that alliances are neither industry specific nor a recourse only of unsuccessful companies. These two firms, situated in much different industries, have employed alliances for similar purposes and with equivalent effectiveness.

We have discerned three key lessons to be learned from the experiences of Ford and Motorola.[42] One, alliance-based strategies evolve in intricate ways over time. Two, there are constant and continuous feedback effects among firms strategies, the role of alliances in those strategies, and the manner in which the alliances are forged, structured, and managed. Three, the artistry of alliance-based strategy lies in managing to best effect the evolution of and interlinkages within a network of alliances.

The starting point for an alliance-based strategy, as Figure 2.1 suggests, is the strategy of the firm. Only after its overall strategy is set can a firm decide what types of alliances to engage in and what role they will play in the broader corporate strategy. Having decided to forge an alliance, a firm must consider its choice of partners and manner of negotiating, undertake the often complex and time-consuming task of structuring the alliance, and commit adequate talent and resources to its ongoing management. Inevitably a firm evolves a network of alliances that demand greater and more sophisticated management attention. This is lesson number one.

Also depicted in Figure 2.1 are two sets of feedback loops. The first loop pertains to the immediate impact each step in the alliance approach has on the step that precedes it, particularly in the case of future alliances. Managers apply the lessons learned from structuring and managing an alliance to the structuring and management of subsequent alliances a company might contemplate and, on the basis of accumulated experience, constantly refine the kinds of roles alliances play within the firm's overall strategy, which may itself remain unchanged.

The second feedback loop refers to how the manner in which alliances are forged, structured, and managed over time impinges on the conception, and, if necessary, a revision of a company's overall strategy itself. This is as it should be. Strategy is not fashion design, intended to change every six months, but neither should it be a tablet of Ten Commandments etched in stone.[43] As alliances progress, they invariably influence a firm's choice of future strategies. More important, the evolution of a network of alliances can affect a firm's strategic posture. The second lesson of alliances, then, is the exigencies of the two types of feedback loops.[44]

The third lesson of alliances concerns managing both the evolution of strategy and the changing role of alliances. That is to say, managers must not only worry about the effects of their alliances on their strategies and the changing roles of different types of alliances employed in particular strategies, but also ensure that changes in strategies and in the role of the alliances associated with them occur in tandem. As a network of alliances develops, this becomes an exacting task that if not executed effectively, can spell disaster for a firm.

Figure 2.1
Evolution of Alliance-based Strategies

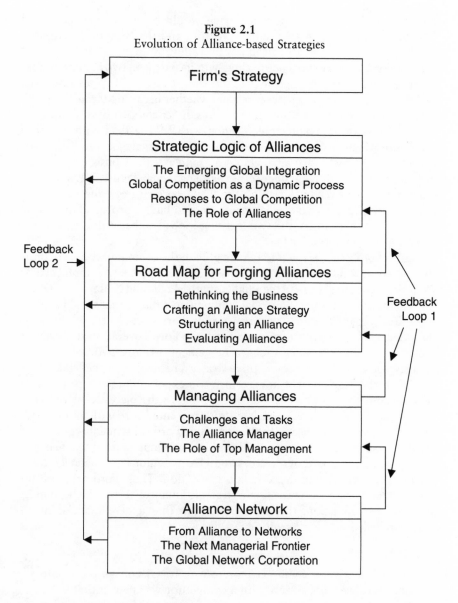

These subtle lessons are best understood through examples. When it first began to experiment with interfirm alliances in the early 1970s, Ford allocated to alliance partners Nissan and Mazda a modest role in its global strategy, which at the time relied largely on the internal, but nevertheless global, network of operations. Established mainly to serve sourcing purposes, the alliance was forged and structured as a three-way joint venture and managed, as any component buying would be, at arm's-length. Ford bought transmissions from the joint venture and that was that. As lesson one would say, the alliances fit into a prevailing strategy.

As Ford gained experience dealing with its partners, two major developments ensued. Ford management found that it could distinguish between the two companies. For whatever reason, whether because Mazda was much smaller than Nissan or because it was a less direct competitor to Ford, Ford executives felt more comfortable dealing with Mazda than with Nissan.[45] Its Nissan-Mazda experience also disposed Ford management to view more favorably the prospect of alliances on a grander scale. Consistent with the evolution of the strategy-alliance nexus depicted in Figure 2.1, Ford top management was ready to rethink the firm's core strategy and the role of alliances in it. These two developments were to have a profound impact on the firm. In other words, the two learning loops emphasized in lesson two could be seen in action at Ford.

Still, Ford's strategy was to remain global; the company would continue to compete around the world and across many products. But emboldened by its successful management of the alliances with Mazda and Nissan, Ford senior management began to plot a global competitive strategy that would supplement the company's internal network of subsidiaries with a network of external alliances. Moreover, the role of alliances in Ford's overall strategy was to move beyond arm's-length sourcing arrangements to more involved and risky alliances closer to its core competitive strategy, hence more beneficial.

With top management in agreement on expanding the scope and role of alliances, it was only a matter of time before the pieces fell into place. Mazda's financial troubles in the late 1970s presented Ford with the opportunity to rework its alliance with the company. Ford subsequently purchased a 25% stake in Mazda and secured the right to name up to three members to the company's board of directors and place a senior Ford manager at the senior executive level in the Mazda organization. Thus, Ford prepared for the eventuality of making the link a strategic alliance. "From the beginning, we were keen on making this relationship more than a mere financial investment," recalled one Ford senior executive.

> We knew we could get more out of it. Of course, the whole notion of working closely with a competitor was new at that time. We wanted to preserve, though, the option of Mazda's playing a progressively growing and more important role in our overall strategy. That is why we insisted on board seats as well as representation at the working level. With our people in place, we could feel secure that the relationship did not become a one-way street with information flowing from us to a potential competitor. We could rest assured that we could monitor the flows of people and information.

Ford and Mazda both benefited from the strategic alliance. Their rivalry in the marketplace notwithstanding, the two firms found ways to collaborate and learn from each other in areas ranging from product design to production-facility planning. The firms worked jointly on the Ford Escort, Festiva, and Probe, the Mercury Tracer, and Mazda's Protégé and Navajo. Ford's top-ranking plant for quality, located in Hermosillo, Mexico, benefited greatly from Mazda's expertise in plant design. Mazda on-site engineers helped Ford's plant designers implement Mazda's production-layout approaches. Ford's marketing team, in turn, shared its highly developed and sophisticated research techniques with Mazda marketers.

Competition between Ford and Mazda remains alive and well amid this close cooperation. Each, for example, has made some products off-limits to the other. Ford refused to help Mazda develop a four-door Navajo; Mazda did not share its sporty Miata with Ford. Even in public policy matters such as U.S. car manufacturers' petition to the U.S. government alleging dumping of minivans by Japanese automakers (including Mazda), the two companies have agreed to disagree, taking opposite sides in the dispute. Thus, the firms have managed to maintain a balance between cooperation and competition.

The third lesson in the evolution of alliance strategies, namely, the creation and management of a network of alliances, could also be seen in action at Ford. The success of its strategic alliance with Mazda had a second round of feedback effects on Ford's strategic-policy evolution. The demonstrated ability to manage a complicated link with a competitor convinced Ford senior managers to forge a new set of alliances with other automobile companies to solve a host of strategic problems.

Ford officials, for example, viewing an alliance as a way to survive in the small, fragmented, but potentially attractive markets over the long term in Brazil and Argentina, in 1986 launched a joint venture with Volkswagen of Germany that rationalized the two firms' production facilities in the two South American countries. The innovative venture, named Autolatina, called for coproduction, sharing of production facilities, and realizing economies of scale of components through commonalities. The firms preserved the competitive element in their relationship by marketing their cars separately. Again, Ford had managed to straddle the line between competition and cooperation in an alliance.

In 1988, faced with the need to commit substantial resources to product development in the areas of minivans and off-road vehicles, Ford again decided to pursue an alliance. Its partner this time, Nissan, established with Ford joint production facilities in the United States and Europe in which the two firms would cooperatively develop the two products.

Buoyed by its success in forging and managing the Latin American alliance with Volkswagen, Ford entered another alliance with the German car manufacturer early in 1990, this time to manufacture minivans in Portugal for the European market. At the same time, Ford began to explore additional product-development efforts with Nissan and expanded its collaboration with Mazda to include marketing of Ford cars in Japan by Mazda and Mazda cars in Europe by Ford.

Such is Ford's confidence in its ability to conceive and implement an intricate, alliance-based strategy that Ford president Harold Poling, in a 1987 memorandum to senior managers, indicated that strategic alliances (referred to by Ford as business associations) with other firms would, in the future, play a critical role in "enhancing the overall competitiveness of Ford." The memorandum identified specific areas in which such alliances were expected to have a significant impact on corporate performance, among them achieving best-in-class quality; securing low-cost sources for vehicles and components; establishing competitive operations; increasing product-development capability; and gaining access to product and manufacturing technology and new markets. This list is so exhaustive as to cover every aspect of Ford's core business of designing, manufacturing, and marketing cars.

Contrast Ford's positive experience with strategic alliances with the experience of other, less successful firms. General Motors, for example, enjoyed the same opportunities to build and profit from a network of alliances as Ford. In fact, GM forged an alliance with Isuzu before Ford established its relationship with Nissan and Mazda. It subsequently established a link with Suzuki and was the first U.S. automaker to experiment with an alliance with a major Japanese rival like Toyota. Additional alliances with such firms as Korea's Daewoo in small cars and Japan's Fujitsu in robotics, Hitachi in electronics, and Nihon and Akebono in automobile components suggest that GM, too, has been pursing an alliance-based competitive strategy for more than a decade.[46] So why did a *Business Week* article find that in GM's alliances with firms such as Isuzu "the potential synergies" have not been realized?

GM's failure seems to be an inability to internalize the lessons of alliances, especially the latter two cited above. GM could not adapt its strategy as it learned about the use of alliances, nor could it manage the evolution of and interlinkages among a network of alliances.

GM's initial strategy, for example, called for casting Isuzu in the role of supplier of small cars. Many of its other alliances have served the same sort of sourcing purpose. In all of these, GM was the center of product design and development and its partners mere implementers of those designs. The evolution of these alliances seems not to have been reflected in the roles GM assigned to them or in any way incorporated in its core strategy. Ford managers, in contrast, as they gained familiarity with their counterparts at Mazda, increasingly ceded strategically critical tasks to their partner, thereby avoiding costly duplication of effort in areas such as product development.

General Motors' top management seems not to have developed a knack for managing the evolution of the strategy-alliance nexus. There has not been much effort to rethink overall corporate strategy and the role of alliances in that strategy. Recall that Ford's president indicated that the company's "business associations" were to play a critical role in all aspects of the firm's competitive strategy. No such articulation of policy appears to exist at GM, although such a formulation may be implicit in the pronouncements of top managers. But in the absence of an explicit statement, middle managers lack the focus needed to make effective use of alliances.[47]

Like Ford's, the Motorola experience, too, illustrates the lessons of forging and managing alliances we referred to earlier. First, Motorola incorporated the alliances as part of its preexisting strategy. Next, as it gained experience in forging and managing alliances, Motorola moved to enlarge their variety and scope even as it made necessary changes in its competitive strategy. Finally, once it became comfortable with the notion of working to achieve its variegated strategic objectives through a variety of alliances, Motorola moved on to become a corporation with a network of alliances straddling every aspect of its business. Through it all, continuous learning and experimenting characterized Motorola's approach.

Ford and Motorola could use their alliances to advantage because their top managers appreciated the close connection between alliances and strategy. They recognized that alliances entail both strategic risks and strategic benefits and struck a balance between the two in their managerial approach. Such rational behavior contrasts sharply with much of what has been written about alliances.

Some observers emphasize the problems, pitfalls, and perils of alliances and conclude, sometimes explicitly but more often implicitly, that alliances are risky and best avoided.[48] On the other hand, observers who view alliances as a panacea for all sorts of problems faced by firms coping with global competition tend to gloss over their very real risks.[49] Astute managers, like those at Ford and Motorola, avoided both extremes; they managed their alliances so as to maximize the strategic benefits and minimize the strategic risks.

Ford and Motorola managements further evidenced recognition of the importance of managing the interaction with their partners in a way that maintained a balance between cooperation and competition. In the forging and managing of strategic alliances, Ford and Motorola also developed a sophisticated set of administrative mechanisms to maintain their alliance relationships on an even keel.

Careful forging, structuring, and management of alliances provides both short-term benefits and opportunities for realizing longer-term gains associated with evolving the all-important strategy-alliance nexus. We turn, in the following several chapters, to the critical tasks of understanding the strategic logic of, forging and structuring, and finally, managing alliances.

PART II

GLOBAL COMPETITION AND STRATEGIC ALLIANCES

CHAPTER 3

Strategic Logic of Alliances: Entrepreneurial Globalization

A number of the companies we studied had entered into alliances as a means of quickly remedying immediate operational problems, often without examining strategic issues or projecting risks and benefits over a longer time horizon. Predictably, some such moves had disastrous consequences.

Alliances are a sufficiently recent phenomenon that most American managers have a limited base of knowledge and experience from which to draw. Academic experts and consultants typically proffer lengthy lists of what to do and what to avoid and treatises on the mechanics of forging alliances: searching for, evaluating, and selecting a partner; managing negotiations; striking a deal; and so forth. Seldom do these detailed checklists address the most basic question: Why a strategic alliance?

To make effective use of strategic alliances, managers must understand their logic. Only then can they understand and benefit from a detailed list of guidelines pertaining to the mechanics of forging alliances. The major driver of strategic alliances, the emergence of intense global competition, has rendered less effective the simple generic strategies that have been the staple of many U.S. firms. Today firms must embark on a path of continuous innovation to keep abreast or, preferably, forge ahead of equally innovation-conscious rivals. Firms must cultivate organizational flexibility in a number of areas, among them technology, marketing, distribution channels, and plant economics, and they must do so in the face of growing market uncertainties and increasing constraints on resources, both human and physical.

Developing a flexible organizational capability lies at the heart of entrepreneurship. It is also at the core of the logic of strategic alliances. Hence, the level of understanding and entrepreneurially recasting the global competitive strategy of a firm is where the forging of strategic alliances must begin. We call this process entrepreneurial globalization.

Over the past decade, the reality of global competition has become manifest to managers in manufacturing industries as varied as automobiles, construction equipment, machine tools, consumer electronics, office equipment and copiers, semiconductors, and telecommunication equipment. Managers in service industries, too, have heard the news. Banking, consulting, auditing and accounting, and advertising, among other service industries, are becoming global.[1]

Managers, even as they accept the inevitability of global competition, are faced with another new development—the notion of strategic alliances. These have not emerged by chance; they are intimately linked to the arrival of an integrated global market in which firms are no longer constrained by national and, increasingly, even organizational boundaries.

Multinational and domestic firms alike are realizing that drawing on the competence of other firms around the world to compete more effectively is not only feasible, but often necessary. Growing numbers of firms are seeking to build external networks of national and international alliances to complement their internal networks of national and international subsidiaries.[2]

That this phenomenon of strategic alliances is both a result of the globalization of and a catalyst of significant change in competition is a key theme of this chapter. Managers must reorient their thinking to take account of the new reality of international competition as the first and most critical step in forging and managing strategic alliances. To do so, they must understand the forces that have led to the emergence of global competition and the rise of new competitive imperatives.

The Emerging Global Integration

Over the past three decades, powerful new forces have been unleashed that have transformed the structure and competitive characteristics of industries ranging from soft drinks to telecommunications. In industry after industry, first demand, then supply, then competition, and more recently the competitive strategies of firms have been globalized.[3] This emerging global marketplace poses daunting strategic and organizational challenges.

Globalization of demand. The globalization of demand has been driven primarily by the postwar emergence of major markets in Europe and Japan. The United States, Europe, and Japan have achieved roughly the same level of per capita and disposable family income and boast large mass consumer and industrial markets. Recent years have witnessed the rapid growth of newly industrialized nations ranging from Mexico and Taiwan to Singapore.

A remarkable phenomenon of the emerging global market is the growing convergence of demand for consumer and industrial products. Youngsters in Tokyo, New York, and Cologne demand the same Walkman, the same jeans and sneakers, listen to the same music, are part of the Pepsi generation. Industrial customers are looking for the same power-generating equipment, machine tools, semiconductors, and pollution-control systems. This convergence is affording unparalleled market opportunities to companies as diverse as Coca-Cola, Sony, Benetton, McDonald's, Toyota, ABB, and Motorola.

What is responsible for such homogenization? For one thing, equivalent education levels among consumers in these regions. For another, achievement of roughly comparable physical, social, and technological infrastructures. Technological advances have reduced the cost of communication and transportation significantly, affording people young and old a high degree of mobility and fostering rapid promulgation of recent fashion and other consumer trends.[4] Readily accessible mass media support extensive advertising by major companies.

Harvard Business School professor Ted Levitt, who was among the first to recognize this trend, dubbed it the globalization of markets.[5] Levitt distinguished between the multinational corporation (MNC) and global firm. "The MNC," he wrote, "operates in a number of countries and adjusts its products in each—at high relative costs. The global corporation operates with resolute constance, at low relative costs, as if the entire world, or a major region of it, were a single entity. It sells the same things in the same way everywhere." The standardization of products and "economies of scale" in production characteristic of MNCs are hallmarks of the emerging global market.[6]

Although many observers of globalization have focused on consumer-end developments, such monocausal considerations fall short as explanations of global competition. There are, in addition to "demand" factors, a number of "supply"-side factors associated with the emergence of global competition.

Globalization of supply. Many of the forces that contributed to the rapid rise of per capita income in the triad and newly industrialized nations have also affected the supply side of global markets. A number of writers have identified structural economic developments in the past three decades that have permitted a new international division of labor across national frontiers (see Table 3.1).[7]

Many of these developments are familiar to managers and academics alike. Perhaps the most far-reaching and fundamental impetus to the global division of labor and hence to spreading prosperity is the liberal trading order established in the wake of World War II.[8] Technology has also helped. Technical improvements, in conjunction with substantial investments in ports, container shipping, and roll on/roll off modular systems, have lowered international transport costs considerably.[9]

Coordinating various activities and communicating with offices and plants scattered all over the globe assumes added importance as the division

Table 3.1
Structural Factors Promoting Global Division of Labor

Macro Trends
1. Development of a liberal international trading order
2. Improved transportation systems
3. Falling coordination and communication costs

Micro Trends
4. The rise of newly industrializing countries
5. Growing technological parity among nations
6. Advances in product design and process technology

Sources: M. Casson, ed., *Multinationals and World Trade* (London: Macmillan, 1986); M. E. Porter, *Competitive Advantage: Creating and Sustaining Superior Performance* (New York: Free Press, 1985); and M. Flaherty, "Coordinating International Manufacturing and Technology," in M. E. Porter, ed., *Competition in Global Industries* (Boston: Harvard Business School Press, 1986).

of labor transcends borders.[10] Here, too, technology has come to the rescue. More powerful computers offer cheaper processing power; telecommunication networks permit ever faster and cheaper communication;[11] and declining costs of travel and evolution of common business practices have made international coordination of businesses easy and effective.[12] Macrotrends such as trade, transportation, and communication are unquestionably important, but other, equally important microlevel developments have played as great a role in the international division of labor. The emergence of newly industrializing countries (NICs) in Asia and Latin America, for example, has provided firms new platforms for situating parts of their manufacturing value chains.[13] Industrial revolution is just reaching the NICs. Rural laborers who would otherwise be unemployed have taken low-wage industrial jobs consistent with their relatively low expectations in terms of living standards.[14] Low wages more than compensate for these workers' somewhat lower productivity compared with that of workers in the industrialized West.[15]

A second microtrend is increasing technological parity among growing numbers of nations in general and the triad countries in particular.[16] This parity has increased the capacity of firms in other nations to develop as well as absorb new technology. Hence, a firm seeking a supply of goods need no longer confine itself to developed nations. Workers in other nations, particularly NICs, can understand the implications of and adapt new technologies and perform to expectations normally reserved for the workers of developed regions.[17] Moreover, knowledge of products and processes diffuses quickly among nations, leading to rapid and widespread adoption of innovations.[18] Firms in other nations, too, having achieved technological parity, are in a position to develop new products and processes and enter the world markets.[19]

Organizational developments in product and process design, a third microfactor, now permit wider specialization of labor around the globe. Instead of thinking in terms of designing a product and "throwing it over the wall" to manufacturing engineers, design engineers nowadays are more inclined to think in terms of designing a product to exploit more fully the potential for division of labor.[20]

Firms that have taken advantage of these macro- and microtrends to foster a new international division of labor have benefited in at least three ways. First, they have been able to take advantage of global scale when setting up plants.[21] Economy of scale is an overriding consideration in some industries. For example, two global firms, Boeing and Airbus, dominate the civilian aerospace industry. Global scale has been achieved by firms in other industries as a consequence of dramatic technological discontinuities. Developments in the field of semiconductors, for instance, profoundly changed the industry economics of consumer electronics, shifting the competitive edge from firms that depended on national scale to firms that relied on global scale.

Second, the new international division of labor has permitted the spatial specialization of activities within industries. That is to say, firms can now locate various parts of their value activities in different parts of the world.[22] In industries as diverse as construction equipment, automobiles, copiers, and industrial bearings, most R&D is concentrated in a few laboratories in key industrialized countries, manufacture of major components in several plants in industrial and less industrialized countries, assembly in even less industrialized countries, and sales and service in almost all countries of the world.

Third, the new international division of labor has spurred innovative companies to divide creatively the job of making a product for a worldwide market. This approach has been particularly effective in industries traditionally perceived as being in the realm of local businesses.[23] Examples abound; concentrates in the soft drink industry are manufactured largely in a few countries, with marketing done in many more nations. Of marketing activities, advertising tends to be more concentrated than distribution. Similarly, packaged-goods firms in Europe have creatively employed the new international division of labor and scale economies to standardize product formulations, package sizes, and even multilingual labels.[24]

Globalization of competition. "Global competition," "global corporations,"[25] "global industries,"[26] and "global businesses"[27]—all are part of modern business parlance, yet there is no accepted definition of what global competition is or why it occurs. Neither is there a clear link between managerial actions and global competition. It encompasses the possibilities of both international division of labor and selling in global markets. Viewed from this perspective, there are neither global nor multidomestic industries.[28]

A definition of global competition is, we believe, best arrived at from a competitor's point of view. The key ingredient of global competition is competitive interdependence. As national firms, often involved in national oligopolies, move abroad, whether through exports, foreign investment, or a combination thereof, they find the same rivals in market after market, suggesting that to counteract rivals' moves these firms must develop the ability to respond globally.[29]

Global competition occurs when a firm, multinational corporation or otherwise, takes a global view of competition and decides to maximize profits worldwide rather than on a country-by-country basis.[30] The globalization of competition in an industry thus is determined by the strategic view of the managers of the firms that comprise it.[31] Only the strategic intent of firms is relevant to it. Global competition is possible even for firms that are merely exporting or whose subsidiaries are self-contained in production and distribution.[32]

Global competition takes shape in the minds of managers. As they recognize the possibility of competing worldwide, they reshape their competitive strategies. If global competition is, indeed, the order of the day in many industries, what does it mean for the strategies of individual firms? What strategic imperatives are imposed on firms seeking to compete globally? These are the questions to which we turn next.

Globalization of strategy. Just as globalization of competition followed firms' recognition of opportunities overseas, global strategies of firms have evolved from simple export-based strategies through foreign direct investment and multidomestic strategies to complex global strategies. This evolution reflects increasing recognition of growing interdependencies among markets.[33] The key basis for the evolution of global strategies has been the recognition by firms of successively more complex levels of dependencies among markets. There are at least three types of interdependence among national markets, although most observers have confined discussion to one or another. Intense global competition such as we see today becomes reality only when firms come to appreciate all three. Moreover, these interdependencies are bound up with the evolution of global strategies. It should be noted that the evolution we are about to outline was not linear in all industries, nor did it occur in all industries at the same time.

Scale interdependence is typically achieved first. Firms that operate across geographic boundaries can realize scale economies by concentrating production of components or products in one location.[34] Operational interdependence is achieved next.[35] Firms with operations in many countries are in a position, as market conditions change, to move production from one location to another in order to exploit differentials in wages, resource costs, and so forth. Ultimately they arrive at scope or knowledge interdependence.[36] Firms that operate in diverse markets, often geographic but sometimes product, can now and then use knowledge of the peculiarities of their markets to develop products and processes that can be successfully adapted elsewhere.[37]

U.S. firms' earliest approach to international competition was based on simple exports,[38] involving either surplus production[39] or production geared especially for overseas consumption.[40] The associated strategy that recognized mainly the first of the three cross-market interdependencies, economies of scale, was termed "export-based international (global) strategy." This phase was short-lived, as many nations demanded local production rather than simple imports, leading firms to pursue foreign direct investment and locate production facilities overseas.

As firms began to realize that they could be driven abroad not only by local demands, but also in response to the moves of rivals (often domestic[41] but sometimes from other nations as well),[42] foreign investment and local subsidiaries followed. Initially the resulting subsidiaries were likely to be managed as autonomous units. But gradually, particularly firms with an extensive overseas presence began to recognize another cross-market interdependence—operational interdependence. Companies that operated in many countries found that they could benefit from country-based advantages.[43] Cross-hauling of components and finished goods by multinationals came to characterize operational interdependence.[44]

The third phase of global competition emerges with the evolution of scope or knowledge interdependence. In this phase, firms come to appreciate the need to learn from their different markets, internalize their learning, and use it to enhance their strategic position in the marketplace.[45]

Failure to recognize management's role in initiating, implementing, and improvising global competitive strategies is at the heart of the problems that confronted many U.S. firms in the 1970s and 1980s.[46] In many industries, those slow to recognize the possibility of competing with a more complex global outlook were outwitted by nimble foreign rivals.[47] In the motorcycle and automobile industries, for example, Japanese firms, serving multiple national markets with standard products manufactured in highly efficient, large-scale plants concentrated in Japan, were the first to develop a more global approach. The advantages to be derived from economies of scale were clearly in evidence to these firms.[48]

While leading Japanese automobile manufacturers pursued export-based global strategies, their U.S. rivals General Motors and Ford, which early on had established major manufacturing facilities overseas, notably in Europe, were slow to recognize the advantages associated with pursuing an integrated global strategy. They neither exploited possibilities for cross-hauling entire cars or large components nor employed their network of subsidiaries to exploit differential country-based advantages.[49]

A global strategic approach is not a prerogative of one country or a group of countries. In many industries, U.S. firms were quick to compete with complex global strategies. Boeing in the aircraft industry, General Electric and Pratt and Whitney in jet engines, GE in medical systems, Intel and Motorola in semiconductors, Caterpillar in earthmoving equipment, and IBM in computers are but a few.

The evolution of global strategies based on recognition of cross-market dependencies is depicted in Figure 3.1. As a firm moves from one level of global strategy to the next, it must manage the newly recognized as well as previously recognized interdependencies. Firms interested in exploiting the advantages of a network-based global strategy, for example, must manage all three types of interdependencies. The complexity of their strategies grows as firms move up the ladder from export-based to network-based strategies.

Firms in an industry do not always pursue the same global strategy. In the automobile industry, for example, Toyota, until the early 1980s, competed with an export-based global strategy while GM and Ford followed affiliate-based strategies. By the end of the decade, GM and Ford were moving to network-based strategies, with Toyota trying to catch up.

Global Competition as a Dynamic Process

The key question, then, is How does global competition affect and, in turn, is it affected by, the strategies of firms? What are the implications of global competition for the firms engaged in it, and whence does the strategic logic of alliances derive?

The answers to these questions must be sought in a view of global competition as a dynamic process rather than as a stable equilibrium punctuated occasionally by the strategic moves of one or more players. It has been

Figure 3.1
Evolution of Global Strategies

Exploited Cross-Market Dependencies

		Scale	Operational	Scope
	Export-based	X		
Global Strategies	Affiliate-based	X	X	
	Network-based	X	X	X

suggested that the significance of global competition lies in the first-mover advantage, in that the "response lag" inherent in initiating a countermove permits the first mover to consolidate its competitive position or at least reap extra profits until its move is matched.[50]

But there is more to global competition than first-mover advantage. Its initiation in an industry has the effect of continual scrambling hitherto stable strategic positions. We assert that such constant churning of policy is the most significant aspect of global competition.

Current views of global competition derive largely from prevailing notions of competitive strategy, which tend to emphasize its static aspects. This is hardly surprising, given that much of our current understanding of strategy derives from research that seeks to explain the success of firms over time.[51] Indeed, some researchers suggest that strategic continuity in organizations, punctuated by brief periods of radical change, is the norm.[52]

A view of strategy that emphasizes strategic continuity has been behind the three core, and related, economic concepts that underlie much of the discussion of competitive strategy, namely, sustainable competitive advantage, strategic groups, and generic strategies. Global competition, a dynamic process with immense consequences for managers, has important implications for all three.

Sustainable competitive advantages. To understand a firm's competitive strategy it is necessary to understand the value chain of its business.[53] Every firm performs a set of discrete tasks related to designing, producing, marketing, delivering, and supporting its products. Value activities are normally physically and technologically distinct. A generic value chain is depicted in Figure 3.2.

Delineating the value chain of a firm enables a manager to understand how market rivalry is linked to the way the firm meets its customers' needs. In essence, a value chain disaggregates a firm into its component activities. While firms in the same industry tend to have similar value chains, the value chains of competitors often differ in emphasis. Identifying these differences is the first step toward understanding companies' competitive strategies.

Consider automobile manufacturers BMW of Germany and Hyundai of Korea. Although both firms engage in a gamut of primary value activities such as product design, process engineering, manufacturing, assembly, marketing, sales, distribution, and service, as well as such support activities as human resource development and financial operations, analysis of their value chains reveals significant differences in product design, process engineering, marketing, and service. "A firm's value chain and the way it performs individual activities are a reflection of its history, its strategy, its approach to implementing its strategy, and the underlying economics of the activities themselves."[54]

Figure 3.2
The Generic Value Chain

Source: M.E. Porter, *Competitive Advantage: Creating and Sustaining Superior Performance* (New York: Free Press, 1985).

Competitive success is not achieved merely by gaining an advantage in one or more value activities, but also by maintaining such an edge. Sustainable advantage is at the heart of successfully implementing competitive strategy.[55] Sustainability must be strived for. It relies on investments in assets related to key parts of the value chain that create entry barriers for new entrants and mobility barriers for competitors in other strategic groups. To provide a sustainable advantage, such investments must be in irreversible assets whose duplication would be uneconomical.[56] Irreversible assets represent a credible commitment that intimidates prospective entrants.[57] Such asset investments lead to the formation of strategic groups.

Strategic groups. In their search for defensible and sustainable advantages, firms pursue strategies based on different asset investments. Firms that choose similar asset investments come to constitute stable strategic groups within their industries.[58] Competition tends to be fierce among firms in the same strategic group.

Competitors in many industries tend to separate into strategic groups that stress different aspects of a business.[59] In so doing, they create mobility barriers that prevent rivals in other strategic groups from replicating the sustainable competitive advantage that characterizes their group. In the automobile industry, for example, Ferrari and Maserati are in one strategic group, GM and Toyota in another, and Yugo and Hyundai in yet another.

Strategically mapping and tracing the moves of groups of similar competitors enables managers to recognize immediate and long-term competitive threats.

Generic strategies. Combining the notions of value chain, sustainability, and strategic groups yields the concept of generic strategies. This describes the way firms compete to strengthen market position vis-à-vis their rivals.[60] Broadly speaking, there are two generic strategies. One aims at achieving a low-cost position by minimizing cost in all activities. The other relies on differentiation, that is, providing customers greater perceived value than one's rivals. Differentiation permits a firm to charge a premium for its products, with the result that cost is no longer a primary strategic target. Competitors separate themselves into distinct strategic groups that, because of the high mobility barriers between them, tend to be self-perpetuating.[61]

Generic strategies can be analyzed through the concept of the value chain. Cost leadership relies on analyzing competitors' relative cost positions by examining the basic determinants of cost (cost drivers, Michael Porter calls them) to assess which value-chain activities have a potential for yielding cost advantage over others. Differentiation, on the other hand, relies on analyzing rivals' value chains to assess which activities might be varied in level or content.

In general, generic strategies are mutually exclusive. According to Porter, "Sometimes [a] firm can successfully pursue more than one approach as its primary target, though this is rarely possible. Effectively implementing any of the generic strategies usually requires total commitment and supporting organizational arrangements that are diluted if there is more than one primary target."[62] Generic strategies are at the core of many current conceptions of competitive strategy.

Collectively, sustainable competitive advantage, strategic groups, and generic strategies offer an implied prescription to managers—that the best way to compete in the market is to analyze the value chain, see where one can add value, and identify and learn how to manage key cost drivers. Following this prescription leads to a general strategy and membership in a strategic group. A firm's strategic position is subsequently defended and its sustainable advantage reinforced by management's constantly fine-tuning operations and making appropriate and necessary strategic investments.

Impact of global competition. The trouble with the approach to strategy described above is that being largely static, it is most successful in a stable competitive environment. It also implicitly assumes that key competitors are predictably busy defending their own strategic positions. Globalization renders the competitive environment anything but stable, global rivals that assail entrenched players being highly unpredictable. Global competition thus puts a premium on the dynamic aspects of strategy.

Global competition affects entrenched firms in two ways. First, firms in different countries have brought to the competitive arena different bundles of competitive advantage that have blurred the distinctions among strategic groups. Second, many firms have followed a sequenced-entry approach to penetrate almost surreptitiously the entry and mobility barriers erected by incumbent firms.[63] While the incumbents were busy fortifying the walls, the prospective rivals were burrowing under it!

With global competition, new entrants can come from anywhere in the world; entry in general, and sequenced entry in particular, often occur initially through systematic exploitation of resources that are well within the entrant's reach. That is, the new entrant exploits advantages it already possesses through presence in a related industry or those that are available by virtue of presence in a geographical area with preferential access to the requisite resources, for example, low-cost labor and cheap raw materials.

New entrants derive strength from their home-market characteristics.[64] With global integration and the corresponding convergence of taste, firms in different countries are in a position to exploit their home-market advantages. In the television set market, for example, Japanese firms, which initially specialized in small sets suited to the small size of Japanese homes, have been able to capitalize on U.S. buyers' demands for portable and second sets. Sometimes technological discontinuities provide needed impetus, as when the 1970s oil shocks triggered worldwide demand for smaller, more fuel-efficient automobiles, which Japanese manufacturers were already positioned to supply.

Indeed, globally oriented firms frequently introduce new modes of competition that transcend simple generic strategies. They develop multiple sources of advantage by exploiting opportunities worldwide and taking advantage of the interrelationships among activities in product segments, geographic segments, technology bases, and industries. Global competitors constantly strive to create new strategic groups superior in profitability to existing ones.

"Constantly strive" are operative words. Unless countered early on by existing firms, the superior profitability of new entrants may erect walls around a new strategic group, thereby threatening the long-term survival of incumbents. To survive, the firms in established strategic groups must abandon their stockades and build and fortify new ones. The scrambling of the old strategic groups will then be complete. But the entire cycle will be repeated as other firms strive to compete more effectively. The dynamic agitation of the competitive battlefield and the need to respond to it are at the heart of global competition.[65]

The major home appliance and power systems industries exhibit the scrambling effects of globalization.[66] Both have traditionally been considered "national" industries fortified by such severe structural impediments to globalization as national standards and national buying preferences. Cross-border economies or dependencies were not seen as feasible. This state of affairs has changed in recent years, with European managers pioneering the changes. U.S. firms in both industries have only recently awakened to the possibility of global competition.

Consider, for example, the Swedish firm Electrolux, which since the 1970s has been systematically working toward a global strategy while such giants as Whirlpool and GE in the United States and Siemens and Philips in Europe remained content to compete nationally or multidomestically. Not until the late 1980s did Whirlpool finally respond by buying a majority stake in Philips's appliance business in Europe.

Electrolux's strategy explicitly recognized the three cross-border dependencies discussed earlier. By the late 1980s, through well-timed acquisitions, Electrolux managed to gain a presence in all major markets in the world, except Japan. Next, it sought to gain global economies of scale at the component level by concentrating production in a few specialized plants and cross-hauling to other markets. Simultaneously, it tried to gain operational flexibility by locating plants with interchangeable manufacturing facilities in different countries. Finally, it sought to gain economies of scope by employing cross-national product-development teams to generate merchandise globally.

Another Swedish firm, ASEA, moved to globalize competition in the power systems industry. In the mid-1980s ASEA engineered a merger with the Swiss firm Brown Boveri. The new firm, Asea Brown Boveri (ABB), has since sought to implement a global strategy by acquiring and integrating firms in various European, North American, and Far Eastern markets. ABB has also moved to acquire controlling stakes in Westinghouse's U.S. electrical distribution business and its Latin American power systems business. ABB's rivals were quick to respond. In early 1989, faced with the sudden threat of globalization of competition, GE moved to form a joint venture with General Electric Company in Europe.

ABB's global strategy also recognized the importance of the three types of interdependencies. ABB rationalized its plan to gain economies of scale at the plant level, reportedly launching a scheme to modularize its product offerings where feasible to achieve economies of scale. The company plans to establish a number of "home" bases for production to afford it operational flexibility, and its R&D is being revamped to ensure that learning in different markets is transferred to ABB's centrally guided research and development facilities so as to benefit the entire system.

Forcing new ways to compete in the global market is the most profound change introduced by global competition.[67]

Responses to Global Competition

If generic competitive strategies based on static sustainable advantages are insufficient in the arena of global competition, how are national firms with no international presence and multinational firms to counter a global competitor that has gained a first-mover advantage? We suggest that the essence of any response should be to build layers of competitive advantage. By spreading value activities around the globe, for example, a firm can reap the benefits of low cost and differentiation simultaneously. Flexibility achieved by keeping several strategic options open to enable a quick response to new rivals with their bundles of competitive advantages becomes a key organizing principle under global competition. Finally, firms need to strive constantly to learn new skills even as they protect, preserve, and build on their existing core competencies.

This is a tall order. How are firms to meet this challenge? A national firm faced with global competition is probably in the most difficult position. With no overseas presence, such competitors face the prospect of being forced to exit their industry unless they can match global firms' lower costs and differentiation advantages.

A multinational corporation (MNC) is perhaps a little better positioned to respond to a global challenge. Its presence in many countries puts the MNC in a position to reconfigure and coordinate globally the value chain among its subsidiaries to match that of a global competitor. An MNC that lacks a presence in parts of the world where such desirable resources as low-cost labor are available, however, may find itself in much the same position as a national firm.

IBM perhaps best exemplifies an MNC that has reconfigured and coordinated its value chain. It has spread its activities all over the globe, located manufacturing facilities in a number of countries, replicated its distribution and service capabilities in every major country, and even situated its research and development facilities on three continents—North America, Europe, and Asia—to take advantage of local talent.

IBM has also pioneered a virtually unrivaled system of managing interdependencies, which has been emulated by the latecomers, among them Japanese multinationals. NEC, for example, which has located research and development facilities in North America and Europe, manufactures key components abroad. Sony and Matsushita have located value activities in multiple locations, and Siemens and Philips, having built autonomous subsidiaries in many countries over the years, are striving to integrate them into a coherent global presence with value activities dispersed among many affiliates.

International competition is not new; the phenomenon of the multinational corporation was widely recognized and well researched in past decades. What is new is that competition is now global, and it is becoming increasingly clear that competing through a string of national subsidiaries is but one of its facets. Moreover, the multinational solution encounters problems by its ignoring a number of organizational impediments to the implementation of a global strategy and underestimating the impact of global competition. Take the notion of global coordination of a network of global subsidiaries. Such an approach relies on organizational changes that may be extremely difficult to implement.[68] Subsidiaries that have come to value their autonomy may be reluctant to relinquish control over key areas in the name of strategic benefit.

Alternatively, an MNC might choose to build a network of subsidiaries. But any exclusively internal response, including an internal-network approach, presumes that globalization can be accommodated by juggling tangible assets such as people and plants. We believe such shuffling may be necessary to compete globally, but because it ignores many of the other vital implications of the globalization of competition—the time element, the technology factor, differing managerial systems, and the role of economies of scope—it will seldom be sufficient. It is because intangible or embedded factors play a major role in global competition, and firms such as IBM are augmenting their internal networks of overseas subsidiaries with an external network of alliances.

The time element. Building an internal network takes time. NEC, Sony, and Matsushita have been at it for more than ten years, IBM and Ford for decades. Once it establishes a presence, a firm must develop organizational capabilities to exploit it. Its global competitors do not wait for a firm to reconfigure and coordinate its subsidiaries into an internal network. Nor does time stand still with respect to other aspects of global competition.

Firms are coming to realize that time is a vital dimension of competition.[69] Product-development cycles, for example, are being compressed, and technological diffusion has become more rapid as the major nations of the world have achieved technological parity. Firms are always on the lookout to adopt, adapt, and circumvent their rivals' innovations as they are forced into an ever accelerating tempo of product development. Sony's general manager in charge of Walkman commented, "As each generation was launched, we stayed ahead of the competition by manufacturing excess. The day we launched the first generation, we were ready to launch the second, and development work was already completed on the third."

The technology factor. The accelerated tempo of global competition is compounded by other demands of technology development, notably the convergence of hitherto distinct technologies. Computers and communications provide an obvious example. Less well known, perhaps, are convergences in the materials sciences, steel with rubber in radial tires and glass with polymers in products used by the aerospace and automobile industries, for example. Such technological convergence poses a dilemma: the technology frontier must be covered more broadly than ever as the cost of doing it is rising.

Global competition has raised another competitive specter: standards. In many areas, technological standards have been left largely to the marketplace, more often than not becoming mere weapons in the arsenals of competitors. A particular standard's failure to catch on can spell disaster for a company forced to spend large sums of money on product development. Witness the demise of Sony's Betamax videocassette recorder and IBM's microchannel standard and OS/2 operating system, both struggling despite their acknowledged technological superiority. To protect its investment, IBM is offering to license its technology at low cost to all comers.

Global competition is forcing firms to attack increasingly complex and costly issues even as they weather heightened competition and cope with growing resource constraints. The problem of resources is compounded by the need for highly skilled researchers and engineers.[70]

Differing managerial systems. Firms from different nations bring to the competitive arena not only such tangible advantages as better products and processes, but also such intangible strengths as their managerial and work systems. These are now recognized as competitive advantages. Rare is an acute observer of international business who does not recognize that different managerial systems can bestow competitive advantage. It is now trite to say that Japan's managerial system enables that nation's corporations to compete in ways different from those of Western corporations.[71] Indeed, even such a corporate phenomenon as the *keiretsu* is the product of a Japanese managerial system. With the rise of Korean *chaebols* and the possible success of Indian family-based business groups, we are beginning to hear more about this aspect of global competition.[72] To compete against firms with different organizational dowries, a global competitor must learn from, adapt, and internalize these new work organizations and managerial systems. For example, Fujitsu of Japan and its British subsidiary, ICL, have begun an exchange program involving midcareer engineers and managers. The purpose is to let each firm learn "management lessons" based on the managerial system of the other.

The role of economies of scope. Global competition demands that entrenched firms respond to new entrants that possess different packages of competitive advantage. Global competition enables firms to alter the competitive arena by combining their resources and advantages in new ways, thereby putting a premium on their ability to imitate newcomers by acquiring their new combinations. Such resources and advantages are frequently associated with the new entrants' presence in related segments, industries, and geographic areas or some combination of them.

This brings us to a discussion of competitive scope, which refers to "the scope of a firm's activities."[73] It encompasses industry-segment coverage, integration, geographic markets served, and coordinated competition in related industries. Three dimensions of scope affect the economics and con-figuration of the value chain: segment scope, geographic scope, and industry scope. Segment scope refers to the varieties of items produced and customers served, geographic scope to the breadth of countries or regions in which a firm competes, and industry scope to the range of related industries in which a firm competes.

Firms can choose either a narrow or wide scope with respect to segments served and countries and industries targeted for competition. Narrow scope, often an indicator of a focused strategy, usually gives way to broader scope as a firm grows. A firm that remains wedded to a particular market niche sacrifices the opportunity to broaden its market appeal. Hence, most firms choose to compete with a wide scope, or at least widen their scope with time.

In general, a broad approach permits a firm to exploit the interrelation-ships between value activities in the three dimensions of scope. Serving both the semiconductor and computer industries, for example, may enable a firm to exploit economies of scale and experience curve advantages in a way not possible for a rival that competes in only one of the industries.

Likewise, a firm that serves one segment of a market may take advantage of its control over the distribution network to serve other segments as well, thereby gaining an edge over a competitor that serves only one segment. A manufacturer of large automobiles, for example, may use its distribution network to serve the small-car market as well. Similarly, a presence in several countries might enable a firm to perform activities such as component manufacture and assembly in different countries according to the compara-tive advantage of the firm in each country, thereby gaining an edge over a single-country firm.[74]

Scope also permits a firm to augment its knowledge base. This in turn leads to greater learning opportunities, which lead to the possibility of new ideas in the areas of product and process technology. Scope advantages have implications for global competitive strategy in that they enable a firm to redefine itself through skillful utilization of competitive scope and the resulting interrelationships. Global competition has contributed to such structural change in many industries. A large number of Japanese firms in the semiconductor industry, for example, were also major players in such user industries as consumer electronics, which has had a deleterious effect on U.S. semiconductor manufacturers. Likewise, Microsoft, with its firm grasp on microcomputer software, particularly operating systems, has been able to redefine the software market and put IBM on the defensive.

MNCs' internal networks can alleviate these problems only to some extent. What is needed is a mechanism that enables a firm to work at the forefront of technological innovation even as it struggles to compete with finite resources, a mechanism that permits learning new methods of work organization, allows access to new developments in the frontier where technologies converge, and fosters the distribution of value activities without sacrificing the firm's competitive edge. In short, firms have to supplement their internal networks of domestic and overseas affiliates.

The Role of Strategic Alliances

Herein lies the strategic logic of alliances—that advantages traditionally gained through internal development must now be secured through external networks. Multinational and national firms alike can strive to compete globally through coalitions or strategic alliances with other independent firms. Coalitions or alliances are, according to Porter, a "way of broadening scope without broadening the firm by contracting with an independent firm to perform value activities or teaming with an independent firm to share [value] activities."[75] Coalitions thus permit a firm with narrow scope to gain the benefits of broader scope without entering new industry segments, geographic areas, or related industries. Coalitions are also a way for a national firm to reconfigure its value activities around the globe to achieve the necessary cost and differentiation advantages vital to meeting the challenges posed by global competition.[76]

Alliances permit firms to react swiftly to market needs. As time-based competition becomes more important, the role of alliances in managing the time element becomes critical. Recall how quickly and forcefully IBM was able to respond to the emerging market in personal computers pioneered by Apple. The response was feasible only through IBM's extensive use of alliances with such diverse firms as Intel, Microsoft, and Epson.

Alliances also allow firms to bring technology to the marketplace faster. Historically, Xerox had depended on its own efforts to introduce products using new technology. Not anymore. A number of strategic alliances with Novell, Lotus, Sun Microsystems, and Microsoft has enabled Xerox to market innovative technology faster. As a bonus, Xerox has also been able to focus its business and strategic efforts better.[77]

In addition, alliances permit firms to confront issues associated with differing managerial systems head-on and enable managers to take the initiative in learning to live with and learn from such systems. Alliances with Japanese carmakers, for example, have let American automakers learn and internalize such approaches as working closely with suppliers to design new components, lower costs, and improve quality.[78] American firms have also learned to accelerate their product-development cycles by using Japanese practices.

The lesson of alliances is simple: they are a new way to compete in the international marketplace. The competitive combination that might occur to rival firms is limited only by the imagination and ingenuity of entrepreneurs. The world is now the arena of competitive interplay, and managers can be expected to change the rules of the game to their advantage. Alliances are a powerful way to redefine the competitive battlefield.[79]

With nearly all industries subject to redefining the rules of the game because of the entrance of newcomers, many firms have begun to rethink what their firm is or ought to be. One of the managers we interviewed had this to say:

> What is so sacrosanct about our doing all the things we have been doing all along? We have been in so many things. We have our own sales force. Our research facilities are extensive. We are into every exotic technology we can think of. We have a service group that is the largest, and perhaps the best, in the industry. We are operating in some thirty countries. Still, these new guys often do better than we in segment after segment. Sure, the new players are not the same ones in each segment; but we were being harassed by different competitors in each. It is like an elephant trying to fight an army of gnats. Our first inclination was to think we could continue to swat at each of them. Gradually it dawned on us that maybe we should cease to be an elephant and become more like a gnat, albeit a large one. That is when we started rethinking the whole system and the way we were doing things. We started asking questions like, Should we be doing it? Should we ask someone else to do it for us? Should we do it with someone else? And so on.

It is out of such gradual rethinking of a corporation that strategic alliances come into being. An alliance might begin with one or two value activities in one or two businesses. The managers relinquish part of the value chain to another firm. Gradually, as managers develop a different mind-set, the alliance option comes to mind earlier and eventually becomes part of strategic thinking.

Strategic alliances are in essence following up such rethinking with an effort to "deintegrate" a business's value activities, "reconfigure" those activities uniquely and imaginatively, and "leverage" a firm's resources through joint efforts with independent firms to gain scope advantages. At the same time, smart alliance makers strive to maintain a safe fall-back position through appropriate arrangements both within the firm and without, to create through a series of related strategic moves multiple strategic options for the future, and perhaps most critically, to innovate continuously through constant reevaluation of the network of alliances in order to stay ahead of competitors.

Rethinking businesses, deintegrating and reconfiguring value activities, and remaining flexible and market-responsive through the creation and maintenance of fall-back positions and strategic options are, not surprisingly, at the heart of entrepreneurship. This is not a coincidence. Globalization has engendered the need to put entrepreneurship back where it belongs—at the heart of corporations. Companies have to become flexible, quick, and responsive, and strategic alliances are their most direct route to those qualities. Alliance-making puts a premium on companies' once again becoming entrepreneurial. The key question then becomes, How are alliances best forged and structured?

CHAPTER **4**

Forging Strategic Alliances: A Road Map

Our research has identified four key activities that tend to be visited by firms that have successfully employed strategic alliances. Although we present these as a sort of conceptual road map, we can seldom trace the step-by-step approach outlined in Figure 4.1, even among firms that have developed sophisticated approaches to alliance formation. Firms usually enter into alliances in an ad hoc fashion, driven by immediate, tactical reasons. The route we plot here reflects best practice in firms that have furthered their strategic goals through carefully considered and effectively executed alliances.

RETHINKING THE BUSINESS

Ideally, firms compelled by the pressures and threats posed by international competitors to consider the use of alliances begin by reassessing the business they are in, evaluating their mode of competing, and searching out opportunities to enhance their competitive position. When the last factor includes alliances, firms are well advised to consider more fundamentally the role of such interfirm relationships with respect to their longer-term strategic goals.

Strategic Reassessment

To illustrate how a firm's managers might, in the context of a reassessment, take a fresh look at how a business could be reorganized, we consider the example of the Appliance Motors Company.[1] AMC has for more than seventy years produced for the U.S. market motors of various horsepower

Figure 4.1
Road Map for Forging Alliances

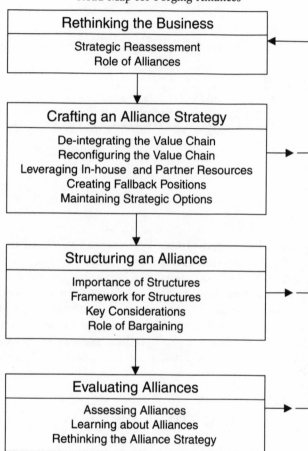

ratings for appliances ranging from refrigerators and vacuum cleaners to pump sets. The company owned the dominant share of the U.S. motor market, a handful of domestic rivals competing for the remainder, and its reputation for technological innovation, quality, on-time delivery, and service, management believed, justified premium prices.

In the late 1970s, when key customers began to move their manufacturing plants overseas and new competitors began to enter from the Far East, AMC's market share began to slide, leading the company to begin what turned out to be a major reappraisal of the business.

A senior manager commented as follows:

> In every segment, we found a few new rivals from Asian coun-
> tries such as Taiwan and Korea. They were gaining market share
> at our expense in the U.S. as well as among the transplants [company
> word for customer plants outside the U.S.]. None of them operated
> with as broad a product line as we did, and each operated in just
> one or two segments. One company, for example, was a maker of
> table fans. Another made motors for small room air conditioners.
> They manufactured motors for their internal use, moved to sell
> their surplus motor production to others, and then expanded into
> a couple of other segments where motors with similar ratings, but
> with some modifications, could be sold. None of these newcomers
> were spending much on R&D. But they began to take the bread-
> and-butter businesses away from us using price as a key competitive
> weapon. Their quality was not as good as ours, but was clearly
> acceptable to our customers.

What AMC faced was a classic case of global competition: newcomers
with neither significant R&D nor broad product lines exploited low labor
costs and scope advantages associated with their presence in customer markets to compete in a new business. As it gathered more data on its new
competitors, AMC discovered that a few were realizing very low rates of
return on their appliance motors business. Another AMC manager said,
"None of my people would have dared come up with a project with such
lousy returns." But a disinclination to discourage low-return projects was,
again, both a symptom and a cause of global competition.

To their credit, AMC managers construed the threat as an opportunity
to rethink their business: the manner in which it was conducted; the nature
of their investment priorities and core competencies and configuration of
the distribution network; how customers' needs might be changing; and the
company's strengths and weaknesses generally. This introspection led to a
decision to continue to compete across the board in all segments of the
appliance motors business. Yet another senior manager remarked,

> The easiest solution would have been to do what many American
> firms in industry after industry were doing: retreat to the high end
> and leave the low end to others. We felt that was both dangerous
> and unnecessary. Dangerous because where does such retreating
> end? What happens when the foreign firms move upmarket? How
> far can we retreat? Unnecessary because why throw away your
> brand equity? In all segments, we had a good name with the channels
> and customers. Our only problem was that our costs and prices
> were out of alignment. We decided to set that right through our
> alliances.

The notion of competing across the board in all segments goes against conventional wisdom in competitive strategy. Specialists who recommend that a firm focus on one end or the other lest it be "caught in the middle" assume, often implicitly, that the firm is self-contained in all aspects of its value chain and cannot identify and separate its segments in terms of product design, production, sales, marketing, and service, leading inevitably to inefficiencies that render it unable to serve any segment well. These assumptions may not hold for firms that compete with strings of alliances; creative relaxation of constraints is what entrepreneurship is all about. Globalization calls for, as well as permits, the employment of alliance-based entrepreneurial strategies.

Although it was defensive reasoning that propelled AMC into alliance-making, offensive reasoning can also occasion the plotting of routes to strategic alliances. Companies need not wait for global competition to threaten before taking steps to meet it head-on.

Establishing a Role for Alliances

Having concluded that an alliance is desirable, a firm must establish more specifically the role it wants an alliance, and alliances generally, to play in its overall business plan. This determination will influence the firm's choice of alliance types. Although establishing a role for an alliance was, at least initially, a trial-and-error exercise in many of the firms we studied, it need not remain so. Most senior managers seem to develop an intuitive sense of the role of alliances in their businesses.

AMC managers resisted an early impulse to source some of the company's low-end motors from a Far Eastern firm, realizing that they would be able to exert little control over an arm's-length relationship based on annual renewable contracts with a supplier that was likely to become a competitor. On completing their internal reassessment of firm strategy, AMC managers were able to approach the examination of the role of alliances in their company more systematically. Ultimately, they settled on a role that one manager termed "hub-and-spoke," AMC being the hub and its alliances the spokes. Collectively, the alliances were to be managed in an integrated manner to enhance the firm's strategic flexibility, necessitating the adoption of new alliance structures and management approaches.

Failure to recognize and define the role of alliances is responsible for much of the criticism of interfirm relationships. When viewed not as quick fixes but as contributors to firms' long-term strategic health, alliances are almost always productive. When the roles of alliances are understood and defined in terms of long-term strategic benefits, the road to crafting strategy is much easier to follow.

CRAFTING AN ALLIANCE STRATEGY

Alliances are, as a manager put it, no more than an effort to "do business differently." We have identified at least five aspects to doing business differently that variously involve (1) deintegrating the value chain, (2) reconfiguring the value chain, (3) leveraging in-house and partner resources, (4) creating fall-back positions, and (5) maintaining strategic options for the future.

Deintegrating the Value Chain

Deintegrating the value chain involves disaggregating and evaluating each of a firm's value activities to determine which might safely, without much undue risk to long-term strategy, be done by other firms.[2] This activity forces a firm to become entrepreneurial in the most Schumpeterian sense of "seeking new combinations" for doing business.

Appliance Motors again yields some interesting insights. The company responded to its new global competitors by assessing which of its own activities added the most value to its products and which might be better performed by another firm. The analysis revealed implications of changes in the company's market that management had not fully recognized. "It was pretty obvious that at the low end—the standard motors that had practically not changed in decades—little value was being added by AMC," said a senior manager. "The designs were old, the inputs were commodities anyone could buy in the open market, and the customers did not value our R&D or delivery enough to pay our premium prices." At the same time, strengths in specialized applications were neither being exploited nor marketed well enough to earn the returns they deserved.

AMC managers, on rethinking the firm's value chain and assessing the company's relative strengths in key market segments, determined that, at the low end, distribution channel access, logistic economies, service capabilities, and brand name were more valuable than manufacturing activities, while at the high end, demonstrated strengths in advanced technological and manufacturing capabilities clearly provided an edge over rivals. Its value activities having been laid on the table, so to speak, it remained for AMC management to rearrange them in the way that made the most sense.

Reconfiguring the Value Chain

Reconfiguring the value chain involves distributing value-chain activities among a parent firm and its subsidiaries (often based abroad) and its alliance partners (again, often foreign firms), and keeping in-house activities from which it derives key competitive advantage and distributing the others. AMC managers, having decided that the company would compete across the board in all segments of appliance motors, needed to determine whether it could do so while focusing on only a subset of its value-chain activities. They decided that product design, marketing, service, and R&D would be retained in-house for all products. Manufacturing, on the other hand, would be distributed, namely, retained in-house at the high end (particularly customization for key customers) and let to overseas alliance partners at the low end.

Leveraging In-house and Partner Resources

"When you do some of the work and get others to do other parts, it frees up resources and lets you do more than you had been doing before," said an Appliance Motors senior manager. "It is just like leveraging your company through borrowing. Here you leverage through other firms' resources." AMC leveraged the resources of partners in the Far East, having secured half a dozen alliances with firms in that region. All were manufacturing-oriented, consistent with the firm's hub-and-spoke alliance strategy. Not all were mere sourcing alliances; some served AMC's entry strategy for new markets.

Much having been written on the topic of partner selection,[3] we add only a few observations. First, we found that firms generally have little difficulty executing a systematic search for and locating potential partners. Then, given that alliances are a way to leverage a partner's as well as in-house resources, firms tend to seek partners with complementary resources. Indeed, the availability of such partners can prompt a firm to revise its alliance strategy. Finally, alliance-seeking firms are likely to attend closely to "compatibility of organizational cultures" when choosing potential partners. Managing relationships is easier when firms share time horizons, decision-making processes, and so forth.[4]

Creating Fall-back Positions

Deintegrating, reconfiguring, and leveraging are often sharply criticized for giving away the future by permitting critical manufacturing skills to migrate out of a company.[5] Moreover, partners can fail to meet expectations for delivery and quality, exploit critical circumstances to try to exact a ransom, and even become direct competitors.

To minimize such possibilities, firms create fall-back positions; for example, they taper integration into manufacturing or establish multiple interchangeable alliances for a particular function. AMC continued for a time to manufacture in its U.S. plants some of the motors it was sourcing from its Korean alliance. "At least in the beginning," explained AMC's general manager, "we did not want to shut down all of our manufacturing facilities that specialized in those types of motors. Also, we needed a transition period to ease the labor union's concerns." Moreover, the company structured alliances in Korea, Taiwan, and Malaysia so that any one, in a pinch, could substitute for any other. "If there was a supply problem in one," the manager added, "we could quickly gear up the other for production."

Maintaining Strategic Options

Firms maintain a set of strategic options as a defense against the eventuality of an ally's turning adversary and, more generally, as a mechanism for coping with future developments. So AMC, having identified product-design investment as a critical area in which it needed to preserve its position as a technological leader, increased the size of its design team. "We saved some money in manufacturing, but a good part of it we plowed back into hiring new design engineers," the general manager stated.

AMC also increased investment in computer-aided design facilities and declared design virtually off-limits to alliance partners. "We felt that keeping the product-design approaches to ourselves and allowing only the results to our alliance partners—and that on a need-to-know basis—served as a way to maintain control over the alliance relationships," AMC's head of research and development told us.[6]

Basic motor design not having changed in decades, AMC, believing that development of environmentally friendly, more energy-efficient motors would enable it to sustain its lead over future rivals, invested heavily in research. When, for example, superconductivity became a hot topic in the late 1980s, the company quietly began funding a small unit within its R&D department to explore possible applications in motors.

AMC did not neglect process development, insisting on full access to partner firms' manufacturing facilities and information gained therefrom. "We were helping them to gain a foothold in business by sharing with them all we had learned over the years," declared a senior manager. "We were not going to be shut out of future developments in the area. Who knows when we might need that knowledge again?"[7] On the other hand, AMC rigorously circumscribed access to service data for sourced products and process developments.[8]

Careful linking of development of future options and alliances is largely an outcome of the first substep in forging an alliance-based strategy, namely, reexamining a firm's business and overall business strategy. Just such an analysis led AMC to focus on design, energy efficiency, and process technology. Alliances free up the resources needed to pursue such options.[9]

STRUCTURING ALLIANCES

There is no one-to-one correspondence between alliance structure and alliance activity or industry.[10] Some examples should make this clear. Nonequity alliances include traditional supplier-buyer links. Prototypes include

Eastman Kodak, which sources, on a long-term contractual basis, medium-volume copiers from Canon of Japan for sale in the United States under the Kodak brand name, and General Electric's (GE) power systems group contracts with Japanese, Brazilian, Romanian, and Indian companies for products such as switch gears.

Nonequity links permeate research and development. The Siemens-IBM alliance's working on the development of advanced chips is one example, the Seiko-Compaq alliance's developing liquid crystal displays for laptop computers another. Philips and Hitachi even exchange researchers under a cooperative agreement with no equity involvement.

Supplier-buyer relationships and R&D coalitions have also been built on minority equity stakes, a familiar pattern in the automobile industry. General Motors (GM), for example, holds a 42% stake in Isuzu and a 6% stake in Suzuki, two firms from which it sources subcompacts to sell under its own name.[11] Likewise, Ford holds a substantial stake in Mazda and AT&T acquired an equity stake in Olivetti when it began to source personal computers from the Italian firm. Ford, when it decided to use outside software firms in connection with its efforts to introduce computer-integrated manufacturing in its plants, acquired minority equity stakes in the vendors it selected, and IBM moved into the specialized software end of the computer market by acquiring minority stakes in small software firms. AT&T's efforts in the multimedia market are similarly supported by minority equity participation in a number of software companies and semiconductor design firms.[12]

Examples of joint ventures in which two or more alliance partners hold equal equity stakes include GM and Toyota in Fremont, California, GM and Suzuki in Canada, and Chrysler and Mitsubishi in Detroit. Fifty-fifty joint ventures have been established by Mitsubishi and Westinghouse to manufacture and supply circuit breakers for the parent firms and by Philips and DuPont for research and development, and in 1984 AT&T and Philips established an equally owned joint venture to manufacture and market telecommunications equipment.

If we conclude from these examples, as well we might, that neither a participant's industry nor the targeted activity seems to determine the structure of a relationship, we are left with a question: Does the structure of an alliance really matter?

The Importance of Structures

According to a group of researchers that has studied alliances, "Managers are too often obsessed with . . . ownership structure. . . . The challenge for Western companies is not to write tighter legal agreements but to become better learners."[13] A well-known business consultant deprecates the alleged "dangers of equity" in alliances, exhorting Western firms to "overcome the popular misconception that total control increases chances of success."[14] The ownership structure of alliances, according to these writers, is not at issue; managers' ability to get what they want from ambiguous relationships is.[15]

Dismissal of the importance of alliance structure is at odds with managerial behavior and thinking. Managers who plan and negotiate alliances devote considerable time to discussing suitable structures. Were structure not important, managers would probably not accord it precious time.[16] Virtually every manager interviewed in our study believed that the success or failure of alliances hinged on their structures.

When, for example, AMC decided to establish a sourcing relationship with a Korean firm, it devoted several months to hammering out a suitable structure. "I was in the second wave of negotiators to hit the shores of Korea," recalled an AMC legal counsel. "The first wave of managers had settled on a particular Korean firm on the basis of managerial competence, technical capabilities, and perceived common interests. Still, it took me and my colleagues months to arrive at a suitable structure for the alliance that was acceptable to all concerned." The structure they arrived at, as can be seen from the stylized rendering presented in Figure 4.2, is quite complex.[17]

By way of another example, General Motors' managers haggled for more than a year to secure a one-third equity stake in Isuzu. "From the beginning, we knew that MITI [Ministry of International Trade and Industry] would not let us gain majority control at Isuzu," a GM manager said. "Therefore our aim was to get 33 1/3% plus one share so that we would have a say in the affairs of the company. We doggedly pursued that goal through seemingly endless rounds of discussions with the Japanese because the structure mattered to us."[18] Having the benefit of its earlier experience with Isuzu, GM went to extraordinary lengths to ensure that the structure of its relationship with Suzuki was to its liking. When it was offered only a 5.5% stake, insufficient even to secure a seat on Suzuki's board of directors, GM pursued a more favorable structure through other means. Ultimately, it persuaded Suzuki and Isuzu to exchange 20% blocks of shares, thereby indirectly controlling 25% of Suzuki's equity through a combination of its direct equity holding and its substantial ownership of Isuzu's equity.[19] The process, according to GM managers, took several months.[20]

In none of these examples was structure an obsession only of lawyers. The line managers we interviewed were often most insistent on securing a favorable structure. According to a corporate lawyer in our research sample,

> Managers want to fix everything through contracts. It is fine as far as it can go. Lawyers, however, cannot specify every possible contingency and provide for it [in the contract]. I do see the point of managers in reducing uncertainty. Sometimes, when I start talking of the evolving nature of relationships and managers start talking of specifying contingencies, I sound like a manager and the managers sound like lawyers!

Figure 4.2
Alliance Structure at AMC

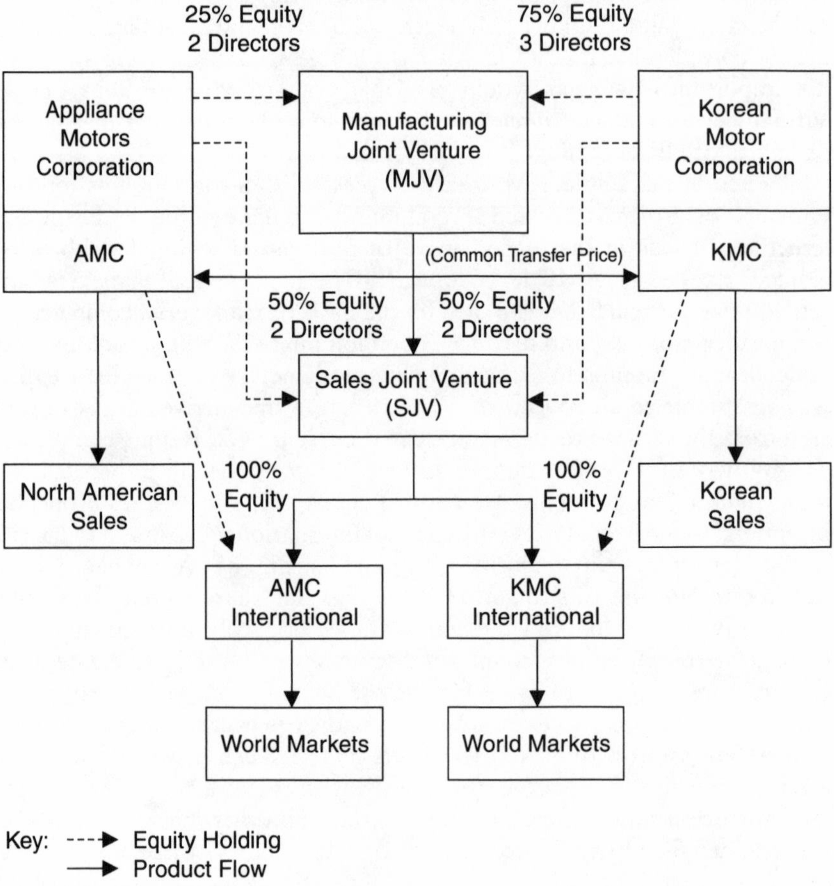

Key: ---▶ Equity Holding
       ——▶ Product Flow

Side Agreements	Key Provisions
MJV Agreement	• AMC has full access to MJV • Unanimous board approval needed for all decisions at MJV • Profit split at 35-65 for AMC/KMC • AMC has option to increase equity to 50%
Technology Agreement	• Technology license fee to AMC • Technical assistance fee to AMC • AMC has full access to technology developed at MJV
SJV Agreement	• Unanimous board approval needed for all decisions • Transfer price will be the same for both AMC International and KMC International • Profits split 50-50

Advice that alliance structure does not matter, if taken seriously, is misleading at best and dangerous at worst. A well-thought-out structure may not ensure an alliance's success, but it vastly improves its chances.

Our research suggests at least two key reasons why structure should matter: it provides the setting for ongoing interaction between alliance partners, and partners' strategic and operational objectives, whether stated or hidden, can be achieved only if the alliance structure permits. Managers we interviewed seemed to be aware of this. "A key reason for seeking the right structure is access to and control of information," said one. "In some instances, the kind of information you are after may be accessed or controlled through simple arm's-length contracts. In others, you may need a more involved mechanism."

If access to and control of information seems too nebulous a concept to support our argument for well-conceived alliance structures, consider the following examples. In a sourcing alliance in which product quality is of more strategic concern to the buying than to the selling firm, the latter has an incentive to skimp on quality control, the former an incentive to secure a structure that will afford access to information about, and some ability to influence, its partner's quality control efforts. Alternatively, in an alliance in which the object is for the partners to learn from one another, the structure chosen determines what types and amounts of knowledge or information are transferred. Whereas the mechanics of quality control can be readily accessed through a factory visit permitted by a simple contract, the transfer of complex ideas related to process technology relies on a structure that affords ample opportunity for interaction.

Structure can also serve to conserve a firm's options for the future. Market and technological uncertainties lead managers to seek as much room to maneuver as possible. Speaking of the choice of an arm's-length relationship for sourcing finished products, a manager at a high-technology firm said, "Why should we lock ourselves into an equity-based alliance when we can retain the strategic flexibility of moving to a different structure as the technology and our strategy evolve?" Another alliance manager emphasized that the firm's choice of a minority-equity-based structure for its link in Korea was based on the need to maintain strategic and operational flexibility: "In a world of evolving global competition, we should be prepared for changes, be they political conditions, exchange rates, or even wage rates. The structure we chose was designed to provide maximum flexibility."

If we accept that structure plays a pivotal role in maintaining strategic and operational flexibility and providing a fertile context for nourishing interfirm relationships, then clearly we want to know why different partners in the same industry, engaged in essentially the same type of activities, choose different alliance structures. The answer lies in a complex web of issues that we will break out in the context of a framework for alliance structures, a framework we developed on the basis of our study.

A Framework for Alliance Structures

Although largely studied as if managers were always confronted with a polarized choice between equity and nonequity arrangements or, more generally, between "market" and "hierarchy,"[21] strategic alliances can in fact be arrived at through a variety of contractual arrangements, some more hierarchical than others. Indeed, most firms end up somewhere in the middle, with arrangements involving both equity participation—at less than 50%—and detailed contracts, which we term "quasi-hierarchies."[22]

So although interfirm arrangements are limited in principle only by the "imagination and ingenuity of entrepreneurs,"[23] for our purposes it is necessary to confine our discussion to some easily recognized categories. In the theoretical literature, the level of equity participation is widely used to distinguish interfirm alliance structures.[24] Ownership is viewed as a key dimension by writers because it often reflects the division of managerial responsibility among partners and thus the extent of strategic control over important decisions made in the context of the alliance. The hybrid nature of most alliances notwithstanding, we begin by considering just one delineating characteristic—equity participation. What factors lead a firm to pursue or forgo equity participation in an alliance?

Consultants and academics frequently offer managers lists of advantages and disadvantages of different types of interfirm links.[25] We believe such lists, because they fail to distinguish clearly between important and not-so-important considerations and provide nary a clue as to where managers might begin or how they might organize their views, have little operational utility.

Finding the right alliance structure involves recognizing and evaluating the various types of structures in light of commonalities and distinctions associated with a particular alliance. Earlier, we posited that managers' recognition of the importance of choosing appropriate alliance structures reflects two sets of considerations, one strategic and the other operational. An appropriate structure should facilitate the realization of a firm's strategic objectives and be operationally feasible.

Key Considerations for Alliance Structures

The strategic and operational factors that bear on choice of alliance structure, although not explicitly identified as such, have been widely discussed by academics, almost invariably as alternative views of structure.[26] The complexities of business reality belie such a simple dichotomous view of interfirm relationships. Executives we interviewed stressed that alliance-seeking was a major "strategic" decision, but were also aware that arrangements must fit the "needs of the occasion," that is, be operationally desirable.

What they seem to be suggesting is a need for balanced consideration of both sets of factors.

Given that these strategic and operational factors can favor either arm's-length (nonequity, contractual, or market) or equity-involved (hierarchical) arrangements, an alliance-making firm's final choice depends on the way its managers strive to balance opposing tendencies. We explore these factors and concomitant tendencies in turn.

Competitive strategy and alliance structure. That growth of a business enterprise influences the way it is organized (or structured) is widely accepted. That is, organizational forms change as enterprises grow,[27] and growth occurs as firms decide "to expand the volume of activities, to set up distant plants and offices, to move into new economic functions, or to become diversified along many lines of business."[28] These activities occur in response to shifting demands in the marketplace, new technological developments, and the actions of competitors. In essence, competitive strategy affects a business's internal organization.

From internal organization to external links is but a short step. A firm's relationships with other firms is likely to be influenced by its competitive strategy; firms do not enter into dealings with other firms except insofar as it enhances the effectiveness of their competitive strategy.[29] An alliance can both amplify a firm's competitive position and render the firm vulnerable to moves by its partners. For example, a sourcing partner that becomes dissatisfied with being an original equipment manufacturer (OEM) may decide to sell directly in its final market.[30] The kind of relationship established by the sourcing firm may determine both the feasibility and probability of success of such a move.

To assess its impact on alliance structures, it is necessary to examine the several dimensions of competitive strategy. We are concerned here with considerations that relate to a subset of these dimensions,[31] specifically whether a hierarchical or market relationship bestows more control for a given dimension.[32]

Foremost among the considerations that determine alliance structure is the role the relationship is expected to play in long-term strategy. Consider the alliances that IBM forged with three companies. IBM's belated early 1980s entry into the personal computer industry via a network of alliances—with Microsoft for operating software, Intel for microprocessors, and Epson for printers—was designed to enable it to gain rapid dominance. IBM chose a different type of alliance structure for each partnership. It established with Epson and Microsoft arm's-length supply contracts, adding to Microsoft's such additional safeguards as a broad cross-licensing of technology. With Intel, IBM secured a 20% equity stake, representation on the company's board of directors, and a technology agreement that permitted it to manufacture microprocessors in-house and sell them, embedded in customized boards, to third-party buyers. Why such a wide array of sourcing arrangements for software, microprocessors, and printers? The answer lies in differences in scope, time horizons, and impact on core competitive advantages.

The Epson alliance was a limited-scope, relatively short-term (less than three years) arrangement designed to afford IBM an opportunity to gear up to manufacture printers in-house. Because the alliance was not perceived to pose any threat to its core competitive advantages in marketing or technology, IBM opted for an arm's-length contract. Although IBM viewed the Microsoft alliance, too, as temporary, planning to bring system software development in-house over the long term, the need for IBM technical experts to work closely with Microsoft engineers would expose the company's core competence in technology development. IBM managers therefore deemed it essential that the company benefit from any technical developments that resulted from the collaboration. Moreover, were IBM to develop its own system software in the future, downward compatibility with previous generations of software might have to be maintained. Such strategic considerations led IBM to include the provision for cross-licensing of software copyrights.

The alliance with Intel was more involved, calling for IBM semiconductor engineers, chip designers, and manufacturing-process engineers to work closely with their Intel counterparts, thereby exposing an important part of IBM's core competence to a partner that could well become a rival. IBM's managers deemed the circumstances to require greater control than could be provided by an arm's-length sourcing agreement. Perhaps also thinking of preserving strategic flexibility by reserving the option to enter the third-party semiconductor market, and no doubt anticipating the need to maintain access to its partner's technology development as microprocessors moved through several generations, IBM sought an equity-based alliance with Intel.

The more critical an alliance to competitive success over the long term, the greater is the contribution in technological resources and shared information, and the greater a firm's contribution to an alliance, the more important it is to ensure that its partner, whether alone or in collaboration with another firm, does not soon become a major rival. As control is typically gained through equity participation, elaborate contracts, or some combination of these, a firm entering into such an alliance is apt to insist on a hierarchical or quasi-hierarchical arrangement.[33]

Alliance structure must also take into account the strategic interdependence of the partners. An alliance confined to a well-defined activity with little spillover into other business areas is likely to be constituted as an arm's-length contractual arrangement. But as an interfirm relationship becomes more involved and interdependent, one or both partners is liable to insist on a hierarchical structure.

Consider, for example, two late 1980s alliances established by Toshiba of Japan, one a three-way relationship involving Toshiba, IBM, and Siemens and the other between Toshiba and Motorola. Although both involved Toshiba and its partners' sharing expertise and developing new chip technology, the alliances were structured quite differently. Strategic concerns played a major role.

The Toshiba-IBM-Siemens alliance was an arm's-length contractual arrangement that called for some exchange of chip libraries and collaboration on the development of next-generation chip technology, with research to focus on chip design. The firms' researchers were to meet and define project scope and domains of responsibility, then work independently in their respective laboratories, meet at regular intervals, and exchange notes on their progress. It was understood that the partners would not have ready access to one another's research facilities or scientists. When the research goals had been realized, the alliance partners were to disengage and go their own ways. Commercialization was to be entirely the purview of the partner firms. This was clearly, in the language of the typology elaborated earlier, a precompetitive alliance. Scope was clearly delineated, interdependence relatively low, with little spillover expected into other areas of the business.

The Toshiba-Motorola alliance, by contrast, cemented an intricately interdependent set of links between the two firms. The alliance came about as the global semiconductor industry was maturing and U.S. and Japanese firms were increasingly recognizing their complementary skills. U.S. firms such as Motorola and Intel excelled at product innovation, particularly microprocessor design, Japanese firms such as Toshiba and Hitachi in process technology. Since Toshiba and Motorola expected to benefit from each other's technological and marketing strengths while continuing to compete in several geographic areas, theirs was a competitive alliance, with accompanying tensions of competition and cooperation.

The Toshiba-Motorola alliance, in calling for strong mutual interdependencies in the areas of user interface with key customers (particularly in Japan), product design, process-technology development, joint manufacturing, and even some marketing as Motorola sought greater market share in Japan, would expose some of the partners' cherished core expertise. Motorola, for example, was to transfer to the alliance its coveted microprocessor technology (the "crown jewels," as a Motorola executive put it), Toshiba its highly prized manufacturing-process technology, perfected over the years ("our family heirloom," according to a Toshiba executive). The success of the alliance relied on both partners' fully meeting their commitments.

Each desiring an organizational arrangement that would permit it to control the flows of knowledge and information to its partner, Motorola and Toshiba opted for a fifty-fifty joint venture in Japan, governed by an intricate legal contract that stipulated the technologies and information to be exchanged. The joint venture was to be controlled by senior managers from the two firms, each of which was to establish an office to deal with the venture and its partner firm.

A third set of strategic considerations revolves around the notion of learning. Alliances, particularly of the competitive type, afford opportunities for learning from rivals as well as from customers, suppliers, competitors, and even other industries. Moreover, learning may relate to any aspect of a business. Learning and its significance for the success of firms has in recent years been widely stressed in the management literature.[34] Transfers of knowledge occur in all types of alliance structures—arm's-length, quasi-hierarchical, and hierarchical. Market exchange of knowledge through licensing of technological know-how is widely practiced, and joint ventures have been used to create as well as transmit knowledge.[35] In the context of alliances, the important question is, Which structures facilitate which types of learning?

In terms of scope, the objective of learning dictates alliance structure. Consider, for example, the NUMMI venture between General Motors and Toyota. Ostensibly a sourcing alliance (the joint venture makes one vehicle, which is sold by Toyota as Corolla and by GM as Geo), the link is primarily a learning mechanism for the partners. GM wanted to gain a better understanding of the famed Toyota production system as adapted for use in North America, Toyota to learn from GM how to deal with North American labor unions and suppliers. The firms seem to have agreed that the best arrangement for acquiring knowledge that is deeply embedded in an organization is a fifty-fifty joint venture.[36]

Strategic considerations clearly play a major role in alliance-structure decisions, but competitive strategy is only half the story. An equally important determinant of structure is the operational efficiency with which an alliance can be consummated. We turn now to a consideration of efficiency-related issues.

Operational efficiency and alliance structure. Alliance management being complex, complicated, and costly, operational efficiency, that is, holding down costs, is a key consideration in structuring alliances.[37] Among the costs of managing an alliance are those associated with negotiating, monitoring, and enforcing contracts. Contracts that must cover a multitude of contingencies or accommodate disagreements between partners regarding relative values of contributions are difficult to write and hence costly.[38] Monitoring the performance of an alliance to see if it conforms to obligations as set forth by a contract also incurs costs, more so if it is difficult to measure partners' contributions.[39] And because contracts are rarely self-enforcing, ensuring compliance with the terms of a contract may add further costs.[40] Coordinating a firm's internal activities with those of a partner increases the cost of alliance management, as does ensuring adequate communication between partners. Finally, there are the oft-neglected costs of making organizational adjustments as an alliance progresses. Individually, such adjustments may impose only a nominal financial burden, but cumulatively they can be enormously expensive.

Contractual arrangements can be used to control the operational costs of alliances. When one partner's control of an alliance relationship increases, for example, the interests of the partners tend to become more closely aligned. This has the effect of reducing operational costs associated with negotiating contracts, but increasing costs associated with coordination and communication as the information gathering requisite to alliance decision making increases. Therefore, total operational costs—contract-related, plus coordination and communication, plus organizational adjustment—must be factored into the contract that governs an alliance relationship.

Operational efficiency, like competitive strategy, embraces a host of considerations related to production aspects, marketing interfaces, and the nature of the alliance-seeking and partner firms.[41] The preferred alliance structure varies with the relative importance of these different facets of operational efficiency. Each may point to a different arrangement, but more important, they may point to an arrangement different from that suggested by strategic considerations. The ideal, that is to say, most "efficient," alliance structure protects the strategic interests of both partners while maximizing the operational efficiency of the relationship.[42]

If strategic and operational dimensions overwhelmingly favor a market arrangement, firms are likely to adopt a market structure; if they favor a hierarchical arrangement, that becomes the structure of choice. Absent a preponderance of support for either arrangement, firms often establish intermediate contractual arrangements that typically exhibit a quasi-hierarchical structure.

In weighing facets of the strategic and operational dimensions that bear on alliance structure, most managers, rightly we believe, accord primacy to strategic issues. Efficiency considerations tend to temper decisions made on the basis of their strategic implications.

The Role of Bargaining

Any mutually agreed-upon alliance structure is a product of bargaining power. But to suggest that bargaining power is a key determinant of alliance structure is to put the cart before the horse. Worse, it confuses means and ends. Firms come together to strike deals only when each believes it has something of value to offer in return for something it wants. Evaluating this give-and-take and the issues it raises is a necessary prelude to negotiation. It reveals the "bargaining sets" that negotiators must recast so that they appeal to all parties.[43] Managers should view the negotiation process as a means to an end and remain focused on the factors that bear on the success of an alliance. They should enter into negotiations having weighed the relative importance of these factors and recognizing the complex interrelationships among them. Finally, managers should recognize the iterative nature of the process; the very choice of one structure over another influences the importance or weight of particular factors and the nature of the alliance, suggesting a need to step back and evaluate how a chosen structure might affect future needs.

EVALUATING ALLIANCES

We mentioned in connection with contract provisions the costs associated with monitoring and reevaluating alliances. The process of forging an alliance does not end with choice of structure, which must be viewed as fluid, subject to change as dictated by continual reevaluation. In addition, within a given structure, managers may have to intervene to obtain optimum performance, especially from the partner.

Assessing Alliances

Both ongoing management and timely intervention play a part in ensuring that an alliance meets expectations. For example, when AMC discovered after a few months that its first alliance partner was not meeting expectations in terms of investment in quality control, company managers interceded to remedy the situation. In a research and development alliance, within the first few meetings of research personnel from both firms, one partner felt that the other firm was not committing its best researchers to the joint effort. The alliance manager took up the issue with his counterpart in the partner firm, and they resolved it quietly within a few weeks.

Assessment of alliances need not be confined to such first-level objectives. In a major, and complex, alliance between a U.S. firm and a Japanese firm, the Japanese firm's senior management regularly reviews the progress of its junior managers in learning from the American firm. Areas covered include the extent to which managers have learned about doing business in the United States.

Learning about Alliances

Learning from alliances is much praised, but learning about alliances can also yield dividends. Assessing alliance performance adds to firms' knowledge base regarding alliances: what they can and cannot achieve; under what circumstances they are most likely to succeed or fail; what managerial actions are most effective in what types of alliances; and so forth.

Investment in quality control having been an issue in its first alliance, AMC made it an explicit consideration in subsequent alliances. Similarly, a major U.S. semiconductor manufacturer, which had determined that its own lax procedures bore some responsibility for its Japanese partner's utilizing alliance-developed technology to compete against it, attended much more closely to internal procedures and day-to-day management in subsequent alliances.

Rethinking Alliance-based Strategy

Ideally, learning about alliances leads to integrated thinking about how alliance-based strategies are best conceived and implemented. Firms' diverse experience with the potential and pitfalls of alliances and strengths and weaknesses of alliance partners positions them to revisit and modify as necessary their original alliance-based strategies. Such a reappraisal led AMC to devise its hub-and-spoke system and pursue different organizational structures for its various alliances. Moreover, the lessons it learned managing its first few alliances led AMC to seek new types of alliance managers. The general manager of AMC remarked, "We realized that we needed managers with a general management mind-set rather than functional orientation as we went along with new alliances."

Another firm discovered that it could further reconfigure the value chain when it assumed responsibility for worldwide purchasing of key raw materials for all its alliances. Centralizing the purchasing function not only was more economical, but also provided another lever through which to exert control over its alliances. Such integrated strategic rethinking of businesses and alliances is far more important to a company pondering an alliance than a listing of do's and don'ts pertaining to partner selection and negotiation.

Indeed, as shown in Figure 4.1, there is a feedback loop in the road map for forging alliances, which is as it should be. As firms learn through their efforts at crafting, structuring, and evaluating alliances, they are able to bring such learning to bear on the way they think about a business—the way it is conducted, configured, and coordinated. This leads to another round of entrepreneurial reexamination of the business. Thus, alliances institutionalize a virtuous cycle of entrepreneurial thinking in firms that employ them.

Ford, for instance, has recognized that it did not have to be as vertically integrated as it used to be, partly as a result of its ability to manage a diverse set of alliances. It sold off its Rouge River steel subsidiary in 1989. At the same time, Ford increased its investment and efforts in new areas of potential future competitive advantage. It now has an active joint research and development alliance with two major aluminum producers, Alcan and Reynolds Metals, to explore the use of lighter materials in cars.

STRATEGIES FOR COPING WITH GLOBAL COMPETITION

We now turn to two examples of global competition and alliance-based strategy that exemplify the myriad issues this chapter has raised. The first is of a company that has creatively configured its various activities into alliances in order to compete in the global marketplace. The second comes from the global earthmoving equipment industry, the scene of one of the major competitive battles of our time, fought over a period of nearly three decades.

Proactive Use of Alliances

Nike, the phenomenally successful athletic, leisure shoe, and apparel company, used alliances proactively, to successfully ride the wave of changing lifestyles, first in the United States and later abroad.[44] From its inception in the early 1960s, long before the term "strategic alliance" became fashionable, Phil Knight, the founder, based his vision of a successful company on leveraging other firms' resources. The entrepreneurial tradition has endured.

In 1963 Knight saw an opportunity, spurred by the pioneering German firm Adidas, to capture rapidly growing demand for athletic shoes. "Adidas shoes were beginning to dominate the U.S. market, and that did not make any sense," commented Knight. "I thought it might be possible to take over the market with low-priced, high-quality, smartly merchandised imports from Japan, as had already happened with cameras and other optical equipment."

Knight entered into a sourcing arrangement with the Japanese firm Onitsuka, the manufacturer of Tiger shoes. He and his ex-athlete partners were to provide designs, and Onitsuka was to manufacture those designs to their specifications. The marketing and other downstream value activities were the responsibility of Nike. The initial strategy took Blue Ribbon Sports (BRS), Nike's original name, to a $2 million market in a matter of a few years. In 1972 BRS faced a crisis. Onitsuka, having seen the company's success, offered to buy out Knight and his partners. Failure to sell, the partners were told, would lead to the termination of the supply contract and consequently the end of the successful franchise. Knight refused the buyout offer, but learned a valuable lesson in alliance management: the need to create fall-back positions and maintain strategic options.

Knight had to find new sources for BRS-designed shoes in a hurry. This time he entered into an agreement with Nissho, a leading Japanese trading company, looking to it to help him develop new sources of supply in the

Far East. To avoid dependence on one supplier, Knight insisted on developing multiple sources. At the same time, he realized that it was important to develop new sources in other parts of Asia, because Japan's competitive advantages of low wages and favorable exchange rate were eroding. Nissho, with its global information network and presence, was extremely helpful in developing such sources. In return, Nissho handled the export of shoes from various suppliers to the United States for a commission.

Nike's big break came in 1972, when the Olympic marathon trials, in which four of the first seven finishers wore Nike shoes, served to promote the new brand name, which was reportedly the product of an employee's dream (the Swoosh logo was created for $35 by a graduate design student). The year 1972 also marked the beginning of Nike's transformation from an importer of Japanese shoes to a shoe manufacturer in its own right; to complement its alliance strategy, Nike opened a small manufacturing facility in the United States near its research facilities.

Over the years, Nike's alliance strategy has become apparent: the company has built a hub-and-spoke system of alliances around it. What is not easily apparent is how systematic the forging and management of an alliance-based strategy at Nike has been in deintegrating and reconfiguring the value chain, creating fall-back positions, structuring alliances, continually assessing alliances, and juggling a shifting network of alliances to its best advantage.

First, Nike took great pains to structure relationships with a network of independent contractors as well as with Nissho. The company's strategy placed a high premium on ensuring maximum flexibility to shift its supply sources to different countries as their competitive positions changed. South Korea, for example, had replaced Japan by the mid-1970s; later the company began to source in other Asian countries, including China. At all times Nike could tap into at least two or three sources. Naturally, the alliance structure Nike chose reflected this strategic imperative. All alliances were arm's-length contracts; Nike held no equity in supplier firms.

To compensate for the lack of direct control through ownership, the company was willing to pay additional "transaction" costs. It assigned expatriates to monitor the performance of the suppliers and to extend technical assistance. Furthermore, it developed expertise in cultivating new suppliers. A senior executive said, "Our people are living there and working with the factories as the product is going down the lines. This is a lot different from accepting or rejecting the product at the end of the line—especially at the end of a three-month pipeline to the United States."

Also telling is Nike's philosophy for dealing with contract manufacturers. "Most of the factories are heavily committed to Nike, and we respect that," stated a Nike senior executive. "We want them to make money, too—though not a windfall, of course—and will do our damnedest, for example, to level production for them. I guess that's part of the company, part of how we want to be perceived. We believe there should be a sense of fairness involved."

The relationship with Nissho was also contractual. Knight understood the unique role a trading company could play: it was excellent in providing local administrative support, arranging for logistics, including ocean transportation and customs clearance, and financing.[45] Nike turned to Nissho for help in these areas. Nissho, with its huge scale and scope, was able to perform these functions much more economically than Nike could itself. In return, Nike paid the company a small commission.

Nike skillfully created fallback positions to minimize the risk associated with relinquishing control over part of the value chain to independent suppliers and a large Japanese trading company. For one thing, it invested a considerable quantity of resources in research and development. "We have the best lab in the business," a company executive announced. "The advanced concept folks, for example, are really out on the edge. They have lots of screwball ideas, but those ideas bring the innovation and the big market."

The company maintained limited manufacturing capabilities close to its research facilities, where advanced technologies were tested and incorporated into the finished products. These facilities served as an important source of learning for executives, who developed an understanding of the manufacturing aspects of the business, including its economics. This understanding proved to be most valuable in negotiating with contract factories and strengthened Nike's hand during negotiations by posing a credible threat to independent suppliers. Nike also afforded future expatriate technicians an opportunity to gain familiarity with manufacturing processes.

In addition, Nike organized an extensive network of retailers to distribute its products. The industry was notorious for unreliable supplies, so Nike decided to use this weakness to its competitive advantage by instituting the Future Sales Program; retailers that ordered five to six months in advance of delivery received a 5% to 7% discount and guaranteed delivery within a two-week period around the target date. While this presented an enormous logistical challenge to Nike, it gave the company important benefits. For one thing, the retailers' advance commitment guaranteed shelf space. It also gave the company valuable information on the market and helped in its production planning. Because almost all the merchandise was manufactured in Asia, the six-month advance notice was particularly helpful for locking in retailers. The strong relationship that Nike enjoyed with retailers also bolstered its negotiating position with foreign suppliers and trading companies, completing a virtuous cycle.

Furthermore, Nike invested a large quantity of resources in building a brand name through active promotion and advertising. One important strategy was to enter into a contract with well-known athletes to endorse its products. Here again, the company sought to leverage its resources by tapping into the assets and capabilities of others, in this case the reputation of famous sports personalities. Nike made a huge investment in building its brand franchise among consumers.

Nike's balance sheet was revealing. The firm owned little in the way of fixed assets. Its working capital was somewhat limited. Suppliers provided the production facilities and working capital needed for manufacturing. The trading company provided logistical services and helped finance the inventory in transit for a commission. Retailers who were eager to benefit from the guarantees for delivery and a discount were willing to accord Nike preferential treatment, which translated into a quick turnover of inventory at the consumer sales level.

Nike saw its main function as acting as the hub of building and maintaining networks of relationships with independent manufacturers, a trading company, distributors, retailers, and well-known athletes. The manner in which Nike divided the margin is quite revealing. It skillfully deintegrated the value chain and kept two critical functions—product development and marketing—for itself. It invested a large sum of money in strengthening its brand. Indeed, one of Nike's core competencies was the ability to manage diverse relationships without relinquishing control over critical functions.

If Nike's is a story of proactive use of alliances, that of Caterpillar and Komatsu is one of the defensive use of alliances in a long-running saga of global competition between two titans, one American and the other Japanese.

Defensive Use of Alliances

Caterpillar Inc., a global competitor par excellence, had dominated the world's earthmoving equipment industry for approximately forty years.[46] The company strategy in the late 1940s and early 1950s was to fully assemble new machines. Caterpillar later established in other countries wholly owned local subsidiaries that assembled machines largely from parts and components sent from its centralized production facilities in the United States. Consequently, the company was able to benefit from scale economies even as it responded to local demand to add value. Moreover, Caterpillar had the foresight to seek affiliates in countries most likely to produce rivals.[47] Finally, it relied on its dealers and technically trained sales force to learn continually from the users of its machines.[48]

Caterpillar's success worldwide derived in large part from its ability to differentiate itself from its rivals in terms of product quality, distribution network, post-sales service, and guaranteed quick delivery of replacement parts. These characteristics, which had enabled the firm to charge premium prices and enjoy superior profitability, relegated all other major players in the industry to the low-price end of the market. As illustrated in Figure 4.3, Caterpillar was alone in the strategic group identified by superior distribution and service network.

Figure 4.3
Strategic Map of Earthmoving Equipment Industry, 1984

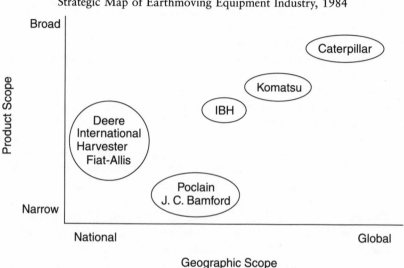

Evolving Global Competition

The arrival in the late 1960s of Komatsu Limited, determined to compete with Caterpillar in the global market, disturbed this cozy arrangement.[49] Komatsu initially specialized in small machines for the Japanese market, later catering to the mining industry and such specialized segments as hazardous waste disposal and underwater operations. Like Caterpillar, it invested in large plants to gain economies of scale at the component level and simultaneously began a massive quality-improvement drive to push its products to the level of Caterpillar.

Komatsu first sought to dominate regional markets in Asia and Australia, then to undersell Caterpillar in its principal foreign markets of Europe and Latin America. Armed with the experience gained in these markets, Komatsu challenged Caterpillar in the United States. Throughout, Komatsu, taking advantage of Japan's low labor costs and favorable exchange rates, substantially underpriced Caterpillar. It matched the prices of Caterpillar's smaller competitors with products comparable to Caterpillar's in quality and service. In essence, Komatsu improved on the value of Caterpillar's offer. The net result of these competitive moves was that between 1979 and 1984, Komatsu's global market share more than doubled, while Caterpillar's dropped by nearly a quarter.

Komatsu's innovative strategy of capitalizing on access to local resources, fully utilizing scope relationships in various segments and geographic markets, effectively rendered the industry's strategic groups obsolete. Caterpillar, which had earlier derided Komatsu's products, was forced to try to match the Japanese firm's price-value combination.

Clearly, as this example illustrates, the rigid dichotomy between the generic strategies of cost leadership and differentiation no longer holds with global competition. Global rivalry permits firms to position their value activities worldwide to gain optimal cost position in each activity and pits firms in different countries with differential access to resources such as low-cost labor against one another. Global competitors are often able to match competitors' sources of differentiation while achieving a low-cost position. (See Figure 4.4.)

Caterpillar faces global reality. In 1981 Caterpillar recorded its highest-ever sales and profits, but in 1984 the company registered its third consecutive loss, to the tune of several hundred million dollars. The competitive battle seemed to be going against Caterpillar in every conceivable way: the company was buffeted by a strong dollar; it endured a serious labor strike; its major markets in the United States and Latin America suffered through a major recession and debt crisis. Caterpillar's strategy of exclusive reliance on in-house design, a high level of vertical integration in parts and components, concentrated manufacturing (mainly in the United States), local assembly, and exclusive dealerships seemed to be working against it. By 1984 Komatsu's worldwide market share was 25%, Caterpillar's 43%, down from 55%.

Figure 4.4
Complex Strategies under Global Competition

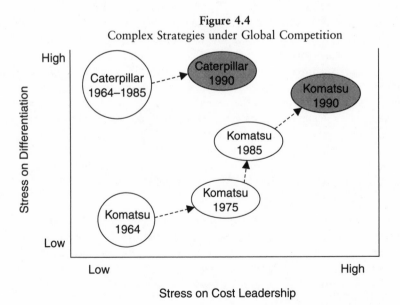

Like those of other beleaguered firms caught by global competition, Caterpillar's initial response was rooted in conventional cost-cutting solutions such as enforced layoffs, plant closures, and demands for wage concessions. The company also sought to source components from other firms, a significant departure from its tradition of vertical integration and in-house manufacture, and a move more tactical than strategic. But with a reported Caterpillar record loss of $428 million in 1984, the stage was set for a more strategic response.

Caterpillar's alliance-based response: 1985–1990. Recognizing that Komatsu had forever transformed the competitive battlefield, George Schaefer remarked in early 1985, when he became Caterpillar CEO, "We have experienced a fundamental change in our business—it will never again be what it was. We have no choice but to respond, and respond vigorously, to the new world in which we find ourselves." Caterpillar responded with alliances, in-house affiliates, and the constituent elements of the reactions outlined earlier.

Even before he took over as CEO, Schaefer, with the support of outgoing CEO Lee Morgan, sought to force Caterpillar managers to step back from their frenetic cost cutting in order to analyze the firm's strategic situation and develop plans to ensure its long-term viability. He made it clear that managers participating in what he called the Business Strategy Conference (BSC) should take no short-term action that might compromise long-term success. BSC participants—all Caterpillar senior managers—were told that "nothing [was] sacred." The BSC's multifunctional teams analyzed various aspects of Caterpillar's social, political, and economic environment, the firm's capabilities, limitations, and new technologies, and the competitive situation. From this strategic reassessment of Caterpillar's businesses and opportunities came a set of thirteen major initiatives that provided the blueprint for a new strategic thrust—to make Caterpillar the lowest-cost, highest-quality producer in the industry. Differentiation through marketing and service excellence was to be maintained. In other words, Caterpillar would mount a challenge in the new strategic group Komatsu had created.

Of the thirteen BSC initiatives, only ten were made public, the other three being deemed proprietary. A number of the publicized elements called for extensive use of strategic alliances, specifically,

- to identify industries and items that might yield *leveraging opportunities;*
- to explore marketing and distribution capabilities through *product branding;*
- to explore in the automated material-handling sector the possibility of entering into *merchandising agreements*, including branding, with one or more manufacturers;

- to aggressively pursue *external funding* for research and development projects that might enhance the company's long-term technical and technological prospects;
- to seek related *external opportunities* for organizing projects and gaining exposure to new developments.

In essence, Caterpillar sought to reduce risk and gain exposure in new industries and technologies through the use of strategic alliances in marketing, product sourcing (in addition to the component sourcing that was already part of its strategy), R&D, and new business ventures. The company's old mantra of self-reliance was to be stilled by its recognition of the new imperative of reliance on the resources of other firms.

The list of strategic initiatives suggests the line of reasoning that characterized Caterpillar's pursuit of an alliance-based strategy. The company undertook a systematic assessment of its value chain to see how it could be deintegrated and reconfigured to permit the leveraging of other firms' resources while maintaining fall-back positions and developing new strategic options.

Caterpillar decided, for example, to deintegrate manufacturing so as to be able to outsource parts and components. Its new policy of "shopping the world" was a major departure from its past practice of vertical integration. The company's executive vice president for manufacturing stated that the philosophy had shifted to buying. "From self-manufacturing almost two-thirds of our parts, we are moving to making only 20%—the vital few we call them—while sourcing the remaining 80%—the trivial many—from least-cost suppliers so long as they maintain Caterpillar's quality standards."

Caterpillar similarly decided that its marketing expertise would be better exploited if it sourced final products, as opposed to parts and components, from other firms and sold them under its own name through its branding program. The company subsequently signed supply agreements with Daewoo of Korea and Kaldnes of Norway (for lift trucks), Eder of West Germany (for small, track-type excavators), CMI Corporation of Oklahoma (for paving machinery), DJB Engineering of England (for articulated dump trucks), and Tanguay Industries of Canada (for forestry equipment).

Mindful of the need to maintain sound fall-back positions, Caterpillar retained design responsibility for many of its sourced products. This permitted the company to (1) retain and further develop in-house design capabilities, (2) ensure control over quality standards so as not to compromise its core strategy, and (3) keep an upper hand vis-à-vis its alliance partners. Finally, should it ever face supply problems, Caterpillar would be able to turn quickly to other sources.

The success of its sourcing relationships led Caterpillar to further develop its strategic options by transforming its thirty-year-old joint venture with Mitsubishi Heavy Industries of Japan. After careful and long negotiations with Mitsubishi, Caterpillar concluded an agreement to create in Japan a Hydraulic Excavator Design Center to develop products for both firms. Forty Caterpillar engineers joined 240 Mitsubishi engineers at the center. Caterpillar retained rights to manufacture the resulting products in any of its plants, but product control clearly rested with Mitsubishi.

To further add to its core competence in manufacturing and product design, Caterpillar initiated a major reengineering effort, called the Plan with a Future, which involved massive investments in plant automation, worker retraining, and product redesign. Again, this is an example of a well-thought-out and integrated alliance strategy relying on increased investment in needed areas, not "hollowing" out the corporation.

Caterpillar has become a formidable and nimble competitor since 1985. By 1990, it had regained its dominant position in the global earthmoving equipment industry with a greater than 50% market share. So vigorous was Caterpillar's return from the brink that Komatsu is currently contemplating radical changes in its strategy.

To a considerable extent, Caterpillar's strategic alliances have been at the heart of its renaissance, permitting the firm to refocus its efforts in the areas in which it most needed to concentrate its resources and reformulate its global strategy to compete effectively with archrival Komatsu. So crucial have alliances been in its rejuvenation that Caterpillar's futuristic mission statement for the year 2000 envisions a major role for coalitions to support initiatives in core businesses and possible new businesses.

Komatsu takes to alliances. Perhaps nothing exemplifies the power of and need for alliances as Komatsu's response to Caterpillar's new strategy. Its 1989 annual report indicated that Komatsu planned to exploit its competitive strengths in its versatile technological base and its tradition of quality first through a combination of internal development, selective acquisitions, and alliances. The stage was set for an alliance-based strategy at Komatsu, too.

Komatsu's first moves were largely either fifty-fifty joint ventures or acquisitions. In late 1988, Komatsu and Dresser Industries of USA combined their Western Hemisphere construction equipment operations in a joint venture in which each held 50% ownership; in 1989 Komatsu acquired 64% of the shares of Hanomag AG, a West German maker of earthmoving equipment.

Further alliances followed in 1992. First, Komatsu purchased a minority equity position in FAI s.p.a., an Italian producer of backhoe loaders, as part of a sourcing alliance. It then concluded an exclusive agreement to import and market FAI's four-wheel-drive backhoe loaders under the Komatsu name in Japan and the Far East. Next, it formed another minority joint venture with Olivlin AS of Norway to produce articulated dump trucks. Again,

Komatsu planned to sell the product under its name. Later in the same year, Komatsu entered into a sourcing alliance with Timberjack of Canada for logging machinery.

Komatsu also seemed to be rethinking the way it configured its value chain in its core activities. It entered into a supply agreement with Korea's Samsung Shipbuilding & Heavy Industries for case steel parts, thus signaling a move away from its previous stance of vertical integration. Indeed, Komatsu announced that it had set a goal to increase the level of offshore material purchases by its Japanese plants to 20 billion yen by the end of fiscal 1992.

Alliances were also to be part of Komatsu's strategy in its related technology acquisition moves. Komatsu expanded its injection molding machinery offerings via an alliance with Husky Injection Molding Systems of Canada. The alliance included a 26% equity participation by Komatsu, technology-sharing agreements, and establishment of a Japanese subsidiary by Husky.[50] The company formed a Japanese joint venture with Cybernation Cutting Systems of the United States for producing turnkey cutting systems for fabrication of HVAC ducting and architectural sign components. It formed another alliance in the area of high-speed, high-precision, image-processing vision systems for automated inspection of integrated circuits with Cognex Corporation of the United States. The alliance was largely contractual, based on OEM and marketing agreements.

Thus, the circle is complete. In just over a decade, the global competition between Caterpillar and Komatsu has moved from being a battle between two giants, largely self-contained entities depending on internal development and an internal network of international subsidiaries, to one between two federations of alliances girdling the globe. Such is the allure of strategic alliances in an age of global competition.

Conclusion

Global competition, by introducing the need to transfer some value activities to other firms through contractual arrangements, provides the raison d'être for a global division of labor achieved through the selective deintegration of activities. Global competitors, particularly firms that are not multinational in scope, cannot hope to gain all the requisite competitive advantages under one roof. Also implicit in deintegration is the option of redirecting investments that would otherwise have gone to manufacturing, as for updating plants. Such investments can go to areas such as R&D and product innovation, where they are more likely to yield sustainable competitive advantages.

Alliances are closely linked to the competitive strategies of firms that must compete in the global marketplace. Indeed, strategic alliances have become a way of life for some firms and have even transformed entire

industries. The factory-automation industry is a maze of intersecting alliances, and in biotechnology they have become the rule rather than the exception. In the computer industry, too, alliances of every kind have come to proliferate in the last several years.

If alliances are such a powerful competitive weapon and if so many corporations have already begun to use them extensively, why do academics and managers continue to be skeptical of their usefulness? The answer lies in the complexity of the task of managing them. Alliances pose unique management challenges, calling for the development of new skills by managers. Moreover, they call for a variety of related organizational innovations. It is to these issues that we turn next.

PART III

MANAGING STRATEGIC ALLIANCES

CHAPTER 5

Managing Alliances: Challenges and Tasks

Even as they are becoming the sine qua non for the emerging world of global competition, global strategies, and global firms, alliances continue to evoke pessimism among business and academic writers. An extensive study of interfirm links led a business school professor in Europe, a region that has seen explosive growth in the use of business alliances in the last decade, to conclude that "strategic alliances are doomed."[1] Respected Harvard Business School professor Michael Porter has pushed the logic of inevitable doom further, arguing that alliances are mere "transitional devices rather than stable arrangements" and hence "destined to fail."[2]

So critical is Porter of alliances that his arguments are worth airing in detail. "Alliances," he contends, "are rarely a solution [to the problem of seeking the home-based advantages of another nation]" because "they always involve significant costs in terms of coordination, reconciling goals with an independent entity, creating a competitor, and giving up profits." Porter concludes that "alliances tend to ensure mediocrity, not create world leadership . . . and *deter [a] firm's own efforts at upgrading*" and that "ultimately, the alliance partner may have to be acquired [or acquire its partner] to yield a sustainable international position [emphasis added]." Do such criticisms doom strategic alliances as a managerial instrument?[3]

Certainly not. We counter that alliances are neither mere "transitional devices . . . destined to fail" nor do they "deter" an alliance-seeking firm's "own efforts at upgrading" its core competencies, but that, to the contrary, alliances enable firms to focus on and invest in a few selected core competencies, leverage the competencies of other firms, and thereby grow into formidable global competitors. That was the thrust of our arguments in the previous chapters.

Why then the pervasive pessimism on alliances? We believe that there are two main reasons why alliances are seen as likely to fail. The first has to do with misinterpretation of observed facts and the second with perceived complexity of managing alliances. Many researchers read press announcements on dissolution of alliances and interpret these as "failures." From there, to infer that all alliances are likely to fail is but a short step. But what is an alliance failure? The NUMMI alliance between General Motors (GM) and Toyota is set to expire in the early 1990s. If the expiration occurs as scheduled, it says nothing about the success or failure of the alliance. In another instance, if an alliance has accomplished its main objectives and the partners decide to go their own way, it hardly connotes failure. In the case of one Corning alliance, the company decided to sell its share of the venture to the partner firm because Corning top management had concluded that the business no longer fit with its strategy. Again, this could scarcely be construed as the failure of the alliance.[4]

Other observers refer to "the sheer complexity of alliances" and the extreme difficulty of controlling and coordinating multidimensional perspectives and dispersed assets across corporate boundaries.[5] Implicit in this criticism is the suggestion that alliances should be avoided because they are difficult to manage.[6] But should managers, on the basis of the difficulty of managing alliances, forswear the use of a potentially powerful competitive weapon? We say no.

The alternative to strategic alliances, insistence on organizational self-sufficiency, reinforces an unfortunate mind-set that too often prevails among managers: if anything is worth doing, it is worth doing themselves. In an increasingly interdependent world laden with opportunity, this mind-set is equivalent to seeking strategic autarky at the firm level.[7] Managers should not be cowed by the complexity of managing alliances but rather strive to recognize their key challenges and find novel, imaginative ways to meet them.[8] Understanding alliances is the first step toward designing administrative mechanisms and organizational responses to deal with them.

Two Examples of Alliance Management

Examples are perhaps the best way to illustrate the intricacy of alliance management.[9] Consider, for example, the case of a leading U.S. manufacturer of industrial products that entered into a sourcing arrangement with a major Korean company. Strategically the alliance was well thought out. The U.S. firm's products, particularly at the price-sensitive low end, had for some time been under serious attack by Asian rivals. Management had logically decided to meet this competitive threat by sourcing some of its low-end products. The Korean company emerged as the partner of choice after much investigation and analysis.

The alliance made sense for the Korean company as well, permitting it to expand exports to the United States without incurring costly and uncertain investments in distribution and marketing. The partners agreed on what was perceived to be a reasonable sharing of value activities; the U.S. firm was to contribute engineering and design know-how, the Korean firm to provide manufacturing support, making available necessary production capacity and developing process technology as needed. The partners also agreed to develop jointly new product models that could be marketed in both the United States and Korea under their respective brand names.

Things began to go awry shortly after the agreement was signed. The Korean company, after appointing a senior executive to manage the alliance interface, was chagrined to learn that its U.S. partner had relegated the task to a midlevel manager in its purchasing department. Moreover, the Korean firm soon discovered that its partner frequently changed at the last minute the quantity and features of the products to be supplied. Finally, the Korean managers found that the market and technical information they considered vital to guiding their manufacturing plans, investments, and schedules was not forthcoming from their U.S. counterparts.

American managers, on the other hand, complained that the Koreans required too much hand-holding.[10] "Our partners came to the table expecting us to turn over solutions for their manufacturing problems on a platter." Some U.S. managers considered their Korean counterparts overly aggressive in seeking sensitive technological and market information and the Korean firm insufficiently flexible to meet changes in the marketplace quickly. Finally, in the post–sales service area, the U.S. company was called upon to solve problems that had not been anticipated when the alliance was formed.

The relationship was on the verge of collapse when the general manager of the U.S. company became aware of the situation. He responded quickly, assigning to the alliance a well-respected senior executive with considerable international experience. The new manager initiated a series of actions intended to alleviate problems with the relationship and turn the situation around. He started with day-to-day activities. "Our problem, I felt," he recalled, "was that the operational guys in the two firms did not trust each other. So my first task was to build trust. To build trust, you need to establish a record of successful collaboration, and for that we needed to begin with some mundane day-to-day tasks."

This U.S. manager urged his marketing managers to provide their Korean counterparts as much advance notice as possible when placing orders and to avoid last-minute changes in product quantities and features. He also sent several teams of managers and engineers to Korea to assess the partner plant's operations, capabilities, and limitations, and he invited managers of the Korean firm to visit and get to know their U.S. counterparts. "You would be surprised to know how much planning went into each of our visits," he said. "I asked my people to make sure that every meeting was carefully arranged, agendas systematically thought through, and even questions thoroughly anticipated."

The new alliance manager simultaneously addressed internal issues, namely, the managers' and engineers' fear that the Koreans were out to steal the company's technical know-how, and the problems of post–sales service for the sourced products. He determined that both were attributable to inadequate communication between top and middle management and the lower echelons. He explained:

> The engineering and manufacturing groups were bitter about the sourcing decision in the first place. On top of that, they were put off by what they thought was an overly aggressive attitude on the part of our partner to acquire our technology. They were all quite critical of our top management for pursuing what they thought was an expedient, short-term solution rather than dealing with basic problems. They were quite fearful that this was just the first step toward mass migration of everything—technical know-how, engineering and design knowledge, and accumulated process technology information—abroad.
>
> The problem with the sales and service people was more complicated. They, too, felt that the Korean company was just using the alliance as a Trojan horse to get knowledge from us to develop themselves as a competitor. They were afraid that sharing more information on after-sales problems with the Koreans would only accelerate the migration of such knowledge.[11] At the same time, the sales and service people did not like selling the sourced products. After all, until now we were the acknowledged technological leader in the field. So they were skeptical of the quality and performance of the sourced products. The problem was compounded by the fact that, in the initial stages, the product experienced minor quality problems. The after-sales complaints increased. That, in turn, reinforced the service people's prior belief that the quality of sourced products would be poor. Obviously our service costs went up. The marketing people started yelling.

Much of the difficulty, the manager soon realized, was due to the fact that no one had told all concerned how everything fitted together.

> Everyone sort of assumed that the strategic reasoning behind the alliance would be known to all the relevant people in the organization. It wasn't so. In the first place, even among the senior managers, only a few people understood the entire game plan. It wasn't right to blithely assume that the strategic rationale for the alliance would percolate downward to all the relevant people. It didn't. And then,

there was the little problem of figuring out who the relevant people were. It was not just the middle managers. If the sourcing alliance was to succeed, the men in the trenches—the design engineers, the manufacturing people, the service personnel—all needed to know how the alliance was supposed to work and what they needed to do to make it all happen.

The alliance manager spent several weeks communicating with the rank and file of the organization, assuring teams of managers, engineers, supervisors, and even floor-level workers that the company had no intention of relinquishing its technological and market leadership position. He explained how the firm, by taking advantage of complementary skills possessed by its Korean partner, would be able to focus on higher value-adding activities, provided, he cautioned, that all worked together to manage the cooperation-competition tension that existed in the sourcing arrangement.

"It took a while, but eventually I did get through to them all," he remarked. "In fact, once they understood the strategic implications, they became most enthusiastic. You see, many of their concerns, especially about creating a competitor, were legitimate. When we validated their doubts and explained the whole picture to them, it was easy to get the problems resolved."

The manager was also able to forge a good personal working relationship with his Korean counterpart.

Initially, I just put it down to my efforts to improve the communication and cooperation between the two firms. Only later did I learn that the Korean manager was more comfortable dealing with me than with my predecessor. My status in the company as a senior manager with ready access to top management appeared to have made a lot of difference to the Koreans. Apparently, it also signaled to them that our company valued the alliance.

Subsequently the two companies stepped up their collaboration, branching into other areas as well.

This alliance went through two major phases—near disaster through inattention to details and rescue through conscious relationship management.

The partners in another alliance took an active approach to management from the outset, leading to an extremely satisfactory outcome for both partners. A major U.S. high-tech firm established an association with a leading European company for purposes of collaborating on basic research in vital components. Even as negotiations proceeded, senior managers on both sides, agreeing that much was at stake, reasoned that it was necessary to plan carefully for the management of the alliance.

Both firms' managements perceived the project to be of immense strategic importance, expected it to last several years, and recognized that the tasks to be performed were complicated and would involve continuous and mutual exchange of information. Commercialization of the product was to be independent of the alliance; that is, once the technology was developed, the firms were to compete independently in the market for final products. Finally, anticipating future opportunities for collaboration, the managements were keen to make their first project a success.

Attention to sound management led to a number of decisions. First, at the contractual level the alliance was to be cooperative and involve no equity participation. This eliminated the need to create a new organization with the attendant staffing, control, and resource-allocation problems. Each firm was to expend the resources necessary to achieve the objectives set out in the agreement and be accountable for its share of the work.

The agreement itself was carefully structured around several specific projects. Some were to be undertaken independently, with the understanding that the partners would have access to the findings; some were to be pursued sequentially, with one firm responsible for the first, the other for the second; and some were to be conducted jointly. This approach promoted a mutually acceptable and equitable sharing of work and permitted the firms to make credible contributions to the alliance's success.[12]

Major organizational innovations designed to ensure success followed. Parallel management structures were implemented to commit both organizations firmly to the alliance. Each company agreed to designate a senior executive, preferably one with international exposure and considerable experience managing large-scale projects, as a "point man" or "interface executive." Each was to lead a small team charged with similar responsibilities, so that each team member had a counterpart in the other firm's organization. These teams were to serve as the key information-processing and management centers for the alliance. As a way of managing the competition-versus-cooperation tension in the relationship, all communications between the firms were to flow through these offices. By restricting information access, the firms hoped to preclude future charges of one's gaining at the expense of the other.

Each firm also agreed to establish two tiers of permanent committees, one within the research and development organization, the other at the corporate level. The R&D committee was to draw its members from senior research staff and include, by design, a few individuals not closely associated with the project. The R&D committees were to be chaired by the respective senior executives in charge of R&D, with the alliance-interface executives serving as ex officio members. The corporate-level committee was comprised of the heads of various functional groups, including R&D, finance, engineering, and marketing, as well as the heads of the key business units that would be the primary users of the technology to be developed.

The R&D committee met regularly to monitor the progress of the projects and ensure that they received sufficient resources and management attention. The committee reviewed with the alliance manager requests for and flows of information between the partner firms and provided advice and counsel, particularly in technical areas. Termed "internal watchdog and facilitator" by one of its members, the committee also met quarterly with its counterpart in the partner firm to review progress on the various projects and deal with operating and policy issues.

The principal responsibility of the corporate-level committee was to ensure that the alliance attained its strategic goals. The committee met biannually to keep the heads of key functions and business areas abreast of progress on various projects. This ensured continued support and cooperation on the part of those who would be most involved in implementing and commercializing the technology. The alliance manager and head of R&D were invited to make presentations to this committee. The partners' corporate-level committees met annually to facilitate communication and coordinate between the firms. The relationship proved quite successful, yielding some very positive early results. Indeed, the firms subsequently explored possibilities for broadening their collaboration.

Both these histories suggest that active alliance management is a prerequisite to success, a point missed initially by the management of the U.S. firm in the first case. Alliance management need not be left to the vagaries of trial and error; as the second case demonstrates, it can and should be actively planned and executed.

The value of an alliance is the product of the joint efforts of the partners. "When a firm enters into a strategic alliance, it must realize that it has nothing more than a contract on a piece of paper," remarked one executive. "It is up to the partners to convert the agreement into a productive relationship." That transformation is the challenge of alliance management.

The Alliance-management Challenge

Interfirm collaborations are plagued by ambiguities in relationships; tensions associated with the need to balance cooperation and competition; managerial mind-sets unacquainted with, and often suspicious of, interorganizational links; myriad details that need to be managed; and lack of recognition of the complex linkages among the strategies, structures, and systems of both the participating firms and the alliance. We examine each of these considerations in turn.

Ambiguities in alliance relationships. Alliance partners are independent firms with their own agendas. Often they are rivals to boot. Firms enter into alliances with different motives, and one can never be entirely certain of another's true incentives for collaborating. The ambiguous nature of the alliance relationship is further complicated by the fact that different managers within the same firm may bring different expectations and commitments to their task.

Even the legal documents that establish an alliance cannot be complete and exhaustive. "No one can write an agreement that completely specifies every possible contingency," observed one lawyer experienced in writing alliance contracts. A contract can outline only broad themes of cooperation. "It is up to the managers to flesh out the details in their day-to-day working with their counterparts in the partner firm." Naturally, this leaves managers with a great deal of uncertainty.

A third element of ambiguity in alliance relationships is part of managerial life. Alliances are typically conceived and negotiated at the higher levels of an organization and their day-to-day management left to lower-level managers and supervisors, "the troops in the trenches," as one manager put it. Lower-level managers and supervisors may be called upon to field sensitive questions on short notice without recourse to their superiors. One lower-level manager of a sourcing alliance, for example, on a routine visit to his firm's Japanese partner, was shown a new product and asked what he thought its probability of success might be in the U.S. market and whether his own firm might be interested in jointly exploiting it. The manager's quandary? He knew that his own firm had developed and was on the verge of introducing a similar product. To say nothing might later be misconstrued by the partner, but neither could he disclose the information.

Ambiguity is inherent, too, in the evolving nature of relationships. Interfirm links, like human relationships, do not always evolve linearly or in a positive direction. Indeed, many are planned tentatively with the understanding that deeper involvement will reflect the relative comfort levels achieved by the relationship. And even this gauge can be misleading, as one U.S. firm discovered. Its managers having come to trust their counterparts in the Taiwanese partner firm, the U.S. firm increased reliance on its associate for the manufacture of a number of key products. The U.S. firm's managers subsequently learned that the Taiwanese were moving to exploit commercially, and in competition with the Americans, the energy-saving technology the latter had been developing for several years. Failure to monitor the evolution of the alliance and adjust its management practices accordingly cost the U.S. company dearly.[13]

Cooperation versus competition. Managerial ambiguity in alliances is further exacerbated by what we earlier referred to as the cooperation-versus-competition tension that characterizes many interfirm links.[14] Even the most successful alliances exhibit this tension, as evidenced by Ford and Mazda, which reportedly have been unable to come to an agreement for extending their collaboration into Europe even after much discussion. Ford's fear of Mazda as a potential competitor in the already highly competitive European market is believed to be a major reason for the slow progress. Referring to an opportunity to collaborate on a specific model, a Ford executive remarked, "There may be a spillover benefit in future products, but there is a downside: we are assisting a competitor to get into a market in much more depth than they would on their own."[15]

Striving to make an alliance successful while guarding against one's gaining disproportionately from the relationship is a difficult balance to achieve. As one manager involved in a complex link with a major competitor put it, "There is such a thing as too successful a cooperation, especially if the other guy walks away with your store." What makes this balancing act so difficult is the need to develop a trusting relationship with the partner organization. "Obviously, it is important to analyze why your partner is interested in forming an alliance with you and to be aware of motives other than just helping the alliance to succeed in its mission," said the same manager. "Once you begin to suspect the partner's motives, there is no end to it. Too much suspicion can immobilize the entire relationship."

Striking a balance between trusting one's partner and ensuring that one's strategic interests and assets are not compromised is particularly difficult across multiple alliances and over time.[16] Commented an alliance manager:

> We are involved in half a dozen alliances. Some are with rivals and some are not. Our plans call for different levels of information flows to different alliances. Sometimes I have meetings with different managers from partner firms. It is so difficult to keep in mind what can be or cannot be disclosed to different partners. The issue is not confined to me. At different levels of this organization we have people interacting with other firms. I have to make sure that every one of my people is consistent. One slip could cause damage to the firm or vitiate the cooperative environment.

Managerial mind-sets. Few U.S. managers are prepared to perform the balancing acts dictated by alliance management. The supervisory culture and systems of Western corporations have gone to great lengths to eliminate situations that would present opportunities to master the requisite skills. Therefore the intrinsic difficulty of the alliance management task is compounded by managers' lack of experience with it.

Almost invariably, today's multinational corporations, during their expansion phase through the end of the 1960s, maintained a strict policy of establishing only wholly owned subsidiaries. A General Motors policy statement for 1966, for example, declared that "unified ownership for coordinated policy control of all operations throughout the world is essential for [GM's] effective performance as a worldwide corporation."[17] Clearly, sharing control through ambiguous links in joint ventures was not deemed a good idea.

This environment has affected managers in two ways. One, it has nurtured a mind-set that holds that any situation in which a firm is not in unambiguous control is bad. Imbuing especially the lower echelons, where the fate of alliances is ultimately decided, with a lack of faith in the efficacy of alliances is hardly a recipe for successful management. Alliances entrusted to individuals who do not believe they can succeed clearly begin with a handicap.

Two, managers are hindered by their organizations' managerial systems and processes. Few perceive the hierarchical bias built into these procedures that militates against alliances. Besides, many middle-level managers are in no position to effect changes that might render the systems more suited to alliance management. Despair is a ready companion to the manager who must struggle to make an alliance work against ingrained prejudices and programs stacked against its success.

The tyranny of details. Even managers who overcome their habits of mind are seldom prepared for what one manager referred to as the tyranny of details inherent in managing an alliance. Management begins only with the agreement that establishes an alliance. "Getting the job done" involves close attention to a myriad of details, many of which are not obvious at the outset, a discovery that often comes as an unwelcome surprise to constitute a source of unending frustration for many managers. That the success of an alliance relies on attention to these details is a truth many of them literally learn on the job.

Consider the following episode from an alliance that called for a U.S. firm to train a number of its Taiwanese partner's employees. This seemingly simple task was not being accomplished several weeks into the alliance, leading the Taiwanese firm to complain bitterly of inadequate effort by its U.S. partner. A frustrated U.S. manager eventually discovered that no one had told the floor-level supervisors responsible for the training about the program!

Even with that omission corrected, the problem persisted. Several more weeks passed before managers realized that the trainers were not taking the task of instructing the visitors seriously, largely because the company's incentive system did not provide for the loss of production that activity incurred. By the time the entire affair was resolved, the alliance schedule had slipped considerably.

Attention to details applied equally to dealings with partners. After the alliance described above had sorted out its training problems and sourcing of products from Taiwan had begun, the U.S. firm's logistics group decided to institute, without telling its Taiwanese partners, a new distribution network that called for a change in the destination. Not surprisingly, this omission wreaked havoc with the supply flow.

Complex systemic issues. As the foregoing examples demonstrate, alliance management involves consideration of complex systemic issues associated with interrelationships among strategy, structure, systems, and staff in the participating organizations. Only recently have researchers and managers come to recognize such links.[18] Hence, some alliances' interrelationships are barely understood, let alone well documented and analyzed. The problems for alliance management range from lack of recognition to active resistance to the implications of these linkages. Consider the following examples.

Recall first the alliance cited earlier in this chapter between the U.S. industrial products manufacturer and the Korean firm that was its source. The message sent by appointing the purchasing manager to be alliance manager was that the relationship was to be a simple buy-sell arrangement. The purchasing manager, for his part, did not see a connection between the sourcing alliance and the firm's long-term strategy, leading him to treat the alliance as a simple purchasing arrangement. Uninformed about the requirements for the cooperation, the R&D and manufacturing managers strove to safeguard the firm's technological expertise and manufacturing know-how. (In another instance, manufacturing supervisors, worried that an alliance was but a prelude to shifting the entire manufacturing function offshore, tried to undermine the relationship through bureaucratic sabotage, evidence that any alliance can be stalled by low-intensity guerrilla warfare deep in the interstices of an organization.)

The service and distribution problems that plagued the alliance between the U.S. and Korean firms resulted from inattention to the need for interfunctional coordination. When a firm's value chain is disaggregated and the value activities transferred in whole or part to another firm, interfunctional coordination, previously internal and taken for granted, crosses organizational boundaries and must be expressly considered. Interorganizational interfunctional coordination is possible with the right mix of systems and policies.

In the case of the collaborative R&D alliance described earlier, both the U.S. high-tech firm and its European partner recognized that the support and coordination of related functional and business areas were crucial to the arrangement's success; consequently its management structure included from its inception key executives from relevant groups.[19]

Related to the problem of systemic issues is the problem of reconciling the systemwide practices of two parent firms. As we indicated above, such systems can create problems of their own, as occurred in the case of training workers from another firm. Indeed, the managerial systems in most firms are instituted not with alliances, but with hierarchical (wholly owned) operations in mind. The incentive systems, for instance, may be structured in such a way that a front-line supervisor may be more motivated to give priority to routine tasks than to fulfill the firm's obligations under an alliance agreement. Here again, attention to system issues is the key to success.

International alliances are subject to difficulties arising from differences not only in corporate but also in national cultures.[20] "We all know how distance, language, and cultural differences can often lead to serious misunderstandings, even between corporate headquarters and a wholly owned subsidiary with a long history of ongoing relationships," said a senior manager of an American firm involved in a number of international alliances. "You can imagine how the same limitations can compound the difficulties in an alliance in which there is little familiarity and trust to begin with. Some of the ugly stereotypes of prejudice we have about certain nationalities can surface quickly if you are not careful and conscious of it."

Managing the interface with an alliance partner is particularly difficult in multinational companies with multiple overseas subsidiaries and diversified firms with alliances in more than one division. Many alliances require the firms to interact with more than one subsidiary or division. A firm exposed to information normally scattered throughout its partner's organization is in a position to piece it together in a way that may yield competitive advantage.

Recall IBM's 1980s alliances with Intel, Microsoft, and Epson. They required IBM's partners to interact with IBM's semiconductor, microprocessor, application systems, and computer peripherals divisions, research laboratories, and presumably, its overseas subsidiaries and research facilities (see Figure 5.1). This arrangement afforded the partners unprecedented exposure to information IBM normally would not have made available to any outside firm. Collated and analyzed, that information might have given IBM's partners a significant edge in the personal computer marketplace.[21]

The challenge posed by multiple interfaces is enormous. They may be essential to the success of an alliance, yet transform an organization into a sieve through which information leaks uncontrollably. One need not attribute unsporting motives to a partner to make a case for carefully managing such interfaces.

The network problem. Related to the challenge of managing systemwide ramifications, but important in its own right, is the problem posed by a network of alliances. As we saw in Chapter 2, Ford and Motorola, among other firms, are building networks of alliances, many involving international partners. Creating and managing such networks, particularly as they expand, poses additional challenges. One problem is that networks tend to occur by happenstance rather than by planning, design, and execution with forethought. A firm enters into an alliance for a specific purpose and, as it gains experience forging and managing that alliance, moves on to establish other

Figure 5.1
IBM's Groups and IBM's Alliances—Contact Points

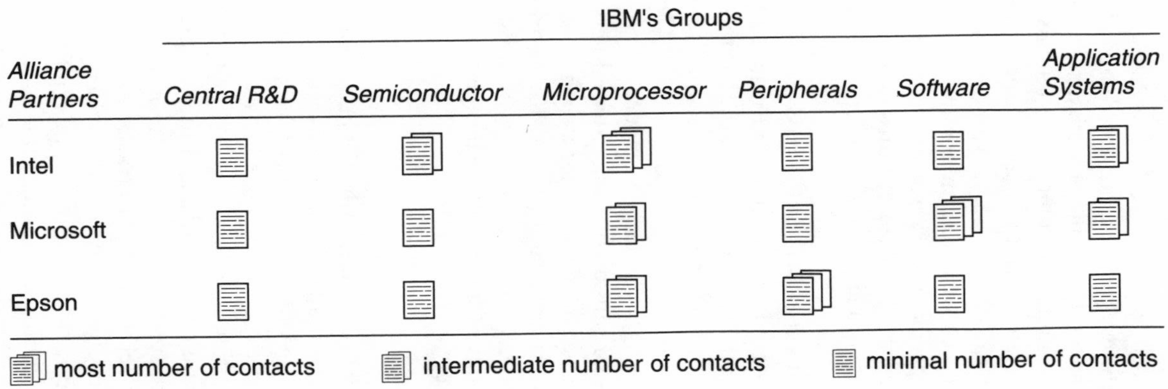

interfirm relationships. Soon the firm is faced with the daunting task of managing not a single alliance, but a network of alliances.

Among alliances that comprise such networks-by-accident are likely to be some that are mutually compatible, but also some that are not. For example, one high-tech firm that established over a period of just a few years a dozen or so alliances, some with companies that actively competed with one another, encountered an administrative nightmare as it tried to ensure that each partner's work was shielded from the other alliances. Moreover, it discovered when it tried to transfer employees among divisions that their involvement in one alliance or another became a bone of contention with its partners.

A network of alliances can also make it difficult to maintain a coherent strategic intent overall, inasmuch as individual alliances are likely to entail compromises in a firm's various strategic objectives. The more alliances, the more compromises, and the more diluted a firm's strategic objectives are likely to be.

Finally, there is the challenge of managing an interface between a firm's internal network of subsidiaries and external network of international alliances. Most multinational companies face this challenge. Managing a multiplicity of interfaces between an internal network of subsidiaries and one alliance is difficult, between a network of subsidiaries and a network of alliances formidable. Adding multiple business divisions and overseas subsidiaries compounds the challenge.

Uniqueness of the challenge. Alliance management poses a distinct set of challenges that sets it apart from supervising either hierarchical subsidiary relationships or arm's-length buyer-seller relationships.[22] Subsidiary management, absent problems of ambiguous links and the tension between cooperation and competition, must however contend with problems of managerial mind-sets, the tyranny of details, and the complexity of systemwide links.

Arm's-length supplier management, on the other hand, relies on fairly detailed, mostly self-fulfilling contracts, the performance of which rarely impinges on or is affected by internal system and process issues. But such relationships are often plagued by ambiguities and the need to manage tension between cooperation and competition.[23]

Figure 5.2 depicts the relationship between a firm and several layers of its interfirm links. At the core are the links, largely cooperative and clearly defined, between the firm and its subsidiaries and other business units. The outer layer comprises arm's-length relationships often characterized by competitive aspects. Between the two lie strategic alliances, which combine both cooperative and competitive elements.[24] It is this combination of the problems of subsidiary and arm's-length relationship management that makes alliance management uniquely difficult.

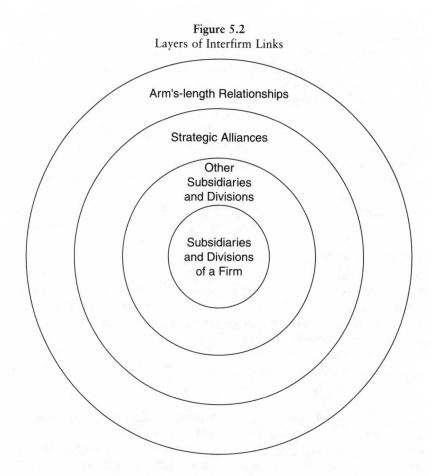

Figure 5.2
Layers of Interfirm Links

Arm's-length Relationships

Strategic Alliances

Other
Subsidiaries
and Divisions

Subsidiaries
and Divisions
of a Firm

Key Tasks in Alliance Management

Alliance management involves a clear and strategic understanding of (1) the nature, scope, importance, and likely evolutionary path of an alliance, (2) aspects related to the protection and augmentation of a firm's core competencies, (3) the need to effect a shift in the mind-set of the managers designated to deal with the alliance, (4) resource requirements, (5) the need to ensure interfunctional coordination, and (6) the potential for a network of alliances to evolve and the extraordinary complexity of coordinating the same. We elaborate on each of these tasks briefly.

Widespread understanding of an alliance. Necessary as it may seem to be, a clear and widespread understanding of the nature, scope, and likely evolutionary path of an alliance is often absent among managers. Such awareness on the part of one or two senior managers will not do; it must pervade all levels of an organization.

The division manager of a U.S. firm who negotiated a sourcing alliance with a Japanese firm intended that the agreement be limited in scope, signing a contract that stipulated that only basic product designs and just the needed process technology were to be transferred to the partner. The relationship had an inherent element of competition in that the partner was not prohibited from selling its own brand of the basic product, leading the division manager to advise his immediate subordinates that the partner's managers were not to have access to the firm's R&D lab. Nor were any new product-development ideas or marketing plans to be shared with the partner.

A significant change in management came on the heels of the forging of the alliance, with the division manager and a few of his key subordinates going to another division. Shortly after the new manager took over, two key executives left the firm. The new management team did not take time to read the contract or talk with the outgoing manager about the alliance. Division engineers were not told explicitly what was to be withheld from the other firm's engineers. Marketing managers were not aware that certain subjects were taboo when meeting with the partner's engineers or that the walls between marketing and engineering tend to be far more porous in Japanese than in U.S. firms. The result was that much of the U.S. firm's core technological and marketing information ended up with Japanese partners.[25]

Protecting and augmenting core competencies. The foregoing highlights two critical aspects of alliance management: the need to protect a firm's core competence and the opportunity to augment core competencies through effective use of an alliance. Successful managers attend to both these considerations.[26]

Consider Honeywell's circa 1960 alliance with NEC of Japan. The latter was to supply computer components to Honeywell, which viewed the alliance as an opportunity to shift part of its value chain, the low end of manufacturing, to another firm. Consequently, it managed the alliance much as it did any other supplier relationship. NEC took a longer-term perspective, viewing the alliance as an opportunity to gain economies of scale. It invested resulting surpluses in augmenting its core skills in R&D, design, and manufacturing. In time, NEC became increasingly indispensable to Honeywell because the U.S. firm fell behind in technology. As it came to fill more of Honeywell's product and component needs, NEC became familiar with the service needs of its partner's customers. Honeywell's core competencies, its knowledge of its customers and their needs, steadily flowed to NEC, which concurrently augmented its own core competencies in manufacturing and design through continuous investment.

U.S. firms are not invariably the losers in alliances. One U.S. firm involved in the manufacture and sale of mobile communication equipment entered into an alliance with a Japanese firm for the purpose of selling some of its equipment worldwide. From the outset, the U.S. firm was determined to both augment its core skills and protect them from its Japanese partner. To protect its knowledge base, it designated specific managers to deal with the Japanese firm, specified that the design technology was not to be revealed to its partner, and established strict guidelines to govern what information could be discussed (e.g., the supplier was not to have complete access to the firm's service records).

At the same time, the U.S. firm's engineers and managers were explicitly told to keep their eyes and ears open when they visited the other firm's factory. This resulted in the acquisition of new techniques in the areas of quality control and manufacturing layout that the U.S. company later implemented in its own factory. Simultaneously, the U.S. firm invested in such key areas as manufacturing and R&D in order to stay technologically on a par with, and avoid becoming too dependent on, its Japanese partner. "We went into the alliance with our eyes wide open," remarked the manager in charge of the link. "We were determined to remain in all parts of the value chain and were not interested in becoming another hollow corporation."

Changing the managerial mind-set. Nothing is perhaps more important to the success of an alliance than the attitude of the managers associated with it. Changing the often negative perspective many of them bring to alliances is a critical task. Too often alliances are seen as quick fixes. Sometimes they are, but more often are not. The trick is to know the difference. It is the senior management's responsibility to ensure the correct positioning of the alliance within the firm's overall strategy and to communicate that positioning to all operating managers.

Many managers perceive alliances as a threat to their jobs; again, sometimes they are, more often are not. Alliances are merely a different way of organizing a business, and managers must be informed of this and made to see how they fit into the new scheme of things.

Alliances sometimes profoundly affect the nature of managers' and engineers' jobs. One manufacturing engineer explained his position as follows:

Before, I was mainly a front-line supervisor. Now, with an alliance in Korea, my job has taken on a whole new dimension. I am called on to do more of troubleshooting. I have to rethink the rationale for a lot of things we used to do in a certain way because that is how we always did them. The new assignment has given me an opportunity to be more creative. I enjoy it. If you had asked me immediately after the alliance was announced, my reaction would have been very negative. Not so now.

It is up to senior managers to ensure that operating managers understand the implications of alliances and rise to the occasion.

Alliances can also give rise to perceptions of winners and losers. In sourcing alliances, for example, marketing is often perceived to have prevailed over production, and R&D and design are likely to construe such arrangements negatively, as assaults on their integrity. Such perceptions must be addressed with sensitivity.

Consider the curious situation that developed when a U.S. manufacturer of medical systems decided to source some basic ultrasonic products from a Japanese firm, which was to receive access to the U.S. firm's imaging technology. When the alliance was announced, with only a few cognizant of its full details, both the ultrasonic division and the imaging group complained that they were the losers under the arrangement! Manufacturing engineers in the ultrasonic division took the alliance as a signal of the company's lack of confidence in their capabilities; researchers in the imaging group perceived themselves to be sacrificial vestal virgins offered up to atone for the incompetence of the ultrasonic division. Neither, of course, was correct. In fact, the move was calculated to strengthen the company's core capabilities in both manufacturing and design by gaining access to its partner's process technology and jointly designing the next generation of imaging cameras in collaboration with key Japanese users.

Expending additional resources. Many managers view alliances as a way to conserve resources. This is sometimes the case, but alliances often incur additional spending needs, some of which are obvious, some of which are not. Obvious needs include additional resources associated with the implementation of an alliance. When a foreign firm is selected as a partner, for example, distance increases the cost of travel and communication. "Suddenly you find your telephone and fax expenses going up enormously," said one manager. "So do travel budgets," he added, sounding defensive. He need not have been; many firms incur these extra expenses. Less obvious resource needs include managerial time commitments to the training of others in the effective use of the alliance and coordination of the alliance's role within the larger context of the organization. These can be considerable.

Need to coordinate among functions. Few firms adequately appreciate the interfunctional coordination needs engendered by alliances, which range from the mundane to the strategic. Recall that in the sourcing alliance between the U.S. and Korean firms, the key issues were ensuring that marketing accurately assessed key demand for particular products, that design engineers delivered accurate specifications in a timely manner, and that manufacturing lent its expertise as needed, distribution attended to logistics, and service correctly anticipated the changing requirements of new products.

Problems of interfunctional coordination are not always so smoothly resolved. In the late 1980s, Caterpillar, wanting to expand quickly into profitable new segments, decided to source forestry equipment and paving-machinery products through alliances with a Canadian and a U.S. firm, respectively. The products, carrying Caterpillar's name, were to be sold through its own regular dealer network. Buyers of these sourced products expected Caterpillar's customary forty-eight-hour delivery and exceptional post–sales service. Unprepared to meet such expectations, Caterpillar decided to discontinue its sourcing of forestry equipment and acquired the paving-machinery company to gain the necessary control to meet market expectations. Clearly, Caterpillar was unwilling or unable to make the systemic changes necessary to make the alliances work.[27]

Consideration must also be given to the links among functional groups and business divisions. In the alliance between U.S. and European firms, the partners recognized that, as in any research program, the full potential of their collaborative effort could be realized only with the close support and cooperation of related functional areas and business units likely to use the technology, leading both firms to ensure representation of these groups early through various committee structures. This action had the added benefit of legitimating the alliance throughout the firm.

Need to anticipate and coordinate a network of alliances. Senior management is responsible for recognizing the potential for an alliance strategy to lead eventually to a network of relationships that poses a vastly more complex management task than individual alliances. We have identified three key tasks in alliance network management. The first is simply anticipation; top management must think in terms of, and prepare for, a network of alliances rather than one alliance at a time. Developing a strategic framework disposes a firm toward a well-integrated network of interfirm links rather than a crazy patchwork of incompatible and unmanageable alliances. Second, management must coordinate among business units to ensure that they act in unison vis-à-vis the firm's various alliances rather than permit themselves to be picked apart, one by one, by a determined alliance partner. Third, management must coordinate among overseas subsidiaries and company headquarters to ensure a shared strategic intent with respect to individual alliances and the network as a whole.

If the challenges and tasks of alliance management are so varied and exacting, how do firms cope with them? What structural mechanisms have been developed to deal with strategic alliances? What is top management's role in the management of alliances? Do the senior managers have a continuing role beyond the formulation and forging of alliances? What is the role of corporate management in diversified companies vis-à-vis alliances? Finally, how do firms deal with networks of alliances? These are among the questions that we ask, and attempt to answer, in the next three chapters.

CHAPTER **6**

Managing Alliances: The Job of the Alliance Manager

Our research suggests that firms which make the most effective use of alliances tend to assign responsibility for their management to a specific manager or group.[1] We have seen widely differing arrangements in terms of both relative importance and patterns of assignment; how the job is viewed and structured depends largely on how seriously the task is viewed within a company and by top management.[2]

ALLIANCE MANAGEMENT: FIVE CRITICAL TASKS

Our study suggests that successful alliance implementation relies on the performance of a number of critical tasks. Although some are idiosyncratic, we have identified a set of generic tasks that seems to fall to most alliance managers.

Establish the Right Tone

"Establishing the right atmosphere is the most important task in alliance management," observed one alliance manager. "Unless your managers have the right chemistry with their counterparts in the partner firm, the alliance will not go anywhere." The manager defined "right chemistry" as organizational trust, that is, trust within a firm and trust between a firm and its partner. The alliance manager is responsible for creating and preserving both. We consider intrafirm organizational trust later in this chapter in connection with managing internal relationships; here we are concerned with interfirm trust.

One alliance manager summed up the need for interfirm trust thus:

> Let's face it, every alliance is plagued by strong suspicions right
> from the start. Senior managers in both firms wonder what the true
> motives of the other firm are. Functional managers wonder what
> the alliance will do to their jobs. Engineers are wary of what the
> other guys want. We step into this charged environment. It is our
> job to make sure that suspicions do not get so out of hand as to
> impede the alliance and to develop working relationships to ensure
> to the extent possible that the people in each firm trust those in the
> other. Believe me, it is not easy.

In the absence of trust, alliance partners' expectations are likely to go unful-
filled, exacerbating suspicion and disappointment and leading to a vicious
cycle.

The alliance managers we studied varied in fostering interorganizational
trust. Some strove to build direct, mostly one-on-one personal relationships.
To encourage the development of lasting personal bonds, Ford and Mazda,
for example, schedule their alliance teams to meet with each other regularly,
alternating between Japan and the United States. Many managers who have
participated in alliances have attributed their ability to solve difficult conflicts or avert potential disasters to close personal ties with their counterparts
in partner organizations.

Close personal ties between the managers of alliance partners also
promote prompt, honest reactions by one partner to new ideas advanced
by the other. One alliance manager's comment is typical.

> Whenever our company wants to make a new proposal, I usu-
> ally test it in advance with my counterpart. Because of the close
> personal ties we have cultivated, we can talk quite openly. At times,
> we decided to retract the request or postpone it, based on his reac-
> tions. More important, based on his inputs we have often altered
> a proposal to make it more acceptable to our partner without sub-
> stantially sacrificing substance. He does the same for me.

Language and cultural differences, of course, can complicate relationship building. "You must be prepared to invest time and effort in this,"
advised another alliance manager. "It requires tremendous patience and
constant effort, but once you build it, it becomes an important asset."

Another route to interorganizational trust is through familiarity with
a partner's strategy, organization, and culture. Managers of a major U.S.
semiconductor firm engaged in a concerted and systematic effort to understand their prospective partner, a Japanese firm, included on the negotiation

team a senior executive who, if the agreement was consummated, was to become the alliance manager.

Tangible results, the earlier the better, can also foster organizational trust. "There is nothing more powerful for cementing a relationship than one or two mutually beneficial accomplishments early in the relationship," said still another experienced alliance manager.

Lack of continuity in management teams is perhaps the greatest impediment to building organizational trust and setting the right tone for an alliance. Managers in foreign firms often complained in our interviews about frequent turnover of their U.S. partners' alliance managers and team members. In the first two years of one alliance, the management team turned over twice on one side and once on the other. One of the firms now insists that prospective alliance partners agree that core individuals remain members of the teams for at least two years. Of course, with individuals' having greater opportunity to switch jobs whenever they want, an American firm can hardly guarantee that its alliance team will remain intact for two years.

Turnover among alliance managers and teams, although not peculiarly an American phenomenon, is only beginning to be perceived as a problem by U.S. managers. Foreign managers, particularly of European firms, have tended to exhibit a greater appreciation for its consequences, and managers of Asian firms have demonstrated an ability to keep their teams intact for longer periods of time.

Monitor Partner Contributions

The value of an alliance ultimately hinges on the respective partners' willingness to make the requisite contributions in human, capital, and material resources in a timely manner. How well a firm meets its obligations to an alliance is the most tangible evidence of its commitment. Monitoring a partner's contributions is therefore critical.

An alliance manager must be in a position, if a partner's contributions are found or, more accurately, judged to be insufficient or unsatisfactory, to initiate appropriate corrective action. Moreover, the monitoring process should take into account the evolving nature of interfirm relationships. The nature and adequacy of a partner's contributions may have to be reshaped and assessed periodically, particularly when a firm's strategies, goals, and priorities are changing.

Accepting that monitoring is a requirement, what then should be monitored? The answer lies with the mission, scope, and role of the alliance. A sourcing alliance, for example, lends itself to assessment along a couple of fairly obvious dimensions, namely, delivery and quality. A partner either meets its delivery schedule or it does not; quality assessment is less straightforward, requiring time to accumulate data on such indicators as customer satisfaction, service calls, and warranty claims. Research and development alliances, on the other hand, are much more difficult to monitor. The caliber of scientists and researchers assigned to such a link is critical to its success. "Partners are not always motivated to commit their best talents to collaborative work," advised one alliance manager. Some firms prefer to keep their best people on internal projects, others are tempted to commit second-string researchers and exploit what they expect will be their partners' top-notch talent. Certainly some firms seek from joint projects the valuable bonus of training their junior people at the expense of their partners. Moreover, researchers themselves may balk at assignments they perceive as diverting them from the mainstream and jeopardizing their career prospects.

Intellectual contributions being difficult to measure at the output stage, control is best exerted at the input stage, as by stipulating requisite qualifications and background in the alliance agreement. But formal qualifications and experience, which are relatively easily screened beforehand, are not the whole story.[3] Credentials are no more important than, among other things, a person's real hands-on technical competence, work style, personality, ability to work with others, particularly those of different cultural backgrounds, and commitment in evaluating the suitability of researchers. Such considerations are extremely difficult to judge. "We have no problem in identifying the extreme cases," explained one alliance manager.

> If the person chosen is a heavyweight in the field, fine. Alternatively, if the person is very inexperienced or lacks the necessary credentials, we can identify him or her quickly, too. But how do you assess those in the middle? The vast majority of people fall there. There aren't any absolute standards. It is all relative to the overall quality of researchers in the other firm. We constantly ask ourselves, "Are they providing the best they have and how do we know if they do?"

Many R&D alliance managers periodically sound out their own scientists about the adequacy of their counterparts from the partner firm. "But alas," said an alliance manager, sighing,

> scientists are not as quick to pass judgment as managers often are. And with reason. More often than not, scientific talent is slow to prove itself. So if you are hasty in your judgment, you may get rid of the wrong guy. The cost of hasty judgment is pretty steep. So I don't blame my researchers for being cautious. It just makes my job that much more difficult, though.

Further complicating alliance assessment are the circumstances that bring firms' requirements together, typically a need for different and complementary skills. This results in alliance managers' being called upon to monitor and assess precisely the areas in which their organizations are weak, leaving many feeling ill equipped to make accurate judgments.

Consider the General Motors (GM)-Toyota NUMMI venture in Fremont, California, intended to afford GM engineers and managers an opportunity to observe, analyze, discuss, and learn about Toyota's production system. These objectives relied on Toyota's managers and engineers' sharing their knowledge with GM representatives. How was GM to determine whether Toyota delivered? To the GM alliance manager falls the unenviable and next to impossible job of evaluating the quality of the Toyota team's "teaching effort."[4] Toyota's alliance manager would have the same difficulty measuring how forthcoming GM is about U.S. procurement and labor practices.

Our research suggests the following approach to monitoring partner contributions. One, identify clearly what is to be monitored, break it down into identifiable elements, and measure those elements. Adopt a disciplined approach that not only recognizes but ensures ongoing consistency in a partner's contributions. Two, monitor continuously. Admittedly, some elements need to be measured only periodically, but to evaluate a process—learning, for example—monitoring must extend over its entire duration. Three, employ informal as well as formal approaches and involve every participant in the alliance. The manager must recognize that close observation of day-to-day interactions requires many eyes and therefore must sensitize and secure the cooperation and commitment of every member of the alliance team. Finally, a manager must be prepared to remedy shortcomings. When a partner is deemed to be falling short of expectations, experienced alliance managers act quickly and diplomatically. "As soon as I conclude that my partner is not meeting a certain commitment," observed one,

> I act immediately. Time is of the essence. Early action is critical. Otherwise you lose momentum and the problem festers. Second, when the partner fails to deliver on a commitment, the thing to do is not accuse but ask why. In my experience, partners often fail to deliver because of poor planning, overcommitment, or competing priorities. So it is wise to try to ascertain the reasons before leveling accusations. A quick but firm inquiry elicits explanations and often remedies. Beset by accusations, the other party will become defensive and then all you get is excuses.

Recognize the Importance of Information Flows

Information is present in every part and created by every activity of a firm. Capturing, retaining, recasting, reformulating, and using information is the business of modern corporations.[5] The conduct of this business bestows distinctive competitive advantage.[6]

Strategic alliances also involve the flow, exchange, processing, and utilization of information. Consider a simple sourcing alliance. The sourcing firm specifies at least product type, quality, and delivery schedules. Frequently the supplying firm lacks some needed product- or process-technology that must be supplied by the sourcing firm. All this information must be identified and packaged—in training manuals, books, oral presentations, one-on-one training, and so forth—and then transmitted between, processed, and absorbed by the partner firms.

Managers who have treated information flow as an incidental and innocuous by-product of alliance-based strategy have paid a heavy price. It is up to the alliance manager to draw the line between the active flow of information that ensures the vitality of an alliance and the unregulated, unmonitored, and unbridled exchange of information that can jeopardize the competitiveness of partners that are also likely to be rivals.

Recall the sourcing alliance between the U.S. and Korean firms. Say the U.S. firm unwittingly passes on to its Korean partner information about changes in design specifications that reveal characteristics about the U.S. market. If it is alert to this information, carefully monitors and studies and augments it with information it already possesses or can gather from other sources, private and public, the Korean firm might be able to draw conclusions that enable it to build itself systematically into a formidable competitor of its U.S. partner. It will have done so without having been unscrupulous in any way and without expending significant sums on market research.

Let us add a layer of complexity. Suppose that after two years in a satisfactory sourcing alliance, these two firms decide to collaborate on joint development of new models of a product to be marketed in the United States. Such collaboration calls for both firms' designers, manufacturing engineers, and marketing staff to work together, affording the Korean firm additional opportunities to learn about competitive trends, changing consumer preferences, price points, and price sensitivity in the various U.S. market segments. It also presents the Korean firm with an opportunity to learn more about its partner's strengths and weaknesses. Quite legitimately, and not through any perfidy on its part, a veritable gold mine of information about its U.S. partner falls into the hands of the Korean firm. Should the Korean company decide to enter the U.S. market, for whatever reason, what it has learned through the alliance could prove invaluable.

This is precisely what happened in the case of an alliance between a U.S. and a Taiwanese firm. The latter systematically gathered information about its U.S. partner during their two-year alliance and then entered the U.S. market in direct competition with that partner. The U.S. firm was further dismayed to learn that its partner's engineers had acquired from its own engineers considerable information about the advanced R&D and product-development projects they were working on. The upshot was that the Taiwanese firm introduced an energy-saving model of the product six months before its U.S. partner did. Eventually, of course, the U.S. firm severed its ties with the Taiwanese firm and forged a new alliance with another East Asian company, this time building better safeguards into the contract and scrutinizing managerial practices as they related to the alliance.

Information flow and learning are not one-way streets. Partners can learn simultaneously simply by observing each other. As firms become enmeshed in multiple complex relationships, information begins to flow through unsuspected and byzantine routes, rendering its management at once more difficult and more critical. One U.S. high-technology company's Japanese partner, for example, learned about a highly sensitive research project from a notice concerning an internal research meeting posted on a company bulletin board.

Similarly, a U.S. firm in a mobile communication equipment industry, as part of a sourcing arrangement, was granted access to its Japanese partner's plants and facilities. Following a plan devised by its alliance manager, the U.S. firm was able to learn a great deal about its partner's manufacturing capabilities, processes, cost structure, and productivity. "The Japanese, our engineers found, were using a process different from ours for quality control and they were getting better results—lower rejects, lower unit cost, and even somewhat lower setup times," the manager explained. "Over a period of several visits, our engineers took the process apart, learned it, and came back and adapted it for our own use. We got excellent results. We would not have learned the process but for the alliance."

The R&D alliance between the U.S. and European firm cited in Chapter 5 involved intense interaction between the two firms' scientists, some of whom worked independently in their respective firms, others as members of joint teams. Through frequent meetings held to share results and exchange information on the progress of their projects, scientists were able not only to assess the caliber of their counterparts, but also to become familiar with their approach to solving problems.[7] One executive with a strong R&D background who played a central role in the alliance offered the following summary:

> Often our people realized that the other group's method was different from ours. There is nothing proprietary about their way of doing things, nor were they necessarily better. But it did stimulate our thinking. Now, after a few months of off-and-on discussions within our firm, our people have come to the conclusion that under certain circumstances the other group's approach is better. We now use it in our own labs. I am sure that our partners learned similarly from us. And we don't mind. Picking up best practices wherever they are found is nothing to be ashamed of.

Information flow thus poses three simultaneous, and often contradictory, challenges. Alliance managers must (1) ensure the smooth and timely flow of information between partners that is crucial to the success of alliances; (2) at the same time, since alliances bring together two firms that are actual or potential rivals, manage the outward flow of information with utmost care, safeguarding their own firms' competitive positions, and (3) exploit the extraordinary opportunities for learning from their partners and manage the inward information flow to advantage.

Much thought has been expended on the management of information flows in alliances.[8] As with so many circumstances with which management must contend, no one approach is universally preferred. Having considered at some length the importance of information flows, we turn now to their management. Our research has revealed some common strands in the way firms handle the flow of information to and from partners.

Direct and centralized control of information flows. Channeling information through a designated person or office affords some measure of control over its content and timing. It also, by making clear what sorts of information a partner is seeking, can reveal a great deal about a partner's motives vis-à-vis the alliance.

Many firms centralize alliance interface activities at the manager level. Outgoing information is collected, incoming information disseminated, all interfirm correspondence screened, and interfirm discussions approved and initiated at this level. This approach permits hands-on management with clear accountability and can foster consistency in the working relationship. It is particularly appropriate to alliances of limited scope in which interactions have to be closely monitored.

A leading U.S. manufacturer of office equipment that agreed to source certain models of a particular type of equipment from a major Japanese rival, which already enjoyed a substantial presence in the United States, was understandably concerned about possible leakage of competitively valuable information. Accordingly, the agreement between the firms included stringent stipulations as to how the relationship was to be managed. It mandated, for instance, that all contact between the two firms be through designated alliance managers. The approach seemed to be working quite well for the U.S. firm at the time of our study.

But direct control is not without drawbacks. It is not well suited to alliances that involve frequent, intense meetings between managers in different functional areas or in which real value is created, as in R&D collaboration. The task of monitoring the extensive information flows associated with such alliances can overwhelm a manager or small staff, eroding the effectiveness of the office and impeding progress in the alliance. Finally, when one partner adopts a centralized control approach, the other often follows suit, with the result that the information flow in both directions dries up.

Decentralized information flow management. Decentralized approaches to managing interfirm information flows vary, but all emphasize a role of guidance rather than control for alliance managers. One manager, for example, categorized information according to whether it might be helpful to a potential competitor or gleaned from public sources. Information in the latter category could be transmitted directly to the firm's partner; transmittal of information in the former category required the alliance manager's approval. To simply require after-the-fact reporting of the dissemination of sensitive information does not seem very useful. A largely decentralized administrative approach that places responsibility for information flow with the functional managers most directly concerned with it facilitates direct and timely interaction between the managers and engineers participating in an alliance, thereby speeding the resolution of alliance-related matters.

Perhaps more important, a decentralized approach can serve to sensitize those with less experience working within an alliance to concerns about information sharing. An alliance manager who invited those who would be closely involved in the alliance to help define the categories of information found the practice to be an excellent way to raise managers' level of awareness concerning issues related to information management. Through the ensuing discussions, the managers came to realize that different functional heads construed the same information to be more or less important to competitors, and that information that overlapped functional areas would be dealt with differently by their different managers. The need to arrive at a consensus as to the level of confidentiality of different types of information heightened these managers' sensitivity to issues related to information flows.

A U.S. firm that wanted to minimize the flow of sensitive information to its East Asian sourcing partners, for example, proscribed access to information pertaining to the manipulation of certain key design parameters and even to its CAD/CAM (computer-aided design/computer-aided manufacturing) facilities. The alliance and marketing managers and service group in another U.S. firm, recognizing that full access to service and warranty data might reveal to their Japanese sourcing partner information about the types and circumstances of common failures, decided to provide sanitized versions of these data sufficient to serve for improving quality of sourced products.

Alliance managers who favor a decentralized approach to handling information flows frequently meet with key managers and engineers prior to scheduled review and examine the reasons for the meeting, goals to be achieved, strategies for negotiating, the kinds of information likely to be sought, and ways to fend off requests for sensitive information without seeming to be too secretive. "In my experience, when project team members are drawn from different functional or business areas, as they often are, the members spend only a limited amount of time preparing as a team for meetings with the people from the partner firm," an alliance manager recounted.

> Each person thinks that he or she has a pretty good idea as to what is expected of him or her. It is an entirely understandable approach. After all, alliances are not their primary job. Moreover, the logistics of bringing together people from different parts of the firm to undertake joint preparation are formidable. My perspective, however, is different. Alliances are my job. I think it is necessary for members to meet as a team and do the necessary homework. In these meetings I encourage them to think through their participation not just from their functional perspective, but also in the context of the overall strategy of the firm. These meetings are also the occasion for us to define the types of information to share or not to share. Equally important is the fact that we discuss what type of information we need to or can obtain from the other firm and how the information is to be processed within the firm once we get it.

Many alliance managers maintain a detailed record of interactions with their partners. One manager complained to us that there was virtually no record of what had transpired between his firm and its partner when he took over. "Everything was in my predecessor's head," he lamented. "I am sure my counterpart took advantage of my ignorance." The manager subsequently insisted that all his people keep detailed records of their dealings with the partner, including topics of discussion, types of information transmitted and received, and so forth. "Not only is the record useful, but the process serves a useful role in instilling discipline," he stated.

Some companies go even further, insisting on detailed debriefings after every major meeting with the partner. Many alliance managers feel that stepping back and reviewing what really went on at a meeting can reveal a great deal about how effectively they dealt with the partner, the true range of information passed on to the partner both formally and informally, and the nature and value of information obtained from the partner. According to one alliance manager, "Because our people are constantly moving, whereas in our partner firm there is little turnover, it is extremely difficult for us to build an organizational memory; debriefing and recording is one way to build our memory base."

Another manager found it useful to show a grid on which any information pertaining to the company could be plotted. The grid then let the manager easily decide whether information could be shared freely with a manager in the partner firm. As Figure 6.1 shows, the two axes of the grid were: Is the information publicly available? and Will the information help a competitor? Depending on where the information sought by the alliance partner fell in the grid, the manager could decide whether to share the information.

Such formal approaches are useful, but insufficient. Alliance managers we met during the course of our study stressed the need to educate managers and engineers continuously about the importance of managing information flows. A complicated alliance requires continuing interactions among large numbers of people in different disciplines and functions, few with any experience working in alliances. "Preventing outflow of sensitive information and at the same time learning as much as you can from the other side does not come naturally or easily to people," remarked yet another alliance manager.

Alliance managers generally do not underestimate the challenge of sensitizing others to the importance of information flows. A major issue, as they see it, is what one termed the "perils of familiarity." Said this manager,

I have observed time and again that our engineers and managers are quite cautious when they first begin to work with their counterparts in another firm. As the relationship develops, however, they become freer in sharing information. Again, remember, American managers tend to be much more open than people in other cultures. When relationships are so ambiguous, and when it is so difficult to draw a precise boundary around what can or cannot be shared or to limit the way people interact in day-to-day situations, my best

Figure 6.1
Assessing Importance of Information

Is the Information Publicly Available?

		Yes	No
Will the Information Help a Competitor?	Yes	Consult Other Managers before Sharing Such Information with Alliance Partner	Do Not Part with the Information
	No	Share the Information Freely	?

hope lies in keeping them constantly reminded of what is at stake. In the end, of course, we must depend on front-line managers' judgment.

Clearly, alliance managers must be adept at cultivating much-needed judgment in the minds of their colleagues, a not inconsiderable task.

Reassess Strategic Viability

We have posited that strategic alliances are forged to bolster the competitive positions of partners. An alliance can augment a firm's bundle of competitive advantages in either of two ways: by enabling it to rectify weaknesses by tapping into the resources of another firm or by permitting a firm to devote less of its own scarce resources to building a particular type of advantage.

Such an interpretation of alliances raises some interesting managerial questions. For example, do the strategic needs of a firm change over time, and if they do, what does this bode for the strategic viability and role of the alliances it has entered into? Who in the organization should be entrusted with the job of continually reassessing the strategic viability of its alliances? Who is best placed to discern opportunities to change the roles of alliances and how is such responsibility best dispatched?

Today's dynamic competitive environment mandates continual reassessment of firms' strategies. The basic thrust of a firm's strategy may not change much over the medium term, but differential emphasis on elements of that strategy very well might. Changes in strategy frequently incur changes in firms' operations, which may imply a need for reassessment of the need for or viability of its strategic alliances. A significant realignment of exchange rates, for example, might render sourcing from a particular nation less attractive and dramatically reduce the strategic value of alliances with firms in that nation.[9]

IBM's circumstances during the 1980s and early 1990s are instructive in how a change in strategic emphasis can affect a firm's alliances. IBM's strategic thrust in the personal computer industry in the early to mid-1980s emphasized offsetting as rapidly as possible its somewhat belated start behind Apple Computer. IBM reasoned that rapid standardization (Apple was pushing its own proprietary standard) and emphasis on its well-known service capabilities (an area in which Apple was perceived to be weak) might shift the competitive battleground to marketing (instead of design or production), where it could exploit its key source of competitive advantage— sales and service. This led IBM to forge critical strategic alliances with Intel for microprocessors and Microsoft for operating system software. So critical were these alliances to IBM that it took a minority equity position in Intel and concluded a strong cross-licensing agreement with Microsoft.

By the late 1980s, IBM's strategic needs had changed. It was no longer the dominant force it had been in the microcomputer market, and the industry itself had changed with the arrival of RISC technology and proponent Sun Microsystems. Consequently, the company changed tack and began to push its proprietary microchannel architecture and OS/2 operating system. Unfortunately, IBM found itself on the defensive as its partners Intel and Microsoft began to exploit their augmented positions at IBM's expense. IBM's strategic needs and alliances had ceased to mesh well.

IBM's response to these threats was to revamp its alliance strategy. To support a new competitive approach that relied on proprietary technology which it could better control, IBM sold off its equity holdings in Intel, commenced work on the next generation of operating systems independently of Microsoft, reduced its dependence on those firms, and in 1991 forged a new and radically different set of alliances with Apple (IBM's erstwhile and Microsoft's future rival), Motorola (Intel's key rival in microprocessors), and Siemens (a major rival of Japanese firms that were pressing hard against IBM in semiconductor technology).

Another vivid illustration of how strategic alliances can be affected by changes in competitive strategy is provided by a large U.S. producer of industrial equipment that sought much-needed efficiency gains by entering into a production-sharing arrangement with a major Japanese firm. As the market was mature, with substantial excess capacity worldwide, the alliance made sense for both companies, enabling them to pool resources and exploit specialization. The U.S. company was to manufacture large equipment, the Japanese firm medium-size and small machines. The two were then to supply each other, taking advantage of economies of scale while remaining full-line suppliers.

The alliance got off to a good start, but after several years both firms felt a need to adjust its terms. The market had improved unexpectedly, partly because a number of firms had either exited the business or drastically downsized their capacities, putting pressure on the partners to resume full-line manufacturing. But attempts to restore full-line in-house production gradually led to tugs of war so acrimonious as to result in an eventual parting of the ways.

Assessment of the viability and role of strategic alliances is the province of top management. But as senior executives charged with the day-to-day affairs of interfirm relationships, alliance managers have an important role to play in discerning changes in the partner firm in a timely manner. Effective managers tend to be proactive rather than reactive, to anticipate and act rather than wait for events to overtake them. They also tend to be less administrator and more entrepreneur, particularly in dealing with potential changes in strategic relationships. Recognizing that such relationships represent important assets that their firms can build upon, they strive to reshape or restructure alliances imaginatively to leverage their firms' investments.

The alliance manager best positioned to initiate smart restructuring is illustrated in the case of a division of a diversified U.S. firm that sought to shore up its competitive position in the U.S. market by sourcing a number of product lines from a medium-size Japanese firm. The relationship worked well for several years, until the yen strengthened dramatically in the mid-1980s. The partners worked closely, initiating major cost-cutting and rationalizing efforts to deal with this change. But the strong yen proved to be more than a temporary phenomenon.

The situation presented a particularly serious problem for the Japanese firm, as sales to the U.S. market through its American partner had come to represent a sizable and significant share of its total sales. Fearing loss of competitiveness, the company began to investigate the possibility of establishing a U.S. manufacturing base and an independent distribution system to gain economies of scale. But the firm's limited size and resources, together with its almost total lack of expertise in setting up and managing a foreign subsidiary with a full panoply of manufacturing and marketing functions, left many of the company's senior managers reluctant to forge ahead.

The alliance manager of the U.S. firm, who had developed close working relationships with the Japanese managers and was watching their thinking evolve, was also aware that corporate headquarters was reevaluating its retention of his division, as it was not meeting corporate profit objectives. Seeing an intriguing opportunity in these developments, the manager proposed that the U.S. firm establish a manufacturing joint venture with its Japanese partner in the United States. After selling the idea to senior division and corporate managers, he explored the possibility with the Japanese firm and went on to fashion a new alliance between the two.

The resulting joint venture met key objectives of both organizations. The U.S. firm was able to rationalize its operations, the Japanese firm to minimize the risks associated with foreign direct investment. The venture was to use the U.S. firm's existing manufacturing facilities, supplied with some new machinery and manufacturing technology by the Japanese firm. To enhance the venture's economic viability, the U.S. firm turned over to it the manufacture of additional products, in return for which it received exclusive rights to market the venture's output in the United States, thereby helping to preserve marketing synergies with other divisions in the company.

Both firms viewed the new arrangement as a major success at the time of the study and conferred credit for it on the U.S. firm's alliance manager. "He not only understood what was happening in the environment but also saw how the whole relationship could be restructured to mutual benefit," commented the division president of the U.S. firm.

> It would have been easy for him to walk away from the alliance once the yen strengthened beyond a point. In fact, corporate kept telling us to get out of the alliance and divest the business altogether.

By recognizing a new opportunity in the changed situation, [he] helped revitalize the business. In fact, he was perhaps the only person in our organization who was in a position to see the whole picture so clearly and pull off what he did.

The Japanese firm's managers were equally effusive in their praise for the U.S. alliance manager. A senior manager told us,

[He] understood our difficulties. During the previous years, he had gained our confidence. True, he was a tough negotiator, but he was always willing to listen. Over the years he had established close working relationships with many of us. He was the one who came up with the idea of a joint venture. He then sold it to us as well as to his own company. But for his patience and commitment, the venture would not have come into being.

Recognize the Importance of Internal Relationships

Thus far, we have focused primarily on the alliance manager's job and responsibilities as they relate to the partner firm and its executives. But just as the importance of managing these external relationships cannot be overestimated, neither can that of managing internal relationships occasioned by alliances.

Alliance-based systems are implemented through the active involvement of people in various functions and at various levels of an organization. An alliance manager cannot "wave a magic wand and expect things to happen." If functional and divisional managers are unwilling to perform the necessary tasks, a manager can accomplish little. Marshaling the support needed to ensure that the contributions expected in the various value activities are made is perhaps an alliance manager's key contribution to the success of a collaboration.

In fact, how effectively managers deal with their own organizations determines to a great extent how effectively they interact with the partner organization. Recall the earlier example of the U.S. firm that assigned the management job for its alliance to a person who was viewed by its partner as being too low in the organizational hierarchy.[10] Even senior people chosen to manage alliances must establish their credibility by securing the cooperation of their colleagues to make the alliance work.[11]

A number of obstacles confront alliance managers who would enlist their colleagues' cooperation. Consider the case of a product-development alliance. New product development calls for close, active, ongoing involvement by R&D, design, engineering, manufacturing, and marketing.[12] Books have been written about the difficulty of assembling product-development teams in-house. Imagine the complexities that emerge when the team is to serve in a collaborative effort with another firm that is more likely a rival. Much the same holds for sourcing, joint marketing, and R&D alliances.

Under enormous pressure, middle managers, who often bear the brunt of the demands imposed by alliances, tend to assign very low priority to demands on their time viewed as peripheral to their core responsibilities.[13] Justified or not, many alliance-related activities tend to be so perceived, leaving the managers in a position of having to compete for the time and attention of their functional and business unit managers.

Moreover, many middle managers resent alliances, viewing them as intrusions. Managers and technical specialists alike are wont to view alliances with competitors as detrimental to their firm's long-term interests, a fear often substantiated by sourcing alliances. Many also see alliances as a prelude to the eventual migration of some or all of a firm's manufacturing activities to a foreign location.

Pride is also a factor. Alliances can be seen as an acknowledgment that a firm lacks the requisite skills or resources to achieve its strategic goals. A U.S. firm that established a product-development alliance with a Japanese office-equipment manufacturer had to contend with a number of design engineers who, although told by top management not to work on the project, had on their own time repeatedly come up with designs they proclaimed superior to the ones being contemplated by the alliance team.[14]

It is not uncommon for middle managers to pay lip service to the importance of an alliance while actively resisting it. Some may be put off by the need to learn a new set of skills; others, accustomed to working with associates in their own firm's laboratories, may be apprehensive about having to worry about sharing information freely.

Alliance managers cannot be overconfident of support from top management. Many senior managers leave the task of selling the importance of an alliance to the middle ranks entirely to the alliance manager, and even senior managers who make an effort to communicate the importance of an alliance to their middle managers tend to leave to the alliance head the job of securing the day-to-day cooperation of functional managers. Finally, alliance managers who continually invoke the power or sanction of senior management to get a job done put at risk whatever credibility they begin with.

Most of the alliance managers we interviewed were keenly aware of these challenges. "There is very little I can do myself," admitted one. "I must rely on various groups of people in my organization. It is part of my job to get the active involvement and willing cooperation of all the people concerned, especially in the middle-management ranks." How do alliance managers secure the active cooperation of their firms' managers and technical specialists? We present below some of the key approaches alliance managers have employed to get middle managers to work with rather than against them.

Be seen as a champion, not a mouthpiece. Successful alliance managers tread a fine line between advocacy and championing. They ensure that the requisite resources, attention, and support are forthcoming without placing the organization's managers and technical people in the awkward position of feeling as if they are acting on behalf of another organization's interests. In other words, they manage to convince skeptics in their firms of the wisdom of an alliance without sounding like representatives of the partner firm.

It is widely recognized that projects in large organizations require enthusiastic championing to stand a chance of success.[15] Alliances, because they are often viewed as new projects in competition for scarce resources, also need champions. It generally falls to alliance managers to fill that much-needed role. In the execution of their championing role, the managers must not lose sight of the skepticism, suspicion (of acting as plants for a competitor), and outright hostility they are likely to encounter.[16] Too forceful a job of championing an alliance might result in its manager's being perceived as a mouthpiece for the partner firm.

The alliance manager for the U.S. industrial products company cited earlier was so consumed by the task of getting sourced products to the U.S. market and generally making the alliance succeed that he was eventually considered as having been co-opted by the Korean partner firm. Colleagues, behind his back, began to refer to him as the Voice of Korea. A number of seemingly innocuous bureaucratic snafus plagued the performance of the alliance, and the U.S. firm's engineers and service personnel in particular were unwilling to honor any kind of request without elaborate paper shuffling.

Nevertheless, we observed a number of effective but careful alliance champions. These individuals tended to check routinely their partners' demands against the original intent of the alliances and the competitive strategy of the firms and eliminate requests they deemed unnecessary or extraneous. Said one, "If you go to your colleagues only when you are fully convinced that your requests are legitimate and fit the needs of [your] firm, you are more likely to sound more convincing and—this is critical—more likely to be believed. If you go to the well too often with trivial or unreasonable requests, you will lose credibility."

Successful alliance managers also tend to be willing to listen with an open mind to managers in their own firms. "I'm not always the only one with the right idea," quipped one. "It is important to listen to other people's concerns. It gives you an opportunity to appraise your own conclusions afresh."

Seek organizational understanding. Fostering organizationwide understanding of a strategic alliance and its role in the overall scheme of things is, in the long run, a more efficient and equitable way of achieving alliance objectives than ad hoc and expedient solutions. But it is also enormously difficult. Nevertheless, we have been able to extract from our interviews with alliance managers a number of approaches that have met with some success.

Successful alliance managers actively shape the expectations of their colleagues and communicate regularly with the people likely to be involved with the activities of the alliance. "Right from the beginning, my approach was to be open with my colleagues," remarked a manager of a major alliance. "As soon as I took the position, I met with them and told them how I saw my job. I indicated to them areas where they could potentially contribute. After that, almost every month I met with a few of them on a rotating basis to keep them posted on the status of the alliance." The manager also sent some of the organization's key people to visit the partner firm.[17] "Nothing," he explained, "helps people to know what a partner can or cannot do for you as much as seeing their plants, talking to managers at various levels, and getting to see the overall context of the alliance." The alliance manager's approach led other managers to begin to take the alliance's needs into account as a matter of routine and as part of their jobs.

Maintain links at all levels. Because alliances both impinge on the jobs and are affected by the activities of managers at various levels, the need to keep all levels of the organization informed and involved would seem to be obvious. Yet only more successful alliance managers seem to strive to do so. Reasons for this lapse are many: a desire to respect traditional organizational lines of communication and authority; underestimation of the time requirements of the circuitous and bureaucratic communication processes that pervade many corporations; control mechanisms that tend to perpetuate outmoded ways of doing business.

A manager who took over an alliance that had run into difficulty described his experience.

> The tendency here was that our job was done if we let the other manager in the company know about our problems, issues, needs, whatever. Unfortunately, more often than not the solutions lay in the hands of people far removed from the person to whom we were sending our memos. Even when our people met with the managers face to face, it did not mean that the people who could really do something about the problem were informed in time or were persuaded to take action in time.

Alliance managers are well advised not to become too dependent on a single level of an organization. By themselves or through their office, effective managers work to develop relationships with front-line supervisors, junior managers, midlevel executives, engineers, and researchers. In one alliance we studied, its manager talked with a factory foreman to learn the reasons for certain of his actions.[18] To be successful at this sort of outreach, managers must avoid being perceived as intruders or as violating normal lines of authority. Rather, they establish links, often informally, with people at different levels in the various parts of the organization, scrupulously refraining from giving the impression of circumventing their managers. They tend to exploit close personal working relationships more often for information acquisition and dissemination than for getting things done. Armed with information, they are able to persuade the other units of the organization to cooperate. "Short-circuit the information processes, but not the lines of authority," is the way one alliance manager put it.

Manage internal demands and expectations. For a given alliance, one can generally find many managers who doubt its relevance or efficacy and many others who make unrealistically high demands of it or have exaggerated expectations of the partner firm's capabilities. "Once we got used to the idea of an alliance with our Japanese partner, it was as though the firm could do anything we wanted with very little advance notice," remarked an alliance manager who termed his managers' enthusiasm the "Asians-with-ten-heads" syndrome. "Managers in my firm were asking the Japanese to do so many things, it looked as though they thought the Japanese firm had unlimited resources."

To ensure that excessive demands are not made on a partner, alliance managers must control expectations within their firms. This is particularly important when a number of projects are involved, as in the case of the Ford-Mazda and GM-Isuzu alliances. Not unreasonably, individual project managers tend to push their own enterprises, which can result in competing demands on a partner's organization. If there is a disparity in the size of the partners, as in the examples cited above, the smaller partner may feel overwhelmed and overburdened. An executive of a Japanese company with extensive ties to a major U.S. firm had this to say:

> One of the problems we have experienced is that our American partner does not seem to understand that our resources are limited. For example, right now we have several very interesting and exciting projects under discussion. Our partner would like us to do all of them, but we know we cannot. We have our priorities, but our partner seems to have a real tough time establishing its priorities. Understandably, each project manager thinks that his project is the most important and makes a demand on our limited resources. We often encounter real conflict as to who gets what.

Similar problems have been voiced by managers of large-scale alliances, particularly among U.S. companies whose project managers are evaluated strictly on the performance of their individual assignments. Under these circumstances, alliance managers must help their companies establish priorities among different projects, a daunting task at best. "One of the most difficult parts of my job," observed an experienced alliance manager, "is to help the company set our priorities among different projects with our partner. Unless we actively manage it, one of two things can happen. Priorities are determined either by the guy with the loudest voice or by the partner. Either way, it is not optimum from our point of view." Foreign partners frequently do not understand the extent of the autonomy strategic business units enjoy in some large U.S. corporations and attribute competing priorities or absence of coordination to management incompetence rather than management philosophy.

A problem related to conflicting priorities is level of expectations. Some alliance managers encourage realistic anticipation on the part of their project managers by sending them to visit a partner's facilities. "Communication alone is seldom sufficient to get people to modify their expectations," the same manager observed.

> We have to make them internalize that attitude. We must also assure them that we are aware of the potential risks associated with an alliance and are trying to deal with them. Often the best way is to get them involved early in the alliance and make sure that their firsthand experience is realistic. I have sent a number of groups over to spend some time at the partner's organization and let them see firsthand what capabilities our partners possess and what they can and cannot do for us. Once we get a few converts in key groups, they can spread the word. But given the frequent turnover in our management ranks, it requires constant effort.

Qualifications for the Job

Alliance managers, as we have seen, must depend almost entirely on others, all but a handful of whom do not even report to them, to accomplish their job. Moreover, the alliance manager can only influence, not order. What are the qualifications needed to perform such a job successfully?

Again, we can offer no clear prescription for who should manage alliances. Consider Kodak's decision to reenter the camera business it had exited seventeen years earlier. The magnitude of investment and ready availability of attractive products in Japan led the Consumer Products Division, charged with responsibility for implementing the strategy, to recommend a sourcing alliance. A careful search and analysis led to the selection of Chinon, a relatively small manufacturer with excellent product and process technology, as a sourcing partner. Quickly recognizing the potential of tapping Chinon's technology for joint product development, and realizing that to do so would lead to extremely close interactions, including sharing of sensitive information, Kodak decided to secure a 25% equity position in Chinon and a place on Chinon's board for the general manager of its Consumer Products Division. The general manager elected to manage the relationship. He explained:

> I decided to assume responsibility myself for a variety of reasons. For one thing, the partnership is a vital part of the division's strategy. It is the first alliance for the division. Also, understandably, some people in Chinon felt uneasy about our taking a stake in their company. I believe my personal involvement has helped us establish a smooth working relationship. In the early stages, until we felt comfortable with one another, I managed the relationship very tightly. A number of different groups are involved now, and even now I watch over them very carefully.

The Kodak-Chinon case is instructive. Granted that a general manager cannot in every case personally manage an alliance relationship, the example nevertheless illustrates some of the issues germane to selecting the right individual for the job. For starters, the manager of a major alliance, if it is not the general manager, must have ready access to the latter. If the mission of an alliance is to be closely aligned with a firm's business strategy, the manager must be in a position not only to understand the firm's strategy, but also to have a voice in its formulation and implementation. To manage effectively an alliance that involves multiple projects and therefore competing priorities, the manager must be intimately acquainted with company strategy.

There is another reason the manager responsible for a major alliance must be part of the general manager's team. Because the many activities associated with a major alliance are invariably performed by different groups, the manager must know which to call upon for particular tasks and be able to orchestrate their activities. An alliance manager's capacity to mobilize the resources of the entire organization must be complemented by a readiness to intervene to resolve competing priorities among different projects. Organizational status alone will not see a manager through these difficult duties; their successful execution relies on intimate knowledge of the organization, extensive personal networks, and above all, credibility with managers at all levels. We saw earlier how foot-dragging by lower-level managers and inattention by those at the top can confound an alliance manager's efforts.

Credibility accrues to an alliance manager who possesses a clear understanding of the business in which an alliance is formed and who is thoroughly familiar with the structure and economics of the industry, the company's position relative to key competitors, and its strategy regarding the business in question. Moreover, an effective manager understands the workings of each of the company's key functional areas and is intimately acquainted with its organization and people.

Personal attributes as well as professional qualifications determine the effectiveness of alliance managers. The three mentioned most frequently are flexibility, interpersonal skills, and the capacity to build trust over extended periods of time. As one alliance manager observed,

> This is one of those jobs for which a job description is meaningless. To begin with, the job is ambiguous, and so is the situation one must manage. One never knows what to expect day to day, but at the same time one must try to anticipate long-term trends and developments. In the course of a day, I deal with issues ranging from the extremely mundane to the very strategic. I must be able to shift my thinking quickly from immediate to long-term issues. A fun part of the job is that there are very few ready-made answers. I have to be creative in finding solutions, often on an ad hoc basis, to many of the problems I face.

"I am constantly negotiating about something with someone either in the partner's organization or in my own," another alliance manager reported. "By design, I have a very small staff and therefore no direct authority over anyone I call on. I must negotiate, persuade, and at times cajole to get anything done. In this job I have learned a great deal about how to get things done through influence rather than through authority."

As ambassador, intermediary, and "point man," the alliance manager sets the tone for the relationship overall. "Some people are very good at managing relationships on a short-term basis, but the real test is whether or not a manager can build trust or credibility with the partner on an enduring basis," observed one of the most successful alliance managers we interviewed. "Over the course of the alliance, your credibility must stand the test of time. To build such credibility or trust with the partner is essential, but to do so most definitely requires a special attitude and commitment."

There is a marked parallel between qualifications and skills that characterize an effective alliance manager and a good general manager. In effect, the attributes required of an alliance manager are similar to those that characterize an effective general manager, except in one respect—alliance managers, unlike general managers, must work with a large number of people over whom they have no direct authority. Not surprisingly, many companies are looking to men and women with general management experience to manage large-scale, intricate alliances. Many are also beginning to view the job of alliance management as excellent training for future general managers.

Motorola Corporation's alliance with Toshiba is instructive in the selection of its manager. Given the strategic importance of the relationship, Motorola top management charged with its oversight chose a corporate vice president who had previously served as head of the microprocessor group in the semiconductor sector, in which capacity he had played a central role in developing strategy and been an important architect of the alliance he was being asked to manage.

Intimately familiar with the sector's strategy, the vice president was ideally suited to the job. Moreover, he brought to his new job a coveted reputation as a pioneer and builder. None of this was missed by Toshiba. The vice president's personal credibility and reputation played an important role in getting the microprocessor group to share its highly proprietary technology with Toshiba in return for memory-related technology. The vice president declared:

> It is critically important for an individual in my position to have an important voice in the formulation of overall strategy. I see this alliance as implementing a part of that overall strategy. Every opportunity I have, I stress to my people why this alliance is so vital to the future of our sector and how it fits the sector's strategy overall. I know I will not be able to perform my job adequately unless I report directly to the general manager of the sector and continue to be a part of the top management group that determines the sector's strategy. My counterpart at Toshiba holds a similar position in that organization. For such an important alliance, it is essential that the partners be represented by members of top management who are familiar not only with the business, but with the core strategies of their respective groups.

Motorola and Toshiba agreed at the outset to create parallel organizations consisting of managers responsible for each of four functions: technology, manufacturing, marketing, and administration. Each manager was to chair a committee composed of key individuals from each functional area whose commitment and support were essential to successful implementation of the alliance. These managers were to interact daily with their counterparts, and the committees were to meet quarterly, alternating between the United States and Japan. Both companies' alliance managers served on the joint venture's board, in which capacity they represented the interests not only of the parent company, but also of the joint venture, affording them yet another opportunity to interact.

The Motorola-Toshiba link is a case in point for choosing the right person for the job of alliance manager. Failure to provide the requisite leadership dooms an alliance to, at best, a bad start and, at worst, failure. The operative word is "leadership." A senior executive of a *Fortune 500* company with extensive interfirm links recalled during our interview a definition of leadership he had encountered in his reading.

A leader is one who gets people to do what he wants, but who at the same time makes them think that it was all their idea in the first place. An alliance manager also has to work along the same lines. He has no battalions of his own, yet he has to get the job done. He has to get people to buy into his vision of the alliance, make it part of their own job assignment, and actively work to make the alliance a success.

Ultimately, excellent managers, like excellent leaders, make their jobs redundant. The idea of working through alliances—and the notion of competing and cooperating at the same time—becomes so ingrained in the organization that there is eventually no need for an alliance manager's "cajoling, coaxing, and controlling."

CHAPTER 7

Managing Alliances: The Role of Top Management

Although the broader purpose of an alliance is often determined by the competitive strategies of the partners, the context, tone, and tenor of the relationship are established by the respective top managers. Top management's involvement in a strategic alliance includes, but does not end with, the appointment of an alliance manager. Just as fast, sure-footed receivers need effective, enterprising quarterbacks, alliance managers must be backed by active, involved top management teams to ensure optimal performance of an alliance and, more important, the success of an alliance-based strategy. But executive participation must extend beyond formulation of an alliance-based strategy that governs the forging and structuring of alliances to personal involvement in the alliance management process.

Top managers' treatment of an alliance signals its importance to lower-level alliance managers and others, thereby setting the context for and delimiting the likely evolution of the relationship. Top managers who view alliances as ad hoc responses to transitory market needs tend to leave their management to alliance managers. Only when an alliance is truly temporary, of clearly limited time horizon and scope and unlikely to affect a firm's long-term strategic posture, conditions that rarely occur, is this a wise course. Even alliances established for tactical reasons frequently have the potential to become crucial strategic links.

If we accept that top management involvement in alliances is crucial, at what level should it occur? Moreover, what precisely do we mean by the personal involvement of top management? Clearly, we are not calling for day-to-day commitment in their management, which is the purview of alliance managers. Top management's participation occurs appropriately at the top. Ideally it takes the form of direct and frequent personal contact between top managers for purposes of understanding how an alliance is likely to evolve and assessing the desirability of that evolution to take steps to shape or influence events related to their respective firms' strategies. Firms pursuing alliance-based strategies that have tried to institutionalize the personal involvement of top managers include Motorola, Ford, Corning Glass, Toshiba, and Mazda. We found Ford's approach comprehensive, instructive, and particularly well thought out.

TOP MANAGEMENT INVOLVEMENT IN FORD ALLIANCES

Among the firms that have been involved in multiple strategic alliances, Ford Motor Company stands out in terms of personal involvement on the part of senior management.[1] We examine specifically how Ford keeps top management involved in its alliance with Mazda in the context of the company's overall approach to alliance management. The elaborate Ford-Mazda apparatus depicted in Figure 7.1 incorporates four levels of interface: senior management; alliance management; functional or operating; and supervisory or team leader. Each performs certain critical tasks, as described in the figure.

A key component of the alliance management apparatus is a three-day meeting once every eight months of executives and a select group of operating unit general managers from each company. This Senior Management Strategy Group, convened to set policy and strategy, establish priorities, and resolve thorny issues, is the apex of interface management between the two firms. Both Ford and Mazda have created alliance management organizations, the Northern Pacific Business Development office and the International Business Development office, respectively, headed by their alliance managers.

Nothing of consequence occurs in the alliance without the approval of these two offices and their respective managers. Many of the tasks associated with alliance management identified in the previous chapter are performed at this level. The heads of these two offices and their key links in their respective operating units (e.g., the heads of the product and engineering divisions) constitute the Joint Steering Committee, presumably the key forum of cooperation between the two companies. All issues are discussed, and most resolved, at this level. The committee is also the key link in the vertical chain between the Senior Management Strategy Group, responsible for strategic direction setting, and the team leaders' group, entrusted with the ground-floor implementation of the alliance.

Day-to-day operational interaction between the partners (e.g., the exchange of information essential to the sourcing relationship) occurs at the functional or operating level. The functional or operating managers themselves meet perhaps three or four times per year.

The base level represents the program-related managers who cooperate to iron out problems, establish routines, and ensure that individual programs

Figure 7.1
Ford-Mazda Interface Management

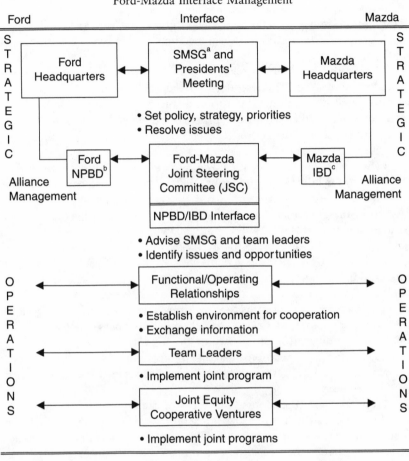

Source: Internal company documents, various years.

function smoothly. At any instant, Ford and Mazda are involved in more than two dozen cooperative programs or projects (e.g., the compact V-6 engine program, MTX/ATX transmissions program, compact pickup cooperation program, Hermosillo assembly program, and Taiwan supplier-based development program). Project-level meetings are convened by project personnel as necessary.[2]

Within this elaborate apparatus for interfirm cooperation, alliance-related tasks cascade from strategic conceptualization at the presidents' level to detailed programmatic efforts at the project managers' level. Top management is embedded in the process in a way that does not involve senior managers in daily routines.

Over the years, Ford senior managers have cultivated personal relationships with their counterparts at Mazda. For example, Philip Caldwell, Ford chairman in the late 1970s and early 1980s, is reported to have established close working relationships with his Mazda counterparts while making his way up in the Ford hierarchy in the 1960s and 1970s, when the linkages between the two firms were still tentative. Donald Petersen, head of International at Ford during the 1970s and Caldwell's eventual successor, and Harold Poling, who later succeeded Petersen, also cultivated relationships with senior managers at Mazda. These strong personal ties contributed significantly to the success of the alliance over the years.

The elaborate mechanisms the two firms have put in place are designed both to reinforce existing ties and to help other members of senior management forge similar ties. So important do Ford and Mazda consider the building of personal relationships that opportunities for informal social interaction are incorporated into the schedules of Senior Management Strategy Group meetings.

Presidents' meetings, which include only the top three executives from each firm, follow the meetings of the Senior Management Strategy Group at intervals of about four months. These meetings accommodate candid exchanges between the firms' top executives on topics ranging from global industry and economic trends to broad strategies and opportunities for cooperation. The meetings stress informality as much as the discussion of important business topics of mutual interest. Ford managers value the meetings as opportunities for freewheeling discussions and for cementing personal relationships.

Exploring the Dimensions of Executive Participation

The good alliance management practice exemplified by Ford encompasses two equally important and closely related dimensions, one external, the other internal. The behavior of senior managers in relationships with partners can have a profound impact not only on the relationships themselves, but also on their own organizations. The balance of this chapter is given over to an examination of these dimensions.

The External Dimension: Top Management and the Partner

We have found that their personal interest in an alliance signals to a partner the top managers' interest in and commitment to fostering reciprocity, deepening personal commitment, engendering organizational commitment, exploring new strategic opportunities, conducting strategic reviews of alliances, and even ending alliances. We examine each of these in turn.

Fostering organizational reciprocity. Frequent involvement by top managers in an alliance suggests that a firm attaches considerable importance to the relationship and encourages reciprocal behavior on the part of a partner. The CEO of a company committed to a number of international alliances remarked,

> When a partner knows you are personally interested in the success of a particular alliance, that immediately raises the stakes for the partner firm. It sends a not-so-subtle message that the senior managers of the partner organization, too, had better pay attention to the alliance. This applies as much to CEOs as to other members of the top management team. When that happens, an alliance takes on an entirely new and important dimension in the partner organization. The other firm begins to reciprocate your efforts toward making the alliance succeed. And that—the reciprocity—is important.

An alliance that lacks reciprocal goodwill is likely to get bogged down in details instead of being carried forward by the overall strategic thrust of the relationship. Top management involvement is a spur to managers at the operating level, an admonition to cease quibbling over minutiae and get on with the work of the alliance.

An alliance between U.S. and Japanese high-tech firms, announced with great fanfare, yielded nothing of significance for more than six months, despite several meetings between middle managers of the two companies to discuss specific plans. In fact, the managers could not reach agreement on a sequence of activities. But when the CEO of the U.S. firm expressed a desire to review the progress of the alliance with his Japanese counterpart, the tenor of the meetings suddenly changed. "All of a sudden," recalled a middle manager of the U.S. firm, "the two sides got busy and resolved many of the pending issues. Even before the meeting, we agreed on a detailed plan and schedule as to what to do."

Top management involvement promotes prompt, effective resolution of differences. The CEO of a U.S. firm allied with a German company recounted how he had been able to resolve some serious issues by simply picking up the phone and calling his counterpart.

> Our close personal relationship has given me sufficient insight into his thinking that I can usually tell where he is coming from on any issue. So can he about my way of looking at issues. We can discuss some issues more openly and candidly than our operating managers. That helps us resolve problems. Also, at our level, we have the ability to detach ourselves from a particular project and view the relationship from the total corporate perspective. Without close personal ties, I cannot imagine these discussions ever taking place or their being so amicable.

Deepening personal commitment at all levels. A CEO we interviewed observed that "personal involvement is often equated [by the partner firm] with personal commitment." Recall the U.S. and Korean firms that got a new lease on life when the U.S. firm's CEO personally reviewed its progress and appointed a senior manager to manage it. "Until my counterpart in the other company got involved personally and made the appointment, we were not at all sure if the Americans were really serious about the alliance," recalled the CEO of the Korean firm. "Once we realized that we could count on his personal interest in the project, I knew I had to show equal commitment to the relationship." Such personal devotion often translates into organizational dedication as managers at lower levels adjust their behavior.

Engendering organizational commitment. Absence of organizational commitment on the part of one or both partners can cripple an alliance. Hence, senior management's personal involvement is more than symbolic; it galvanizes support at lower levels, from the alliance manager down to the rank-and-file operating managers.

An alliance manager involved in a number of alliances explained that he took top management's level of involvement as a measure of how much importance he should attach to a particular alliance.

> Obviously, if top management shows more concern for one alliance than for another, I'm going to pay more attention to the former. Let's face it, it's an organizational fact of life that what the CEO spends his time on becomes important to the rest of the organization. Nobody can be blind to that fact. Take our alliance with [a particular partner]. Everyone involved with the various projects knows that our CEO meets at least twice a year with the CEO from the other company to discuss substantive issues. Naturally, everyone strives to meet the needs of the alliance.

Top management participation, beyond encouraging organizational commitment to an alliance, can foster more active involvement between managers at various levels of the organization and their counterparts in the alliance. Close interaction at multiple levels of the partner firms makes for a stronger alliance.

Exploring new strategic opportunities. Top management's close personal interest in alliances can also afford opportunities to discern areas of cooperation.[3] A senior manager in the Ford-Mazda alliance commented,

> After all, we bring to the meeting a firmwide knowledge and understanding of what is going on in major functional and business areas. Our personal discussions often trigger new opportunities for further collaboration. The two of us discuss new ideas tentatively in our meetings and then turn them over to our staff for further exploration. Of course, some ideas die quickly. That is fine. Others blossom into major projects.

There is another reason meetings between partners' top managers tend to be fertile ground for new ideas and projects—familiarity. Top managers comfortable with their mutual assessments of one another's capabilities are apt to think of one another when new projects are first conceived.[4] Working with known partners is often deemed preferable to seeking new ones for new projects.[5] Again, the Ford-Mazda alliance is instructive. According to a Ford senior manager, whenever either firm conceives a new project for collaboration, it usually gives first consideration to the other.

Conducting strategic reviews. The discipline that drives partners to assess an alliance periodically almost invariably is imposed from the top. According to one alliance manager,

> In a large company like ours, once some action is initiated and set in motion, there is a great tendency for everyone to keep on doing it whether it makes sense or not. Alliances are no exception to this rule. Unless someone, especially someone at the top, asks hard questions, an alliance can become part of the bureaucratic routine. When that happens, a basic premise on which alliances rest—flexibility of response in a changing world—is forgotten.

Hard questioning of the utility, desirability, and efficacy of an alliance is what we call strategic review. Although alliance managers play a major role in the review process for alliances, much of the task necessarily lies in the domain of top management. Alliance managers are positioned to assess change in the conditions and circumstance of an alliance, top management to assess it in the overall context of a firm's strategy.

How do personal relationships between the senior managers of alliance partners facilitate the critical task of strategic review? For one thing, the need to formalize personal relationships invariably puts the review on senior managers' agendas. One CEO remarked,

> I consider alliances to be part of our overall strategy and, as a result, try to meet with my counterparts in all key partner firms once or twice a year. The meetings are not meant to be ceremonial. We take up real issues. These meetings have forced each of us to review the status of the alliance. I feel it is important to make certain that both partners are satisfied with the alliance because, in my experience, only a real win-win relationship can survive over the long run. I just want to make sure that both of us are getting what we want out of the alliance.

When partners' top managements jointly undertake a strategic review, it quickly flows down to lower management. Nothing so concentrates the minds of lower-level managers and staff people as having to brief top management on an item in the latter's agenda for a meeting with another firm's senior managers!

Senior staff in one firm we studied had to do a great deal of work before meetings between their CEO and his counterparts in partner firms. According to a senior manager in the corporate strategic planning group, what began as routine briefing exercises burgeoned into major appraisals in the course of which the planning group asked a great many questions of those directly involved in managing relationships with alliance partners. This, in turn, entailed delving into individual projects in each alliance. In effect, the briefing opportunity for top management had evolved into a strategic review opportunity for the entire corporation. The vice president of the strategic planning group recalled,

> When we undertook the exercise for the first time, we were amazed by what we learned—how extensive our relationship with a particular partner had become, how many people from our firm were involved, and how much interaction was taking place between us and the other firm. As we solicited views from people directly involved in the joint projects, we found out that a lot more of our people were participants in these projects on an occasional basis . . . Until we undertook that exercise, there had not been a systematic firmwide assessment. Since then, we use the annual CEO meeting as an occasion to review the total relationship with each of our partners.

Such annual reviews serve not only to surface specific issues, but also to assess the overall relationship between the partners. "When I meet with my counterpart in a partner's organization," explained one CEO, "it provides me with an opportunity to see the issues relating to our alliance from a different perspective altogether. Sometimes our meetings even permit us to devise new solutions to some long outstanding tricky issues."

Perhaps the greatest dividend of senior management involvement in alliances derives from the law of unintended consequences, meaning that such involvement often fosters organizational learning. Let us explain. The need to prepare strategic reviews of a firm's alliances and the projects within them forces the senior managers who are preparing briefings for top management to meet with the various alliance managers and project leaders. The consequent interaction among all of them promotes widespread information sharing about how alliances function and what alliance-related management practices work best under specific conditions.

Such unplanned organizational learning can be quite helpful, as one alliance manager discovered.

> At first, I did not particularly care for the annual review the headquarters staff conducted of our relationship with our partner. I considered it another high-level staff review that typically took up a lot of my time with little immediate or tangible benefit to me. I was wrong. The headquarters people shared with me the information they had collected and their analysis of the different alliances and projects. That was an eye-opener. I was surprised at the number of projects within all those alliances and the number and types of interactions that were going on. Earlier, I talked to other alliance managers and project leaders only occasionally. Now I talk to them more often and have learned quite a lot from them.

Ultimately, alliance managers in this firm arranged to meet regularly to exchange information and relate lessons they had learned.

Ending alliances. A natural consequence of strategic reviews of alliances is the occasional necessity to end one. Here the role of top management is paramount. For one thing, with it rests the ultimate responsibility to decide when and how to discontinue an association. Top managers are able to rise above the day-to-day diversions of running an alliance and assess whether it has outlived its promise, especially in the context of changing strategic priorities of the firm. Moreover, the top managers' interactions with their counterparts in the partner firm permit them to better assess how the usefulness of the alliance is being viewed by the other firm. Such an input is critical for the timing and manner of ending alliances.

Second, while both alliance managers and top managers need to distinguish carefully between making an alliance work and achieving the strategic goals it was designed to promote, in practice top management needs to exercise an independent judgment. Again, top management is often ahead of middle-level managers, from whose ranks most alliance managers are drawn, with respect to changes over the horizon vis-à-vis changes in the industry and corresponding changes in the strategic objectives of the firm. Thus, an alliance that may be working well may be falling short of the strategic objectives that top management might have set for it. Top management has to provide a clear signal as to when an alliance must be terminated.

Finally, the manner of bringing an alliance to an end is as important as the decision to end it. Whether an alliance ends in acrimony and bitter recrimination or in a peaceful parting of ways with the possibility of future alliances preserved is critical. The manner in which an alliance ends sends powerful signals about the partner firms to others, affecting the reputations of the firms. Therefore, top managers have to be aware of their responsibility in ensuring that the windup of alliances is accomplished without impairment of the firm's ability to form future ones.

The Internal Dimension: Top Management and Its Organization

The message top management sends to its own managers and line people is as crucial to the success of an alliance as the message it sends to the top management of its partners. Internally, as externally, the message is one not of words but of deeds. It is read in the selection of a manager for, and the allocation of resources to, an alliance, as well as in the way senior management shapes shared strategic intent and whether it exerts the considerable effort required to recast reward systems and catalyze cultural change.

Selection of an alliance manager. Earlier, we discussed the important role alliance managers play in day-to-day relationships with an alliance partner. It is top management's responsibility to ensure an appropriate infrastructure for the interfirm relationship and to designate a qualified person to manage it.

Ford top management, as we saw, created the Northern Pacific Business Development office to manage the company's relationships with Mazda of Japan and Kia of Korea. The alliance management office, which reported to a senior executive in charge of strategic planning who was effectively the executive in charge of all alliances, was to be staffed by six key people based in Dearborn, Tokyo, Hiroshima, and Seoul (see Figure 7.2). The office was initially headed by an executive director with extensive operational experience and later by another Ford veteran with considerable experience in Europe.

Figure 7.2
The Ford Alliance Management Office

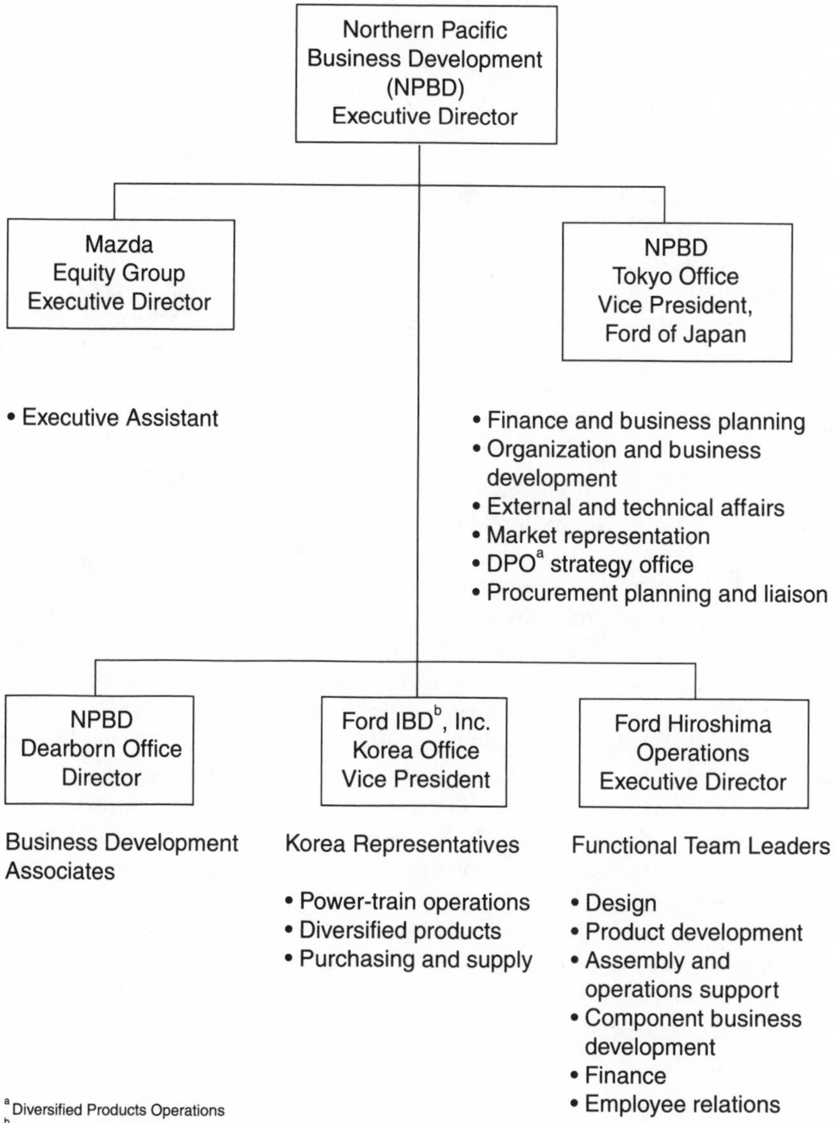

```
                    ┌─────────────────────────┐
                    │   Northern Pacific      │
                    │ Business Development    │
                    │        (NPBD)           │
                    │  Executive Director     │
                    └─────────────────────────┘
```

┌──────────────────────┐   ┌──────────────────────┐
│   Mazda   │   │   NPBD   │
│   Equity Group   │   │   Tokyo Office   │
│ Executive Director │   │ Vice President,   │
│   │   │   Ford of Japan   │
└──────────────────────┘   └──────────────────────┘

• Executive Assistant   • Finance and business planning
                                            • Organization and business
                                              development
                                            • External and technical affairs
                                            • Market representation
                                            • DPO[a] strategy office
                                            • Procurement planning and liaison

┌──────────────────┐   ┌──────────────────┐   ┌──────────────────┐
│   NPBD   │   │ Ford IBD[b], Inc.│   │ Ford Hiroshima │
│ Dearborn Office │   │   Korea Office   │   │   Operations   │
│   Director   │   │ Vice President │   │Executive Director│
└──────────────────┘   └──────────────────┘   └──────────────────┘

Business Development   Korea Representatives   Functional Team Leaders
Associates
                        • Power-train operations • Design
                        • Diversified products   • Product development
                        • Purchasing and supply • Assembly and
                                                   operations support
                                                 • Component business
                                                   development
                                                 • Finance
[a] Diversified Products Operations   • Employee relations
[b] International Business Development

Source: Internal company documents, various years.

Careful selection of alliance managers signals to internal managers as well as to partners the importance top management attaches to a relationship. The CEO of a U.S. firm that established an alliance with a Japanese company related how his choice of an alliance manager played out internally.

> When we signed the deal, there were a lot of questions. After all, the partner firm was one with which we have competed for years. In fact, in several product areas we still do. It was fascinating to observe how many of the concerns were allayed once we appointed a highly respected senior executive to head the alliance management effort. He, in turn, put together a first-class team to help him manage the alliance. We have let it be known that the alliance manager has ready access to the COO and myself. Over time, many of the managers in the operating divisions have come to me to express their happiness over our alliance manager choice. They felt that they could trust his judgment.

Resource allocation for alliances. Alliances, as large-scale, complex, ambiguous relationships, can require a substantial commitment of resources. Top management decides the level of resource allocation for an alliance, a decision, like the selection of an alliance manager, that sends powerful signals.

A few months after a division of a diversified U.S. firm entered into an alliance with a Korean firm, difficulties led to the replacement of the division head. His successor, to improve the division's performance, initiated relentless cost-cutting measures, one of the first being to reduce the number of management layers from three to one, and soon the alliance manager himself was given a major additional responsibility. The result was that the alliance ground to a halt over the next several months. The alliance manager later lamented that other managers in the division, interpreting the new division head's actions to signal a low priority for the alliance, felt there was no need to respond expeditiously to any of his requests for help.

Ford's alliance managers, by contrast, were not only visible, but enjoyed access to significant resources as well. The same was true of the U.S. firm that established an R&D alliance with a European firm; top U.S. company management strove to ensure that its alliance management team was appropriately structured, adequately staffed, and provided with resources.

Shaping shared strategic intent. It is frequently suggested that for alliances to work well, the partner firms must share a common strategic vision. We noted in the course of our study an increasing number of companies' developing joint vision statements to guide their actions. One such, issued by Ford and Mazda, for example, advances the goal of creating a close working relationship without jeopardizing either firm's independence. The statement sets forth basic understandings regarding coordinated efforts to improve resource utilization.[6]

The process of developing a joint vision is as valuable as the statement that results from it because it forces the managers in the partner firms to conceive, communicate, and commit to common goals. Of course, in the absence of a commitment to live by the vision, the statement is construed to be empty and serves only to foster cynicism.

Like the development of a shared vision, the development of a shared strategic intent is vital to building internal support for an alliance. By shared strategic intent we mean a common understanding of the roles and limits of the alliance with respect to the overall competitive strategy of a firm. Managers in a company that employs alliances as part of its competitive strategy must understand how these relationships fit into the firm's overall strategic framework.

Shaping and communicating shared strategic intent is perhaps top management's most critical role.[7] The concept of strategic alliances remains new and alien in many firms. Managers and supervisors are accustomed to a more traditional organizational ethos, that is, working with friends (read subsidiaries or suppliers) and against foes (read competitors). The rules of engagement are clear: cooperate with the former; compete with the latter. Strategic alliances blur the distinction between friend and foe. Educating employees about this change in an organizational ethos is the responsibility of top management and the function of shared strategic intent.

Shared intent elucidates an alliance's fit with a firm's overall competitive strategy, the risks as well as the benefits associated with an alliance-based strategy, and the steps employees must take to minimize these risks while they advance the work of the alliance.

The experiences of the growing number of firms taking steps to articulate and communicate strategic rationales for the alliances they have established offer several important lessons. One is that communication must be extensive, permeating the entire organization. One senior executive stated, "An alliance is an unnatural act; we are simply not used to the concept. Also, we have not had much experience with it. We tend to suspect the worst in things that are unfamiliar to us."

For alliances to work effectively, top management must dispel a host of fears and concerns regarding the exporting of jobs, loss of precious skills and experience, and slighting of internal creative abilities. A senior executive in a firm that has made effective use of alliances declared,

> The day-to-day implementation of details is totally in the hands of our middle and lower management. It is ludicrous to think that we can have an effective alliance strategy without first obtaining total buy-in from the people who must carry on day-to-day tasks. But too often we forget or ignore the obvious at great expense.

When top management fails to articulate and communicate a shared strategic intent for an alliance, the relationship almost invariably falls under a dark cloud of suspicion and is probably doomed from the beginning. Top management's failure in this regard can have another unintended consequence. Managers who do not understand the strategic rationale for an alliance may approach the relationship too cavalierly, for example, leaking vital information to a partner, at considerable long-term cost to their companies.

Extensive communication efforts aimed at informing all levels of an organization about an alliance are becoming more common. Information about alliances with other firms is becoming an integral part of many CEOs' general communications to employees about their companies' overall direction and strategy. General Electric chairman Jack Welch, for one, has frequently appealed to employees to support particular alliances, and Corning CEO James Houghton makes it a point to communicate regularly with the firm's employees about its use of strategic alliances. Toshiba CEOs have made a practice of communicating to employees the reasons for the company's extensive use of alliances, and Ford CEOs have consistently talked about the firm's alliances in their annual letters to employees.

Such CEOs are keenly aware that occasional public announcements are only the beginning of what one called "an internal education effort." Many acknowledge that continuing attempts to enhance organizational understanding of their companies' alliances are necessary. During the formation of an alliance, a number of companies we studied communicated its background, rationale, and anticipated benefits. In a company that was involved in several alliances, top management had developed an extensive communication program with different elements aimed at different levels of the organization. The program came into being through trial and error after the company encountered considerable resistance to its initial forays into alliance-making. The current approach takes a variety of forms.

At the most basic level, a bulletin signed by the CEO, containing considerably more information than traditional corporate bulletins about the alliance and the circumstances that occasioned it, is sent to all employees. Next, the company prepares and distributes to relevant parts of the organization a fifteen- to twenty-minute videotape that provides even more background information, including a profile of the alliance partner and selected shots of its factories, research facilities or sales outlets, and products. It also features interviews with the CEO and relevant executives and managers who participated in the formulation of the alliance and will be actively involved in managing the alliance. Finally, senior managers meet personally with small groups of employees in the business or functional areas that will be most directly affected by the alliance or whose support and cooperation are strongly required.

This three-pronged approach appears to have worked well for the company. "We are not, however, resting on our laurels," said one senior executive. "We are trying to fine-tune our approach to match it to the needs of each alliance and its likely impact on our organization." Here the executive was referring to the different kinds of alliances his firm has entered into. An alliance that involves rationalization of a business, for example, may include reductions in head count. Simple acts of communication do not allay real fears of job loss and consequent lowering of morale in affected business units.

We noted an interesting approach to creating shared strategic intent in a major U.S. manufacturing firm that established a highly visible and important alliance with a Japanese rival, one which has been hailed by the press as exemplary of how alliances can be made to work to the benefit of rival firms. A conversation with the firm's senior management was revealing. One member offered the following assessment:

> Everyone, especially at the senior management level, knows that alliances are an extremely potent competitive weapon. We also, of course, recognize that there are serious downside risks to alliances as well. That is where extensive communication to as many in the organization as is feasible becomes critical. Our intention in communicating to people at all levels is as much to seek their cooperation in making the alliance work as to make sure that they are aware of the fine line we, in this corporation, are walking between tremendous potential payoffs and significant risks. Sure, we want our people to make the alliance effort succeed, but we also want them to be on guard to protect our interests.

It is in the context of acquainting the organization's rank and file with the balance top management is trying to strike between the benefits and risks of competitive alliances that an interesting managerial practice of this firm stands out.[8]

The same U.S. firm developed an extensive weekend orientation program designed to afford affected managers greater understanding of the rationale for an alliance and acculturate them to work with their counterparts in the partner organization. Various levels of middle managers are briefed in detail on the history of the alliance. Among the thick confidential briefing books managers receive on arriving for the program is a file containing an elaborate competitive profile that details the evolution of the partner's strategic moves in such areas as product offerings, technology development, and marketing channels, provides extensive comparative data on both firms, and outlines projections of possible areas of cooperation and conflict (or competition) between the two firms. These data are elaborated in the classroom.

The effect of the program is to make lower-level managers aware of the competitive nature of the alliance.[9] "The idea," a senior manager explained, "is to make everyone in the firm realize that they have to walk a fine line between cooperation and competition." We subsequently discovered that the U.S. firm's Japanese partner has a similar in-house training program for managers involved in alliances.

Recasting reward systems. Successful implementation of alliances imposes new demands on managers. Corning's Houghton contributed this appraisal:

> By forcing my senior managers to spend a lot more time worrying about alliances, I have broadened and complicated the scope of their work. My managers have become responsible for operations over which they do not have full authority. They are accountable for results over which they have only partial control. This means they have to use influence to shape priorities. They have to be comfortable negotiating rather than just deciding on important issues.

How can top management encourage managers to meet new demands of their jobs at a time when most are already under enormous pressure as a result of corporate restructuring?

For one thing, it can make the incentive system congruent with the nature of the tasks managers are asked to perform. The need to realign traditional incentive and reward systems to the new reality was not widely recognized in the companies we studied. Most managers tend to deal only with the symptoms of alliance-related problems that have their origins in incentive systems that do not reward alliance-related activities.[10]

Bizarre incentive mechanisms are often built into alliance-related work. If a sourcing alliance works smoothly and well, for example, the sales manager is most likely to benefit. When low-cost, low-price quality products flow in a timely manner through a firm's distribution channels, it is the sales manager who looks good. But the manufacturing and engineering groups are the ones that typically must put the most effort into a sourcing alliance. Yet not only are they not rewarded commensurate with their contribution, but the success of the alliance could lead some to conclude that in-house manufacturing is inefficient and more sourcing alliances are needed.

Consider a product-development alliance between two firms. The more successful the alliance is in creating new products that do well in the marketplace, the more likely it is that the company managers will compare it with the projects undertaken solely in-house. A superficial comparison, however, may be misleading. The success of the alliance project may depend significantly on the progress made in the in-house projects. As these linkages are often invisible on the surface, managers may decide to shift resources away from in-house R&D to alliances. This is the first step on the slippery slope to becoming a "hollow" corporation.

Incentive systems deeply embedded in the fabric of organizations are built over the years in response to past needs. Alliances are too recent and too unique to be easily incorporated into traditional incentive systems. We saw in an earlier chapter how a floor supervisor in a manufacturing plant was rewarded for increasing output, not for training an alliance partner's personnel. Such a manager is not liable to and in fact did not pay much attention to the needs of the alliance. Nor can an alliance manager unilaterally change reward systems without thinking through the ramifications of such action. "It's easier to recognize a perverse incentive problem than to do something about it," remarked one supervisor. "Most operating managers are reluctant to make ad hoc changes in order to make my job easier. I can understand their reluctance. After all, another manager may come along tomorrow and ask for some other change. Where is the end to this tweaking of incentives?" Moreover, the alliance manager, although best positioned to recognize perverse incentive structures, lacks authority to initiate major changes.

The existence of different types of alliances further confounds the issue of incentives. It calls for different changes in incentive systems. Take the interface between manufacturing and R&D in a firm with two alliances, each with a different firm, one for sourcing and the other for product development. From the point of view of the sourcing alliance, it is best if manufacturing engineers quickly transfer new ideas relating to product extensions to the alliance partner for incorporation into the products. However, the partner in the product-development (R&D) alliance may not appreciate the transfer of ideas from the R&D alliance to a third party (here the sourcing-alliance partner). Indeed, if marketing managers are brought into the picture, their short-term interest may support the needs of the sourcing alliance, which enables them to bring new and improved products to the market sooner; but their long-term interest may support the needs of the R&D alliance because it continues the flow of new and fertile ideas to the joint product-development collaboration.

Finally, there is the question of designing appropriate measurement systems for those required to take part in an alliance. Effective participation often relies on a special set of skills. Consider the attitudinal and behavioral changes required of scientists in an international research and development alliance. National differences in scientific training and education introduce complications. European- and Japanese-trained scientists' tendency not to challenge colleagues' ideas directly initially comes as a shock to U.S. scientists, who thrive on adversarial intellectual debate. Moreover, U.S. scientists tend to be more individualistic than, for example, Japanese scientists, to say nothing of the inevitable differences in language and culture. A U.S. scientist told us,

> We are much more open to sharing ideas and information with others. We have been trained that way. It is not that our Japanese colleagues are secretive, but they tend to be much more cautious and in many ways much more conservative. Moreover, there is also a subtle language factor. Since many of our Japanese colleagues have a real language handicap, they often cannot articulate their views clearly. But most of them understand English much better than they can speak it. Therefore, they tend to understand most of what we say, but their language handicap and our inability to understand Japanese makes it really difficult to engage in meaningful discussion with them. Our corporate incentives for scientists reward a high degree of specialization and individual accomplishments. Their corporations do not appear to contain this incentive. Herein lies a real conflict for us to be able to work effectively as a team. I do not know what the answer is, but somehow we need to change behavior, and I am sure that means we need to alter our traditional incentive system.

Changing a long-cherished incentive system is not easy. The firms we studied continue to struggle with this issue. But although none have yet found a satisfactory solution, some tentative approaches are evolving. Top management in one company that employs alliances extensively includes in its annual appraisal system an assessment of how effectively executives manage their alliances. "In appraising the performance of our executives," a senior executive in the corporation informed us, "we make certain that we look at how they are managing their alliances. It is difficult to quantify many of the criteria, and we must be extremely careful in identifying and rewarding appropriately those behavioral characteristics that are conducive to successful implementation of alliances. It is not easy." Another added, "The mere fact we raise these issues has certainly helped raise the consciousness throughout the organization."

A CEO we interviewed had this to say:

> We have given a great deal of thought to this issue. After all, the traits and behavioral patterns that are essential to be successful members of an alliance will be required in all future managers anyway. These traits include flexibility, teamwork, willingness and ability to learn from others, negotiating skills, and so forth. For that reason, I am trying to encourage our organization to figure out a way to measure these characteristics generally, not necessarily only for those who are directly involved in alliances.

To make our network come alive, people at several levels have to move across invisible borders. This requires managers with a flexible style and a broad portfolio of skills. Such individuals are normally in very short supply. Both joint-venture partners have to recognize that moving bright, energetic people in and out of alliances is not only acceptable, it is vital. We can't tolerate opportunistic practices like cherry-picking bright people from alliances, or worse, filling them with parent company rejects.

Catalyzing cultural change. The business approach historically favored by most firms, particularly U.S. companies, which stresses unambiguous control over resources and clearly delineated responsibilities in dealings with other firms, has occasioned an extraordinarily complex web of interrelated policies, procedures, and practices. The result has been the development of what might be called a corporate culture of self-reliance characterized by clear lines of demarcation between the firm and its environment, between suppliers and competitors, between information that belongs within a firm and information that can be shared with outsiders, and between what is and is not essential to the success of the organization. Alliances straddle all these neat dichotomies, hence the need for cultural change within organizations.

Personal involvement in alliances, fostering organizational commitment and reciprocity, deepening personal commitment, seizing new strategic opportunities, conducting strategic reviews, appointing the right persons as alliance managers, ensuring proper resource allocation, shaping shared strategic intent, and reworking reward systems—all the tasks of top management that we have enumerated thus far must be part of any effort to change organizational culture to accommodate alliances. But additional steps are required to catalyze cultural change, and they, too, must be taken by top management.

Our research suggests that there are three areas of corporate culture which top management should seek to alter by direct action: the us-versus-them attitude with respect to cooperation that prevails at most levels of organizations; the not-invented-here syndrome with respect to organizational learning; and the inability to strike a strategic balance between cooperation and competition.

How does a firm that has difficulty getting people to cooperate across functions get managers, supervisors, and workers to collaborate with their counterparts in an alliance? U.S. firms have often been criticized, for example, for failing to get their marketing, manufacturing, and research and development people to collaborate for the common good.[11] Multibusiness companies have difficulty getting their business units to collaborate, multinational companies to effect interorganizational cooperation; subsidiaries and headquarters do not always work toward the same goals, nor do different national subsidiaries. Clearly defined responsibility for profits and costs relies on autonomy of action, which tends to encourage independence and unwillingness to collaborate. Alliances are an anomaly in this historically noncollaborative culture. They call for close association not only within firms, but also between firms, often those that compete.

Faced with considerable resistance to and misunderstanding of a new alliance-based strategy, the top managers of a major U.S. company, recognizing that middle management was clinging to the old culture, decided to mount a major educational effort. They assembled a team of outside experts, consultants, and academics to design a one-week educational program to communicate to middle managers the strategic logic of, risks associated with, key management issues related to, and the skills needed for effective participation in alliances. Top management also brought in executives from other companies involved in alliances to talk to program participants about the managerial changes required to cope with alliances. Finally, participants were exposed to cross-cultural learning experiences designed to acquaint them with the cultural differences that inevitably come into play in international alliances. Top management has institutionalized the educational program as part of an ongoing effort to render the organization's culture more hospitable to alliances. Another firm includes topics related to alliances in the curriculum of its extensive in-house management-development program.

Perhaps the greatest opportunity and challenge posed by alliances relates to organizational learning.[12] As we have seen, alliances afford a unique opportunity to learn from partners in such areas as process technology, marketing-related skills, and even inventory management. Many observers have suggested that Asian companies tend to be ahead of U.S. firms in terms of having a learning culture, some going so far as to assert that because Asians tend to be good learners and Americans better teachers, alliances are invariably to the detriment of the U.S. partners.[13] Such assertions imply that the cultures of U.S. firms are not conducive to organizational learning and will remain so forever. It may not be so. The not-invented-here syndrome, however, is alive and well in many firms.

The educational program discussed at some length earlier also emphasized the need to develop skills necessary for learning from partners. It emphasized that learning could be institutionalized through regular briefings of people who visit partner firms and debriefings on their return. Moreover, the program stressed that learning was not imposed from above, but was a product of individual effort and organizational sharing.[14]

Perhaps the most difficult cultural change top management must make is to inculcate in lower-level managers the ability to strike a balance between the spirit of cooperation required to ensure the success of the alliance and the element of competition required to preserve the partners' independent competitive positions. Cautioned one senior manager,

> It is so easy to go overboard with this idea of cooperation. Sure, we want our people to work harmoniously with the people in our

partner firm. It does not mean we want our company to be an open book for the other firm. After all, we are still competitors in many product markets. The alliance does not change that fact. Getting our managers to remember this is not as easy as you might think.

Surely, it is contrary to human nature to maintain the contradictory impulses of cooperation and competition simultaneously.

The difficulty of teaching notwithstanding, managers must learn to navigate the treacherous waters between overenthusiastic cooperation and counterproductive competition. Here, top management can lead by example. Lower-level managers are often present when the senior managers of alliance partners meet. Their observations of how senior managers conduct themselves with respect to information exchange can guide their own efforts to balance cooperation and competition.

CHAPTER 8

Managing Alliances:
The Multibusiness Firm

Thus far, we have considered strategic alliances in the context of single firms or units of multibusiness firms. Industry's being the arena in which the struggle for competitive advantage is fought, and strategic alliances' being, by definition, part of the effort to win that struggle, we have emphasized the managerial imperatives of alliances for general managers who compete in a single industry.[1]

Our research suggests, however, that alliances should be examined from the perspective of corporate as well as single-business-unit management. This distinction, not clearly defined in the current academic or managerial literature, is particularly important in the case of diversified corporations. In the latter, alliances may be established by corporate management in any of the businesses in which the organization participates; an alliance could come at the initiative of corporate management or by management at the level of the strategic business unit. Obviously, the question arises, Does the job of managing interfirm linkages change from one level of management (the corporate level) to the next (strategic-business-unit level)? The answer is intimately related to the two concepts of strategy—business, or competitive, strategy and corporate strategy.[2]

BUSINESS AND CORPORATE STRATEGY

That two types of strategy are generally at work in most organizations is widely recognized. The distinction between business-level and corporate-level strategy is perhaps most relevant to senior management in diversified corporations.

Consider General Electric (GE) chairman Jack Welch and General Motors (GM) CEO Jack Smith, whose respective corporations participate in a host of alliances at the division level (see Tables 8.1 and 8.2). Are their jobs identical in terms of forging and managing alliances? The answer is bound up in the distinction between business and corporate strategy.

Business strategy refers to the competitive course a firm charts relative to its rivals in a particular industry. It is therefore confined to analysis of that industry and the competitors within it.[3] The identification of business strategy with industry as the unit of analysis has led diversified firms that compete in more than one industry to organize along the lines of individual divisions known as strategic business units (SBUs). SBU general managers plot business strategy, subject only to corporate approval and capital constraints imposed by corporate management, as if they headed independent firms in their respective industries.[4] In response to these circumstances, a second level of strategy, which we term "corporate strategy," has emerged; it is concerned with the composition of the portfolio of businesses in which a firm competes.

The responsibilities of chief executive officers who head diversified firms are appreciably different from those of their single-business counterparts.[5] That is to say, the jobs of Welch and Smith are different. General Motors is largely a single-business firm, automobiles accounting for more than 80% of its sales and profits. Smith's job is to make sure that the company remains competitive relative to its rivals, domestic and foreign. His menu of choice for investments, like that of the head of GE's Medical System group, is circumscribed by the largely one-business nature of the organization.[6]

On the other hand, Welch's charge, General Electric, is the largest diversified multidivisional firm in the United States today, with operations ranging from basic manufacturing to high technology to services. No single GE division contributes more than 15% of the firm's sales or profits. What does the job of GE's CEO entail?

The CEO of a diversified firm has four major concerns: (1) optimal deployment of corporate resources among the divisions or SBUs; (2) the efficacy of the business-level competitive strategies of the division or SBU managers; (3) exploitation of the synergy among various businesses; and (4) the impact of multipoint competition from other diversified firms.[7] The general manager of a single-business firm is concerned almost exclusively with setting competitive strategy and deploying resources to support its implementation. Neither interbusiness synergy (as distinct from interfunctional synergy, which is subsumed under competitive strategy) nor multipoint competition is relevant to the single-business manager.

Table 8.1
Major General Electric Alliances Since 1980

	Partner Firm	Industry	Purpose	Structure
1.	Hitachi, Japan	Nuclear power	Joint R&D	Contract
2.	Hitachi, Japan	Nuclear power	Joint product development	Contract
3.	Chrysler	Robotics	Joint product development	Joint venture
4.	Electric Power Research Institute	Power systems	Joint R&D and product development	Contract
5.	Mitsubishi, Japan	Consumer electronics	Sourcing	Contract
6.	NTN Toyo Bearing, Japan	Bearings	Sourcing	Contract
7.	Fujitsu, Japan	Computers	Sourcing	Contract
8.	Snecma, France	Jet engines	Joint product development	Joint venture
9.	Stone & Webster	Nuclear power	Joint distribution	Joint venture
10.	Japan Servo	Major appliances	Sourcing	Contract
11.	Fiat, Italy	Helicopter engines	Joint product development	Contract
12.	Tabuchi Electric, Japan	Power systems	Sourcing	Contract
13.	Matsushita, Japan	Consumer electronics	Sourcing	Contract
14.	Ungermann-Bass, Germany	Factory automation	Joint product development	Joint venture
15.	Nachi-Fujikoshi, Japan	Robotics	Sourcing	Contract
16.	Toshiba, Japan	Power systems	Sourcing	Contract
17.	Rolls-Royce, United Kingdom	Jet engines	Joint manufacturing	Joint venture
18.	Sanyo, Japan	Major appliances	Sourcing	Contract
19.	Hitachi, Japan	Robotics	Sourcing	Contract
20.	Mitsui, Japan	Plastics	Joint manufacturing	Joint venture
21.	Thorn EMI, United Kingdom	Lighting systems	European entry	Joint venture
22.	GEC, United Kingdom	Major appliances	European entry	Joint venture
23.	GEC, United Kingdom	Medical systems	European entry	Joint venture
24.	Toshiba, Japan	Lighting systems	Joint R&D	Contract
25.	IBM	Microelectronics	Joint product development	Contract
26.	Babcock & Wilcox, United Kingdom	Power systems	Joint product development	Joint venture
27.	Ansaldo, Italy	Power systems	Joint product development	Joint venture

Table 8.1 *(Continued)*

Partner Firm	Industry	Purpose	Structure
28. Fanuc, Japan	Robotics	Joint development and production	Joint venture
29. Yokogawa, Japan	Electronic components	Sourcing	Joint venture

Table 8.2
Major General Motors Alliances Since 1980

Partner Firm	Industry	Purpose	Structure
1. Akebono, Japan	Automotive	Production of brakes	Joint venture
2. Daewoo, Korea	Automotive	Production of ignition coils and starters	Joint venture
3. Mitsubishi, Japan	Automotive	OEM supply of parts	Contract
4. Nissan, Japan	Automotive	OEM supply of parts	Contract
5. Toyota, Japan	Automotive	OEM supply of parts	Contract
6. Ishino Gasket, Japan	Automotive	Sourcing	Contract
7. Isuzu, Japan	Automotive	Sourcing	Minority equity participation
8. Suzuki, Japan	Automotive	Sourcing	Minority equity participation
9. NHK Spring, Japan	Automotive	Sourcing	Joint venture
10. Fanuc, Japan	Factory automation	New venture	Joint venture
11. Pioneer, Japan	Automotive	Sourcing	Contract
12. Toyota, Japan	Automotive	Joint production	Joint venture
13. Jaguar, United Kingdom	Automotive	OEM supply/sourcing	Joint venture
14. Isuzu, Japan	Automotive	Joint production in United Kingdom	Joint venture
15. Suzuki, Japan	Automotive	Joint production in Canada	Joint venture
16. Pininfarina, Italy	Automotive	Sourcing	Contract

THE ROLE OF THE CEO IN A DIVERSIFIED FIRM

We now consider the unique responsibilities that fall to the CEO of a diversified company. Because competition occurs at the business-unit, not the corporate level, formulation of business or competitive strategies for individual SBUs is critical. The CEO typically does not become involved in details of strategy formulation at the level of individual SBUs, but rather provides direction, guidance, and discipline.

The principal contribution of the CEO to strategy formulation for SBUs is the articulation of a corporate philosophy. An example is GE's announced goal of being "number one or two" in any business it participates in, which establishes an overarching theme within which SBU strategies are set. The need to provide firmwide strategic consistency leads the CEOs of diversified firms to attend closely to the formulation of strategy for new businesses, whether internally developed or acquired. Once an SBU has established a long-term strategy, day-to-day involvement by the CEO is usually occasioned only by poor performance or a demand for radical redirection in the face of a changing environment.

Beyond articulating corporate philosophy, Jack Welch provides a common framework for GE's fourteen business-unit heads by requiring them to consider the following questions.[8]

- What are the current market dynamics globally, and where are they going over the next several years?
- What actions have your competitors taken in the past three years to upset those global dynamics?
- What have you done in those three years to affect those dynamics?
- What are the most dangerous things that your competitor could do in the next three years to upset those dynamics?
- What are the most effective things you could do to bring your desired impact on those dynamics?

These broad, yet essential questions provide a common framework within which to formulate individual SBU strategies. "After the initial reviews, which we update regularly," explains Welch, "we could assume that everyone at the top had the same playbook and knew the plays."

Another important role for a CEO of a diversified firm is to motivate business managers to make optimal use of the resources allocated to them through regular performance evaluations supported by a system of reward and punishment. More broadly, the CEO must manage the mix of businesses so as to ensure an appropriate allocation of resources corporatewide. This is consistent with the view of a diversified firm as a bundle of businesses, related and unrelated, that mimic a portfolio of assets held by an investor.[9]

Again, GE provides a useful example. Since Welch became CEO in 1981, General Electric has exited mining, consumer electronics, small appliances, and semiconductors, among other businesses, collectively worth more than $9 billion, and acquired a number of new businesses, chief among them RCA. Welch ascribes these moves to the need to redirect the firm's resources to fit its strategic priorities.[10]

Managing multipoint competition and interrelationships (synergy) has become a significant responsibility of top management with the growth of diversified firms that compete in a number of related or unrelated industries. Because General Electric, Hitachi, and Siemens, for example, compete against one another in a variety of industries, a competitive move that makes sense for one SBU might provoke retaliation aimed at another. Competitor analysis at the level of individual SBUs must be augmented by equivalent analysis at an aggregated corporate level. Top management in a multibusiness firm must, moreover, coordinate the strategies of its SBUs relative to all its multipoint competitors, a daunting task.

That "horizontal interrelationships" among the SBUs of diversified firms can be exploited to enhance competitive position—the venerated notion of synergy—has been doubted by some who have contended that extraordinary organizational effort is required so as to make the process impractical for most firms. But according to Michael Porter, "The failure of synergy stemmed from the inability of companies to understand and implement it, not because of some basic flaw in the concept."[11] Porter cites a number of reasons why managing interrelationships is becoming increasingly important. One is the growing emphasis on performance as diversified companies in the developed part of the world contend with a slow-growth environment. Another is technological change, which is a facilitator as well as supporter of synergistic interrelationships. The convergence of computers, communications, and microelectronics, for example, is sundering traditional industry barriers and making it easier to share activities across SBUs.[12] Top management must help individual SBUs overcome their reluctance to cooperate with one another and to compete as a team. Prodding each SBU to succeed in its business even as the SBUs cooperate to benefit from their strengths is critical to the success of the diversified firm.

General Electric, as we noted earlier, has for more than a decade attended closely to managing interrelationships among its many businesses. GE's research and development synergy is a critical competitive strength for many of its SBUs. Its gas turbine business benefits by working with the jet engine business in high-temperature engines. Its major appliance group benefits by working with the plastics division on materials subject to a great deal of wear and tear. Welch himself has said of management review and incentive systems in GE's SBUs that it is top management's job "to transfer best practices across all the businesses. We want to know which programs are working and immediately alert the other businesses to the successful ones."[13]

Differences in the responsibilities of CEOs who head diversified firms and those who head nondiversified firms, or manage SBUs, stem largely from differences in strategic point of view. These disparities are an important clue to the nature of the alliances they are apt to be asked to manage. We examine this range of alliances next.

SINGLE-BUSINESS VERSUS CORPORATE ALLIANCES

Alliances, as we observed earlier, can further the strategy of a strategic business unit or a corporation. The motives for targeting one over the other are quite different. Single-business firms generally enter into alliances—sourcing or technology alliances, research and development links, distribution coalitions, or logistics-related relationships—to enhance their competitiveness. Such alliances tend neither to be transitional nor to lead a firm to exit an existing or enter a new business. The objective of corporate alliances, on the other hand, tends to be to enhance the attractiveness of a portfolio of businesses. To this end, they tend to serve all the purposes that single-business alliances do not, for example, to help an SBU make the transition to a new competitive strategy, to manage the exit of an SBU from an industry, or to serve as a route to developing a new business.

The categorization of corporate alliances as competitiveness-enhancing, rationalizing, transitional, and new-business, particularly in a corporate or diversified setting, is largely a matter of perspective. Two partners may rank a given alliance differently (see Figure 8.1). What is important about the classification scheme is that corporate management recognize the type of alliance it is pursuing and whether the partner perceives the relationship in the same or a different light.

Competitiveness-enhancing Alliances

Toshiba is a major player in a number of businesses, among them consumer electronics, major appliances, personal computers, industrial machinery, power systems, and semiconductors. A senior executive declared,

> We are an outstanding company with strong technological capabilities. But in the marketplace, we have not always done well. We have suffered from the so-called number two syndrome. We have seldom been number one in any of our businesses. Surely we are in the top tier in all these areas, but often find ourselves in second, third, or even fourth position in a particular industry. Moreover, in

Figure 8.1
Corporate Alliances and Partner Perspectives

Partner B's Perspective

Partner A's Perspective	(1) Competitiveness-enhancing	(2) Rationalizing	(3) Transitional	(4) New-Business
(1) Competitiveness-enhancing	Toshiba-Motorola (semiconductors)	GE-GEC (appliances)	Whirlpool-Philips (appliances)	Boeing-MHI (aircraft)
(2) Rationalizing	GEC-GE (turbines)	Asea-Brown Boveri (power systems)	Dresser-Komatsu (earthmoving equipment)	Siemens-Corning (fiber optics)
(3) Transitional	GE-Bosch (motors)	Asahi-Corning (TV glass)	Ciba-Geigy–Corning (diagnostics)	Corning-Dow (silicone)
(4) New-business	Kodak-Matsushita (batteries)	Fanuc-GE (factory automation)	PPG-Corning (construction glass)	Multimedia alliances

Notes: 1. In all examples, Partner A is mentioned first, then Partner B.
2. The industry in which the alliance competes is shown in parentheses.

most of our businesses we must compete against truly world-class rivals. In power systems our competitors include Hitachi, GE, ABB, and Siemens. In major appliances we are up against competitors like Matsushita, Sanyo, Hitachi, and Mitsubishi. In consumer electronics our competitors include Sony, Matsushita, JVC, and the like. In semiconductors and computers our competitors include NEC, Hitachi, Fujitsu, not to mention foreign suppliers. Many of our competitors can outspend us in each segment of the industry.

Toshiba's semiconductor business, which is not only a leading supplier to the global merchant market but is also charged with supplying state-of-the-art chips at competitive prices to such other core businesses as personal computers, communication systems, and industrial machinery, has been a major contributor to company revenues and profits over the years. Yet the capital-intensive nature of the business is problematic for the firm. Additionally, the senior executive explained,

> In a diversified company like ours, how to allocate limited resources among different businesses presents a real challenge to the top management. In our company, given the relative position of many of our businesses, this is a particularly serious problem. We have to be especially careful, not only in making the right bets, but we have to do our best to stretch our limited resources.

Viewed in this light, Toshiba's alliance with Motorola in the semiconductor business made sense. It afforded Toshiba, which was believed to lag Hitachi and NEC, access to Motorola's highly prized microprocessor technology, while providing for the sharing of resources and risks in research and development. But the value of the alliance went beyond improving the competitive position of the semiconductor business, itself no small accomplishment. Another Toshiba executive observed,

> For one thing, the alliance has strengthened the sector's ability to supply semiconductor devices to our internal customers. There has been a definite synergy there. In addition, the partnership has enabled us to shift our resources—financial and technical—to other core businesses, particularly in high-technology areas.

Toshiba's arrangement illustrates how competitiveness-enhancing alliances can satisfy the needs of both SBU and corporate levels. Part of a corporate CEO's job is to ensure that the benefits of alliances accrue not only to the target SBU but, as at Toshiba, to other SBUs and to the corporation as a whole.

Rationalizing Alliances

Our research suggests that a significant number of corporate collaborations are rationalizing alliances, that is, they reduce the number of competitors by combining what were previously industry rivals. Such an alliance permits one partner to exit the industry gracefully by stages.

For an illustration, we turn to the U.S.-based Dresser Industries, a diversified firm that experienced considerable difficulties in the late 1980s and was forced to undergo a major restructuring. One of Dresser's businesses was earthmoving and construction equipment, an industry facing overcapacity and tremendous price pressure. Moreover, long neglect by corporate management had left the business far behind such committed competitors as Caterpillar and Komatsu.

With prospects for the industry dim and an enormous investment needed to revitalize the business, corporate management sought an alliance with Komatsu. By then a global player second only to Caterpillar, Komatsu was experiencing difficulty locating a manufacturing plant in the United States. A fifty-fifty joint venture between the firms enabled Dresser to take advantage of Komatsu's resources and afforded Komatsu immediate access to Dresser's manufacturing and distribution facilities in North American and several major Latin American markets.

That the partnership, Komatsu Dresser Company (KDC), was largely dependent on Komatsu for long-term viability was easy to see even when it was formed. According to KDC's chairman and CEO, Ralph Ytterberg, Komatsu spent $240 million a year on R&D, ten times Dresser's construction-equipment R&D expenditure.[14] Clearly, Komatsu's contribution of technology would continue, and Dresser's contribution was a one-time offering. Indeed, confirming its exit from the industry in 1992, the Dresser company announced plans to divest itself of ownership in KDC and other industrial equipment units through a stock spin-off to Dresser shareholders.

We have another example of a rationalizing alliance in a well-known manufacturer of special glass, which by the early 1980s had diversified into four major businesses: special materials, consumer housewares, laboratory sciences, and communication products. Color television, a core business in special materials, became increasingly unattractive to Corning in the 1980s. As the manufacture of television sets became more concentrated and integrated, and as the industry came to be dominated by the Japanese, competition among television glass suppliers had intensified; with the exit of U.S. television set manufacturers, Corning's traditional customer base virtually disappeared.

Corning responded to these changes by rationalizing its operations. But despite selling 80% of its European television glass business to Thomson and closing all but one U.S. plant, the business continued to founder, partially because of its difficulty in selling to U.S. transplants of Japanese manufacturers.

Asahi Glass, Japan's leading producer of specialty glass, faced a quite different strategic problem. A key supplier to Japanese television manufacturers, which were major contributors to the company's revenues, Asahi had to follow its customers as they shifted assembly, and even manufacturing, operations to the United States. This proved to be a formidable challenge to a company that had virtually no nondomestic manufacturing experience.

Long-standing partners in a number of other businesses, Asahi and Corning perceived complementary interests. For Corning, an alliance would facilitate further rationalization and immediate access to Japanese transplants, for Asahi, quick entry into the United States.[15] The timing was particularly critical for Asahi, because its major domestic rival, NEG, had built a plant in the United States. The final agreement, which called for Corning to sell 49% of its U.S. business to Asahi, afforded Corning an opportunity to remain in the business with a partner that brought excellent technology, manufacturing processes, customer contacts, and a cash infusion of $100 million, which Corning invested in the development of liquid crystal display, an area of considerable strategic importance.[16]

The final example concerns two alliances established in the major appliance industry in recent years. One was between Whirlpool and Philips, the latter a once-powerful European multinational that was experiencing considerable difficulty by the late 1970s. Philips's management, seeking to give priority to its far-flung businesses as part of a restructuring effort, decided that the major appliance business was not essential to the company's long-term survival. Among the major problems with the business were a mature European market with little growth potential, an outdated, highly inefficient, and scattered manufacturing capability, and a threat posed by the major Swedish firm Electrolux, which was aggressively pursuing a strategy of creating a highly efficient and rationalized network of manufacturing capabilities in Europe by acquiring weak, poorly performing national companies. The considerable resources it would have to expend to rationalize its operations, Philips believed, could be better utilized elsewhere. Whirlpool, meanwhile, also contending with a mature market, was seeking an opportunity for global expansion. It had already sought to counteract Electrolux's aggressive moves in the United States, acquiring White Consolidated, a U.S. major appliance manufacturer.

Ultimately, their divergent strategies brought Whirlpool and Philips together in a joint venture in which the former gained majority share and management control. The alliance offered Whirlpool an opportunity to enter the European market while marrying its formidable skills in product and process technology and knowledge of the appliance business with Philips's widely recognized brand names. Philips, for its part, had swapped its floundering appliance business for a minority stake in the new venture. The net result has been a reduction by one company in the number of players in the global appliance business.

The Whirlpool-Philips alliance occasioned another important joint venture between GE's fledgling European appliance business and that of Great Britain's General Electric Company (GEC).[17] Here again, the partners entered the alliance with different objectives, GE to counter Whirlpool's move by expanding one of its core European businesses and GEC to partially divest itself of the major appliance business.

Perhaps the ultimate rationalizing joint venture was between the two power-generating and transmission-equipment companies, Asea Brown Boveri of Sweden and Brown Boveri Corporation of Switzerland. The 1987 alliance rationalized capacity in a fiercely competitive industry by reducing the number of competitors.

In each of these alliances, a company—Dresser, Corning, Philips, and GEC—used its presence and accumulated customer knowledge or manufacturing base in a specific product or geographic market to gain a stake, often a minority position, in a new firm that enjoyed an improved competitive position to some extent because a competitor had been eliminated.

Another point to be taken from these examples is that rationalizing alliances are rarely global in scope. In other words, they tend to be confined to one geographic region or another. The locus of the alliances entered into by Dresser and Corning was the United States, that of the alliances established by Philips and GEC, Europe. Moreover, in each of them, one partner put into the venture all or almost all its assets related to a particular business while the other did not. Two of the companies cited, Whirlpool and Komatsu, were essentially single-business firms. Asahi and Corning were both diversified, but their strategic priorities were different, which led one to use the alliance to expand and the other to contract.

Transitional Alliances

Rationalization alliances also tend to be transitional. In three of the foregoing examples, the contribution of one partner was a one-time event. Dresser, Philips, and GEC each had little beyond an entire business to contribute to a newly formed alliance. Their partners, on the other hand, can expect to benefit handsomely from the acquired facilities and experiences. Only the Corning-Asahi alliance is an exception. Corning, which excels in specialty glass technology and possesses excellent research and development capabilities, is in a position to make continuing technical and financial contributions to the alliance, if it deems them in its strategic interest to do so.

A transitional alliance must not only preserve the dominant partner's options for the future, but also provide incentives for the other partner to act in good faith to maximize its value during the transition. Again we refer to Whirlpool and Philips. The original agreement stipulated that Whirlpool could buy out Philips's interest, which it eventually did. Whirlpool implemented a carefully crafted plan first to introduce its own brand jointly with Philips, then replace the Philips brand with its own. From the beginning, it was clearly to ensure Philips's help during the transition that Whirlpool predicated the final sale price on how well the joint venture performed.

GE, like Whirlpool, was seeking an opportunity to learn about a partner's market and organization, and GEC, like Philips, wanted a graceful way to exit what it considered to be a nonstrategic business. Alliances such as these are really "strategic" only to the extent that they advance the strategy of the diversified company at the corporate level. They clearly do not meet our criteria for shared control and continuing contribution. Moreover, for a diversified firm that relies on a "horizontal strategy" of exploiting linkages among SBUs, management of such alliances requires considerable effort, as we illustrate later.

Market uncertainties related to technological developments, standards, customer preferences, timing, and so forth, also lead firms to pursue transitional arrangements. Corning's alliance with Switzerland's Ciba-Geigy in the field of medical diagnostics is an example. Corning, having developed the technology of porous glass in the mid-1970s, sought to exploit it in the medical diagnostics field. The company faced tough competition— pharmaceutical firms with extensive R&D capabilities and biotechnology firms with focused skills in biological reagents—and uncertainty about which technologies and marketing channels would become dominant in the future. Desiring additional R&D to keep abreast of technological developments, in 1985 Corning sought a partner in the Swiss pharmaceutical giant Ciba-Geigy. "We were a good strategic fit," recalled Martin Gibson, a group president of Corning. "We approached them to form a joint venture—mesh our proficiency at manufacturing and marketing with their biological research capabilities, and together crank up R&D expenditure in the operation." Ciba-Geigy paid $75 million for a 50% share in Corning's medical diagnostics business.

Both firms made continuing contributions to the alliance—Ciba Corning Diagnostics (CCD)—in technologies and personnel, and both exploited its synergies within their respective firms, but neither was sure which would become the dominant partner. The possibility that, as market uncertainties diminished and CCD's strategy evolved, Corning's role might diminish and Ciba-Geigy could become the dominant player, was reportedly discussed by the partners before the alliance was formed. But neither firm seems to have wanted to foreclose its options. To ensure that neither company withdrew its support while CCD was weathering the market uncertainties of the first few years, the alliance provided for no termination procedures. Thus was a transitional alliance born.

Occasionally, for reasons such as synergy with the rest of its businesses, neither firm wants to relinquish control and the transitional arrangement becomes permanent. Dow Corning Company, an alliance between Corning and Dow Chemicals, is an example. Formed in 1943 to develop silicone products invented by Corning, but for which Dow had appropriate manufacturing technologies and distribution channels, the fifty-fifty joint venture was a transitional arrangement that afforded Dow access to a new business and Dow and Corning synergies by association. As the venture prospered, neither wanted to relinquish control, with the result that over the years it developed into a separate company with its own identity and culture in which Dow and Corning share control and to which they make technology transfers. Dow Corning has become a truly strategic alliance.

Indeed, as early as 1937, Corning had established an alliance with PPG Industries to provide the latter technology and access to the construction industry. For Corning, the alliance was transitional, for PPG a means of entering a new business. The alliance continues to prosper as a freestanding joint venture to this day.

New-business Alliances

Given that entry into a new business is greatly facilitated by interrelationships between a target industry and industries in which a firm already competes, a diversified firm that competes in multiple industries has a potential advantage, both in entering new industries and in being sought out as a partner by other firms that wish to do the same. Alliances that target entry into new industries facilitate access to complementary resources and reduce the risk of failure, as evidenced by the following examples.

Mitsubishi Heavy Industry, a highly diversified firm engaged in the shipbuilding, heavy machinery, power systems, transportation, and construction equipment businesses, among others, concerned that a number of these core businesses were in mature industries, had been eyeing the commercial aircraft sector. The industry was appealing because it was one of the few in which Japan had virtually no presence, it was a high-technology field, and global demand for commercial airliners, although cyclical, held considerable promise. Moreover, the aircraft industry would mobilize the entire Mitsubishi Group, ranging from new materials to electronics.

Even for Mitsubishi, the large commercial aircraft business posed formidable entry barriers. The industry is notorious for huge capital requirements for research and development and manufacturing, and to be a viable player requires an extensive worldwide marketing and service network. But perhaps its most serious entry barrier was that Mitsubishi lacked technology. As an alliance seemed to be the only way to enter the industry, Mitsubishi, with two other Japanese firms, formed an alliance with Boeing to develop projects, the most notable being the Boeing 7J7, a new generation of commercial airliner scheduled to be introduced in the late 1990s. Mitsubishi entered into an alliance with Pratt and Whitney to gain access to a second, complementary new business, namely, the design and manufacture of a new generation of jet engines.

Multimedia—the integration and manipulation of computer, audio, video, and other types of information—having captured the imagination of virtually all the major diversified electronics companies, is on the verge of blossoming into a multibillion-dollar industry with potential applications in such areas as entertainment, education, advertising, and scientific research. Major Japanese firms with widely diversified electronics businesses, in particular, perceive multimedia as a major growth area. But given the diversity of the relevant technologies, even the most broadly based electronics firms do not possess all the requisite expertise. Not surprisingly, they have turned to complementing their technological capabilities. Matsushita Electronics, for example, established an alliance with Sun Microsystems to craft multimedia workstations; Sony entered into a joint venture with Apple and Motorola to develop operating systems and communications software for personal digital assistants; NEC, Toshiba, and AT&T are working jointly on a pen-input, palm-size computer capable of transmitting information by radio signal, and Matsushita Electronics and Gain Technology have entered into an agreement to jointly develop software that will enable UNIX workstations to interact with high-definition television.

For an example of a diversified firm that used an alliance to enter a new business, we turn again to Corning. After spending an enormous amount of money to pioneer optical fiber technology, Corning found it difficult to gain customer acceptance. AT&T, which controlled 75% of the cabling business, was intent on developing its own optical fiber, and independent copper cable suppliers, which controlled the remainder of the market, were reluctant to switch to the new technology.

Anticipating its huge market potential, Corning decided to forward-integrate into cable manufacturing. Lacking in-house expertise in this area, Corning discerned that the only way to do so was to find a suitable alliance partner. It subsequently established a fifty-fifty joint venture with Siemens of Germany to produce cables in the United States. The forward-integration strategy proved extremely successful in the wake of the breakup of AT&T, which opened the hitherto closed market to outside suppliers.

When Kodak, faced with a mature and increasingly competitive business, began to look for new commercial opportunities, one of its managers proposed that batteries for consumer electronics and related products might offer an excellent strategic fit, since they are sold through the same channels as film.[18] Kodak top management concurred, but the company lacked the technology to manufacture batteries. The solution was an alliance, a fifty-fifty joint venture with Matsushita of Japan to make and market batteries in the United States. At Kodak's insistence, the joint venture is time bound;

at the end of seven years Kodak, having gained access to the requisite technology, may opt to manufacture batteries on its own. The architect of the alliance strategy and first CEO of Kodak's joint venture, said,

> We could not have done it but for the alliance. We got the product as well as the process technology. A number of Kodak people went over to Japan to learn from the Japanese. We were able to lower the capital demand on us as Matsushita shared in the start-up costs. Part of our capital contribution came by way of company-owned land that would otherwise have not been put to use. Our distribution network is pleased with our entry. In fact, we have already gained a substantial share in the marketplace. We are confident that when the day comes for us to go into our own manufacturing, we will be ready. What else can you ask for?

CULTIVATING AN ALLIANCE-FRIENDLY ENVIRONMENT

Top managers, like coaches, are looked to for guidance and support. Their role, as it relates to fostering environments that are conducive to the formation of effective alliances, encompasses at least four activities: participation in SBU strategic reviews; support for searches and assessments; assistance with alliance negotiations; and assistance with alliance management at the SBU level. Corporate management's regular reviews of SBU performance typically include evaluations of financial performance and strategy. The latter tends to receive closer scrutiny if performance falls short of expectation. In a number of diversified companies we studied, alliances were first suggested by corporate management as a way to bolster SBU competitiveness. A number of alliances at GE came about as a result of such a regular review process. Jack Welch stated, "Our job in the executive office is to facilitate, to go out and negotiate a deal, to make the acquisition, or *get our businesses the partners they need.*"[19]

For example, GE's motor business group, plagued by poor performance, reportedly was encouraged by corporate management to forge a number of strategic alliances, retaining in the United States only such core functions as design, research and development, complex and custom manufacturing, and distribution. Focusing its efforts in that direction has rendered the group a profitable operation and led to a major alliance with Bosch of Germany.[20] GE's success in using alliances to rejuvenate its motor business is in sharp contrast to the failure of the other major U.S. motor producer, Westinghouse. Corporate management proposed no imaginative use of strategic alliances to regain competitiveness, and the underperforming motor division was ultimately divested.[21]

Corporate managements that suggest strategic alliances for SBUs can also assist with the selection and evaluation of partners. Corporate managers are well positioned for this task. For example, alliance partners are frequently sought in related industries, of which top management is likely to have considerable knowledge as a result of involvement in SBU reviews and its general broad exposure.

As top managers accumulate experience with alliance negotiations on behalf of their SBUs and gain knowledge of potential pitfalls, they become increasingly adept advisers. Again, GE is exemplary. GE's top management, recognizing the importance of alliances to global competitiveness, has not only actively assisted in the negotiating process, but also helped SBU-level managers share their negotiating experiences. Welch personally keeps abreast of, and sometimes becomes actively involved in, negotiations with potential partners when a major alliance is in the offing. Vice chairman Paolo Fresco, the only non-American member of GE's board, actively guides and assesses SBUs in formulating alliances. Particularly in Europe, Fresco has been a key player in every major alliance and acquisition. Such strong support from the corporate office for alliance-seeking SBUs has been at the heart of GE's success.

Top management can also play a role in the management of alliances. Again, accumulated experience with partners can yield a valuable base of information from which alliance-seeking SBUs can profit. Top managers' personal relationships with their counterparts in partner firms can also stand their SBUs in good stead in extraordinary or complicated situations. Finally, alliances that involve multiple SBUs with a given partner demand top management attention to aggregate benefits and costs.

As corporate alliances multiply, top management can effectively become a clearinghouse for transferring alliance-related skills among SBUs. GE top management ultimately mandated, for example, that alliance management become a key component of the company's management-training process, thereby institutionalizing the exchange and transfer of ideas among and between SBU managers.

THE ALLIANCE ROLES MATRIX FOR CORPORATE MANAGEMENT

The multiplicity of management roles and alliance types that emerged from our research provides a starting point for structuring our ideas about the tasks associated with alliance management. Figure 8.2 identifies the key roles of top management in each of several types of alliances. Some roles loom larger than others for particular types of alliances.

Corporate management involvement in setting strategy is warranted for all types of corporate alliances—competitiveness-enhancing, rationalizing,

Figure 8.2
Alliance Types and Key Roles Matrix

| Alliance Type | Top Management Roles | | | |
	Strategy Setting	Synergy Maintenance	Resource Allocation	Multipoint Competition Coordination
Competitiveness-enhancing	■			
Rationalizing	■	■		
Transitional	■	■	■	
New-business	■	■	■	■

transitional, and new-business. Moreover, in *competitiveness-enhancing alliances,* this task takes precedence over all others.

Corporate management's responsibility to a business unit's forging a *rationalizing alliance* includes making certain that the association is the most effective way to bolster the business's competitive position. Given that rationalizing alliances almost invariably incur a loss of control, corporate management must weigh issues related to interrelationships or synergy with other business units and the possibility of exposing other profitable businesses to competitive attacks. The more tightly controlled an SBU, the easier it is to ensure synergy.

If synergy is an important attribute of an SBU's entering a rationalizing alliance, top management must take steps to ensure its preservation. For instance, if the rationalized SBU shared R&D synergy with another SBU, corporate may have to increase R&D funding to the second SBU to compensate for the loss of access to the R&D efforts of the first. Alternatively, as we saw in one multibusiness company, the second SBU was encouraged to form a separate R&D alliance with the joint venture created through rationalization so that it could continue to benefit through its access to the research efforts of the rationalized SBU.

Transitional alliances call for top management attention to the financial and managerial impact that eventual absorption of an alliance will have on a firm. Whether absorption occurs gradually or all at once, additional financial investment and management commitment will almost certainly be called for, occasioning renewed consideration of resource allocation, strategy setting, and synergy.

For *new-business alliances,* top management's most immediate tasks are to ensure that new-business opportunities are strategically sound, assess the benefits and risks associated with them, and attend to the fulfillment of their resource needs. Top management must also help to develop a long-term strategy for new ventures and, as new businesses are almost invariably based on expected synergies with existing SBUs, ensure that alliances benefit from such synergies. Finally top management must ensure that what constitutes a competitiveness-enhancing alliance for one SBU does not adversely affect the stability of multipoint competition with its many rivals.

Top management of diversified firms, just like its counterparts in single-business companies, must adapt performance measurement and control systems to reflect the SBUs' involvement in different types of alliances and correspondingly differential contributions to profits, technology development, and synergy with other SBUs. Many firms are only now coming to grips with this highly complex task.

WHAT CAN GO WRONG?—A CAVEAT

We were struck by how few of the senior corporate executives we encountered in the course of our research had given any thought to how alliances might eventually transform their companies and thereby significantly alter their jobs. We see in the inability to appreciate the strategic change that slowly overtakes an organization the danger of a diversified company's becoming largely a collection of minority holdings in some changing set of alliances.

Consider General Electric Company (GEC) of Great Britain, long a plodding, stodgy, not very profitable diversified firm engaged in a wide array of businesses ranging from consumer electronics and semiconductors to home appliances to power systems and defense electronics. It is largely a federation of independent subsidiary companies or strategic business units. Its SBUs held relatively strong positions in the domestic market, but performance in other national markets, particularly in Europe, was less than stellar. Most of its businesses having become global in recent years, GEC has been under intense competitive pressure.

GEC responded in 1989 with a bold new corporate strategy described by managing director Lord Weinstock as adapting the firm's "shape and style according to the circumstances in which it finds itself." The core of its strategy called for GEC to become a decentralized company linked by a web of strategic alliances with other firms—often erstwhile competitors—in order to achieve a global presence, particularly in Europe. The strategic pattern seemed to be GEC's sale of 49% of its British lighting company to Siemens.

Most subsequent GEC alliances have been joint ventures or minority equity stakes. Specific alliances include a fifty-fifty joint venture with France's Cie Générale d'Electricité (CGE) in power engineering; fifty-fifty joint ventures with, or minority stakes in, Siemens's telecommunication, semiconductor, and related businesses; a forty-nine–fifty-one joint venture with France's Matra (holding a 51% stake) in space technology; and fifty-fifty joint ventures with, or minority stakes in, General Electric's home appliance and power system businesses. GEC justifies this approach on the basis of reduced dependence on the British market, higher earnings, and shared costs and lowered risks in areas such as R&D—all frequently touted benefits of alliances.[22]

What is missing in these alliances is an appreciation of the corporate metamorphosis the alliances themselves are working on the company. Almost all of GEC's alliances are in the rationalizing category, designed to bring GEC together with former competitors. But GEC is largely a passive investor in these ventures; its partners are in the driver's seat.

A typical scenario in rationalizing alliances is initial contributions by both partners of technology, money, markets, and personnel, giving way gradually to continuing contributions by the dominant partner, the other firm typically devolving into a collection of minority investments in a variety of businesses, essentially a shell or hollow corporation.

Consider GEC's partners. CGE, a major global player in power engineering, possesses the in-house technological expertise that is the basis for its joint venture with GEC. Indeed, GEC had put nearly a quarter of its assets—its electrical distribution and transmission, robotics, and rail transport businesses—into the joint venture with CGE-Alsthom to get a 50% stake. In GEC's alliances in semiconductors and telecommunications, Siemens is in the driver's seat, and in space technology, Matra, as premier French contractor to the European space program, is clearly in a position to direct its joint venture with GEC. Its global strategy and dominant global presence affords the U.S. General Electric control of joint ventures with GEC in power systems and home appliances. GEC depends on the technological and strategic superiority of its partners for continued success in nearly all its alliances.

What are the managerial implications of the transformation we anticipate in GEC? Its corporate managers will find themselves managing what is essentially a portfolio of investments, with little control over their destiny. And as former operating managers of GEC's SBUs come to identify more and more with the dominant partner, corporate managers' ability to influence the direction of the businesses will diminish rapidly.[23]

That our view on loss of control (and eventual divestiture) is not idle speculation is backed by GEC's own experiences in the past. In 1978, GEC formed a fifty-fifty joint venture with Hitachi in consumer electronics. At that time, GEC hinted that it was a move to strengthen one of its core businesses. By 1984, GEC, having contributed nothing except its initial input to the venture, divested itself of its share to Hitachi. In 1986, GEC formed a similar joint venture in its lighting business with Siemens. That too turned out to be a rationalizing alliance, although GEC did not realize it in the beginning. In 1990, GEC sold off its half interest to Siemens.

Even a firm that maintains a presence in some businesses without engaging in alliances faces new challenges. To the extent that it has relinquished its managerial role in its other businesses, the firm's center of gravity will have shifted,[24] necessitating major changes in organization and management, perhaps even the dismantling of the current power structure, rejection of parts of the old organizational culture, and development of new management systems. Diversified firms engaged in multiple rationalizing alliances that are unaware of these requirements are undoubtedly heading for trouble.

Again, consider GEC. Even as it was entering into various alliances, it sought to become a major player in the defense electronics sector by acquiring the radar business of Ferranti International PLC.[25] This gave GEC a near monopoly of British airborne radar business. But this reorientation away from private-sector to public-sector users, namely, the defense establishments of various countries, clearly signals a further need for accompanying cultural change.[26]

Managing interrelationships among SBUs is particularly difficult when rationalizing alliances are employed. In competitiveness-enhancing and new-business alliances, a corporation continues to be a strategic partner. When it becomes a passive investor, as it does in a rationalizing alliance, its control is apt to diminish to the point that it can exert little, if any, influence over the destiny of its former business. Rationalizing alliances have a place in a diversified firm, but not as the association of choice for most of its businesses. The effect of an overabundance of rationalizing alliances, as we have observed, is to make a firm a clutch of unrelated businesses, thereby rendering it an attractive takeover target for asset strippers.

U.S. General Electric exhibits good judgment on this score, having entered into only a few rationalizing alliances—factory automation and microelectronics come to mind. Most of GE's alliances are competitiveness-enhancing (motors, jet engines, and power systems) or transitional (medical systems). We suspect that this is by design rather than by accident, GE's top management seeming to have consciously thought through many of the issues raised above.

We end where we began. Strategic alliances can be used to further either business-level or corporate-level strategy. The best alliances improve SBU performance even as they enhance corporate strategy. As a means of helping SBUs become more aggressive, competitiveness-enhancing, transitional (at least from one company's point of view), and new-business alliances are preferable to rationalizing alliances, which are more usefully viewed as way stations on an exit route.

Alliances are not a panacea for SBUs' competitiveness ills; they can help or hinder, depending on how well or ill they are conceived and managed.

PART **IV**
FROM ALLIANCES TO NETWORKS

CHAPTER 9

The Next Frontier: Managing the Global Network Corporation

References to the global network corporation, which we believe represents the next major challenge of international management, are best understood in light of globalization of competition and strategy and the strategic-alliance response. Here we consider the roots of globalization, the rationale for the alliance response, and its inevitable evolution into the global network corporation. We examine first the factors that underlie, and the impact on industry of, the globalization of competition.

GLOBALIZATION OF COMPETITION

Two trends, one macro, the other micro, are responsible for what is routinely termed "the globalization of industries." The favorable and liberal macroeconomic trends in world trade and monetary regimes, coupled with improvements and technological advances in transportation systems, afford consumers wide-ranging options for acquiring products from different parts of the world. Then the microtrends in products, technologies, and competition translate this potential into reality. It is with respect to the latter that managerial ingenuity has had the greatest impact on globalization.

Let us begin with products. It is widely conceded that products destined for consumer and industrial markets the world over are becoming more standardized as consumer preferences converge.[1] Sony's Walkman, for example, is the same the world over. So are nuclear reactors, commercial airliners, jet engines, mainframe and personal computers, semiconductors, soft drinks, radios, television sets, and watches. Growth in the universal acceptability of products is perhaps the first step in the globalization of markets.

A second critical, but less well recognized microelement supporting globalization is the widespread and rapid development and diffusion of technology. The United States is no longer the unrivaled fountain of technological development that it was during the first half of the century. Increasing technological parity among nations, particularly those in the major regions of the world, the growing ability of less-developed nations to absorb new technology, changes in the nature of technological knowledge (from the more organizationally bound to migratory or separable from its developer), and the accelerated pace of diffusion of innovation have combined to largely eliminate constraints on where the development of new products and processes that are competitive worldwide can occur.

Universalization of products, when coupled with technological parity among nations, fosters the participation of firms in countries that were previously considered to be internationally noncompetitive in the global competitive fray. So we have the globalization of competition.

Many managers in U.S. industries had been slow to appreciate the growth in technological parity. Caterpillar CEO Lee Morgan remarked in 1983 of Japan's Komatsu: "They sell their products at 10% to 20% discount; that says something about their quality versus ours." Two years later, Komatsu was introducing huge new machines at international expositions while Caterpillar reeled from significant losses in market share and revenues. So advanced were some of Komatsu's machines that the firm's designers, much to their delight, discovered Caterpillar engineers surreptitiously inspecting and measuring them. "Just a few years ago," said a Komatsu engineer, grinning, "it would have been we who were doing that." Such is the speed of globalization.

GLOBALIZATION OF STRATEGY

The globalization of competition has been accompanied by the globalization of strategy. Simple export-based strategies have given way to strategies based on foreign direct investment, which in turn have given way to simple, then complex global multinational strategies. This evolution has been steady and continuous.

Firms have increasingly come to see in the globalization of competition four critical cross-border dependencies—economies of scale, in various parts of the value chain, that span national borders; competitive moves that have implications in more than one national market; opportunities to arbitrage country- or location-based advantages; and scope interdependence that permits firms to leverage across national borders learning related to products, markets, and technologies that have an impact on their competitive strategies. Traditionally, competitive strategy has been construed to be a generic one built around a singular source of competitive advantage applicable around the world. The entry into the market of firms from different countries with different parcels of competitive advantages drastically alters the heretofore stable competitive arena.

As firms have responded to redefinition of the competitive balance by securing as many competitive advantages as possible, distinctions among generic strategies have blurred. Gone are the days when rivals pursuing simple generic strategies would separate themselves into mutually exclusive strategic groups. This pattern can be seen in every major industry. Toyota and Honda in the automobile industry, Sony and Matsushita in consumer electronics, and Komatsu in construction equipment strive to serve all market segments. This phenomenon is not confined to Japanese firms. General Electric and Siemens serve every segment in the medical systems market, ranging from ultrasonics and X-ray equipment to service-intensive nuclear magnetic resonance imagers and CT scanners. In the power systems industry, GE and Asea Brown Boveri strive to serve every segment in steam- or gas-powered turbines.

THE STRATEGIC-ALLIANCE RESPONSE

Building multiple layers of competitive advantage is in essence to globalize competitive strategy. Firms spread their value activities worldwide in hopes of simultaneously realizing the benefits of low cost and differentiation, the two basic generic strategies.

We have observed two approaches that firms that must compete globally—and that includes most major firms—employ to achieve the layering of competitive advantages: (1) development of extensive *internal networks* of international subsidiaries in major national or regional markets and (2) forging *external networks* of strategic alliances with firms around the world. These approaches are not mutually exclusive, and increasingly firms are striving to build both types of networks.

Ford, Motorola, IBM, General Motors (GM), and GE are among the diverse firms building complementary networks, but Corning perhaps most clearly articulates such a twin network-based strategy. According to its mission statement,

Corning is an evolving network of wholly owned businesses and joint ventures. We choose to compete in four global businesses: specialty materials, consumer housewares, laboratory sciences, and communications. *Each segment is composed of divisions, subsidiaries, and alliances* [emphasis added]. Binding the four sectors together is the glue of common values, a commitment to technology, shared resources, and dedication to total quality and management links.[2]

The strategic-alliance-based *external network* solution affords important advantages for aspiring global firms that lack networks of international subsidiaries and even for firms that have foreign subsidiaries, inasmuch as their organizational and administrative heritages may impede their mobilization in an integrated manner. Time being of the essence in competition and increasingly so in the global arena, it is often faster to work through external alliances than to try to change the organizational mandates of subsidiaries. Coupled with the time element is the resource constraints firms face. As technological breakthroughs demand even greater resource commitments, alliances that spread cost and risk become more desirable.

A firm's managerial systems can be a key competitive advantage in meeting global rivalry. Global firms must internalize at least some aspects of the managerial systems of firms in other nations.[3] Subsidiaries molded around the culture and managerial systems of parent companies are far less likely than partner firms in an alliance to yield competitive advantage.[4]

FROM ALLIANCES TO NETWORKS

From a strategic-management perspective, two major trends have characterized business in recent years. One is its seemingly inexorable internationalization, or globalization. The other is the growing reliance on strategic alliances to create "networks" of intricate business relationships among major corporations. Many researchers have taken note of one or the other, few of both. Moreover, reactions are varied. Some see globalization's vanquishing all borders, effectively rendering corporations "anational."[5] Others, with much more faith in the resilience of the nation-state as the critical unit of the corporation, emphasize the competitiveness of nations.[6] Of networks and their growth, most suggest only that they are not apt to be permanent.[7] Commentators on the growth of alliances have largely split into two camps—those who consider alliances to be important primarily in the context of domestic corporations and those who acknowledge alliances in the context of international competition but view them as quick fixes that address immediate market needs or as temporary ruses for learning from competitors or for helping U.S. and European firms penetrate key triad markets, notably Japan.[8]

We firmly believe that the collective effect of these two trends—globalization and networking—will be to change the nature of the corporation as we know it. We further believe that the emerging phenomenon of the global network corporation presents unique opportunities at the same time that it poses formidable challenges to managers. We believe that it constitutes the next frontier of management challenge in an age of "entrepreneurial globalization."

Strategic Links, Not Tactical Fixes

Recent trends in the international competitive arena suggest that strategic alliances satisfy long-, not short-term needs. Alliances and networks of alliances are thus destined to be indispensable for all firms, large and small, not temporary fixes as some commentators have suggested and, perhaps, some managers hope.

Consider the three key dimensions that tend to define firms—technologies, products, and markets.[9] In an era of rapid globalization, firms must cope with increased variety within each of these dimensions. For instance, a firm may have to master more than a few technologies simultaneously and serve a variety of product niches in more than one national market.[10] With technology and product-development costs ballooning and product cycles becoming more abbreviated, serving as many national markets as possible is one way to recoup costs relatively quickly.

Globalization dictates that firms pursue economies of scale in technology, product development, and manufacturing, even as they struggle to contain costs and reduce risks. Moreover, they must manage their way through competitive minefields as new rivals emerge in likely and unlikely nations. Alliances are a natural response to these pressures, partly because they enable firms to focus on a few core areas, be they technologies, markets, or products, by engaging other firms to perform other aspects of the business.

Alliances permit firms to shift resources to competitive advantages that they expect to become the bases for future competition.[11] General Motors and Ford, for example, were able to shift resources to technology development and distribution by engaging partners to deal with certain segments of the automobile market on their behalf. Similarly, Motorola conserved resources for core technology development by allying with Toshiba for manufacturing and distribution. And Corning, through alliances with firms such as Siemens, Ciba-Geigy, and Genentech, has been able to shift much-needed resources toward strengthening its core technological base, the "glue" that binds its varied businesses.

Moreover, alliances afford managers flexibility. Properly structured and administered, they enable global firms to hedge their bets as to the desirability of bringing in-house or shifting to an alliance partner particular value activities. A network of alliances is critical to maintaining such flexibility. Such networks, by enabling corporations to become involved with a multiplicity of technologies, managerial systems, and markets, foster an entrepreneurial culture. What better way to encourage managers to think constantly of better ways to accomplish tasks than to expose them to a mélange of experience that leads them to question the usual means of operation?[12] A Corning executive recalled of the participation of other companies' managers in Corning's management meetings, "Their presence expanded our horizons, their entrepreneurial spirit enriched us, and I guess they learned from us as well."[13]

Boundaryless Management

The rapid growth of alliances has led managers such as Jack Welch, one of today's foremost business leaders, to call for the creation of boundaryless corporations.[14] Welch recognizes, of course, that just as the nations from which they emanate cannot be altogether divorced from firms' operational effectiveness, so firm boundaries cannot simply be wished away.[15] Legal considerations and a desire to maintain an independent existence militate against such wholesale disappearance.[16]

The boundaryless management Welch is calling for considers the strategic interests of both parties and tries to ensure that alliance structures achieve a balance between the needs of cooperation and competition. It eschews the not-invented-here syndrome, promoting instead a climate that fosters organizational learning. It permits firms confronted with problems to devise win-win strategies and to enjoy the fruits of cooperation without compromising core technological and managerial competencies. Boundaryless management enables firms to retain their independence even as they leverage one another's strengths to compete effectively in their respective markets.

Boundaryless management is difficult to conceive, plan, execute, and above all, maintain, particularly when it involves firms from different nations. In fact, the evolution of the global network corporation poses quite different managerial challenges for Japanese firms and their American and European counterparts.

American Multinationals versus Japanese Networks

"We do not have a high tolerance for the ambiguity inherent in the relationship created by an alliance," observed a senior executive of a major U.S. corporation, voicing a concern shared by many U.S. alliance managers. "Nor are we terribly skilled in managing such a relationship. We are getting better, but we still have a strong predilection for total ownership and control." Historically, U.S. firms were among the first to pursue international markets.[17] Over the past several decades, many of them have located various value activities in different parts of the world, and an increasing number have developed the organizational competence to manage their far-flung operations as cohesive networks in order to exploit their systemwide advantages.[18] That the overwhelming majority of these affiliates are either wholly owned or majority controlled has facilitated the process and given rise to relationships that are best characterized as hierarchical.[19]

Japanese companies have a quite different administrative heritage. Multinationality in terms of value activities is alien to them, their traditional strategy having been to serve international markets from assets and resources based largely in Japan. These Japanese firms, particularly those belonging to the same *keiretsu*, have extensive experience cooperating with one another, affording them a core competence in managing collaborative relationships.[20] Japanese managers, acculturated in a highly homogeneous, stable, and particular culture, have developed a special knack for managing the ambiguity in such relationships.[21]

To exploit the advantages of the global network corporation, U.S. companies with experience managing networks of wholly owned or majority-owned international subsidiaries must develop the skills needed to effectively manage the ambiguity inherent in such relationships, sans hierarchical control, whereas Japanese firms must learn to manage their far-flung operations cohesively as they disperse value activities throughout the world, requiring adjustment to different mores and cultures. Moreover, as they expand their external networks to include foreign partners, Japanese firms must learn to apply skills developed in a highly homogeneous environment to a heterogeneous one. "Dealing with our [keiretsu] partners has never bothered us," explained a Japanese manager. "We have done it for years. We know how far we can go with our [Japanese] partners. Our American partners? That is a different story. They have a different way of doing things. We need to learn a lot before we can deal with American partners as comfortably as we do with our Japanese partners."[22]

Figure 9.1 traces the evolution of a global network corporation (GNC) from its uninational roots. U.S. firms are coming at the GNC from a multinational perspective, their Japanese counterparts as network companies, albeit

Figure 9.1
The Race to Become a Global Network Corporation

Familiarity with Managing External Network of Alliances

	Low	High
Low		Japanese Corporations
High	U.S. Multinational Corporations	Global Network Corporations

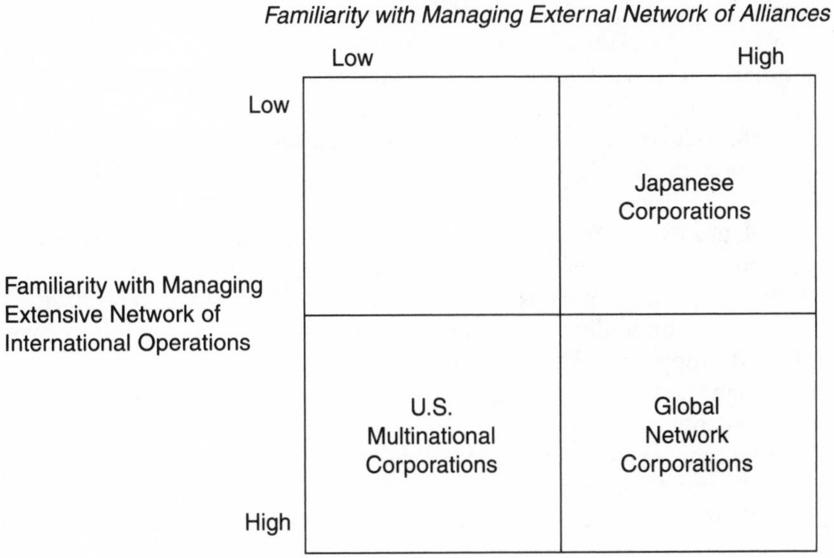

Familiarity with Managing Extensive Network of International Operations

in a domestic context. Which path will prove to be shorter remains to be seen.

THE NEXT MANAGERIAL FRONTIER

Managing in the global network corporation of the future will require both a multinational mentality and a network-oriented mind-set. Development of such a combination of skills, we believe, defines the last frontier of management challenge. Perhaps the key challenge in this new environment is the management of both internal and external networks. Few observers have explicitly recognized the two types of networks and the distinctly different management challenges they pose.[23] None of the characteristics of internal networks of subsidiaries—a common corporate vision, centrality of direction, clarity of roles of subsidiaries and headquarters, and unambiguous lines of control—are shared by external networks, which tend to be, at best, patchworks of common understandings that vary from alliance to alliance. Implicit in these differences is the need for managers to develop different ways of dealing with the respective types of networks.

Take Asea Brown Boveri (ABB), the world's largest maker of power generation, transmission, and distribution systems and a leading world supplier of process-automation systems, robotics, high-speed locomotives, and environmental and pollution-control equipment, as an illustration. Created in 1987 by the merger of ASEA of Sweden and Brown Boveri Limited of Switzerland, ABB in 1993 operated a network of 1,300 wholly owned subsidiaries around the world.

Overall direction for the corporation is set by ABB CEO Percy Barnevik and an executive team of eleven, based in Switzerland. The mandate for the subsidiaries is to work as part of a global team with local responsibility for profit making, the role of headquarters to ensure global coordination in terms of products and technology development. From these organizing principles come the various organizational devices that ABB uses to achieve its corporate goals.[24]

In late 1987, Barnevik set about establishing a shared corporate vision by distributing the "policy bible," a twenty-one-page booklet that described organizational relationships, emphasized commitment to decentralization and strict accountability, and articulated the company's approach to change, to his 300 top managers. He asked them to translate its message into the local language and convene interactive forums to promulgate it to another 30,000 people worldwide.

A key part of ABB's management system is the uniform reporting system Barnevik introduced in 1988, less than a year after the merger. The system, called ABACUS, provides Barnevik, the executive committee, and the various operating managers with timely, detailed, accurate information about sales, orders, margins, and other activities vital to decision making.

ABACUS enables ABB managers to exploit economies of scale and scope by focusing on such specific issues as cash flow, asset utilization, inventories, and investments down to the smallest reporting unit. Analyzing manufacturing costs in all markets, for example, led teams of area business managers to designate certain plants as specialized production sources for major products around the world and to introduce cost-saving measures such as component outsourcing, overhead cuts, and inventory reduction.

Internal network management evolves slowly. The goal of global optimization, however, is always dominant in the minds of managers, even as they grapple with the need for changing and updating mandates for their international subsidiaries. A good example is the evolution of the relationship between Xerox of the United States and its fifty-fifty joint venture, Fuji-Xerox, with Fuji Photo Film of Japan. Historically given much operational autonomy, Fuji-Xerox over the years has emerged as a major source of product design, manufacturing, and marketing capabilities for the global Xerox system. Xerox, recognizing the unique capabilities of its Japanese subsidiary, has sought to take advantage of it by continually redefining the latter's manufacturing and marketing mandates to suit Xerox's global interests.

Much of the redefining was done through a series of agreements relating to management, finance, technology transfer, royalties, sales territories, transfer pricing, and so on.[25] In its most recent such agreement, Xerox let the joint venture serve all of Southeast Asia and Australia. Mainland China, however, was to be Xerox's own responsibility. Xerox also formed a new joint venture called Xerox International Partners, owned 51% by Xerox and 49% by Fuji-Xerox, for sale of certain products made by the latter in the United States. In all such efforts, Xerox has ensured, however, that it has the ultimate say and that its efforts at global optimization are not compromised by the autonomy it has granted to its Japanese subsidiary.

Contrast this working of an internal network of wholly owned (and some majority-owned or co-owned) subsidiaries with an external network of alliances comprising unrelated and independent firms. Barnevik would not have been able to impose an overarching corporate vision on a huge external network of strategic alliances (contracts and minority participation ventures) because each alliance would serve a different strategic purpose. Neither would ABB have been able to impose a uniform mandate for all alliances or introduce a reporting system analogous to ABACUS, alliance partners being independent companies (often rivals), not satraps beholden to the central power of Persia. Similarly, Xerox's manner of dealing with its alliances would be quite different from the way it deals with such of its subsidiaries as Rank Xerox in England and Fuji-Xerox in Japan. It can impose systemic solutions to its advantage on the latter, but not on the former.

Ambiguous relationships, as we have emphasized throughout this book, are best managed by people, particularly alliance managers, not by systems. The ideal manager possesses a mind-set motivated less by global optimization and local maximization and more by a cooperative spirit that emphasizes building for the future without sacrificing the present. To manage an external network effectively, a manager must be able to exercise power without authority, accomplish more with fewer resources, and influence direction without giving orders. This comment came from a Corning manager:

> Operating successfully in a network requires a new mind-set. Our organization has come to be more team oriented. People rely less on formal power. . . . Many levels have been eliminated, and we have a structurally more efficient, flatter organization. I have become more conscious of the highly interdependent nature of my work. Earlier, I used to deal with six to eight people. Now I have direct-line or dotted-line relationships with about fifteen. We now live very well with apparent contradictions. For example, I am the worldwide manager for a business in which no operating manager reports directly to me.

Moreover, operating in a network requires a markedly different perspective from operating in a hierarchy. "A network is egalitarian," stated Corning chairman James Houghton. "The parent company does not dominate its offspring units. All operations are part of a family, some more distant cousins than the others, but all possessing some shared ethics and values." Managers in such an environment have to develop different ways of accomplishing their goals, even as they seek to preserve the interests of their individual organizations.

Table 9.1 summarizes the key differences between internal and external networks in terms of structure, procedure, and personnel.

THE GLOBAL NETWORK CORPORATION

Even as we recognize the diverse challenges inherent in administering internal and external networks, some nagging questions remain. Is the global network corporation (GNC) the solution of choice for all firms? Are there alternative approaches for firms that must compete globally? Is not alliance management inherently difficult and troublesome, and do not alliances, in any event, become unstable as the interests of partners diverge? Is it not preferable to develop one's own capabilities rather than those secured by means of shaky alliance networks? As managerial solutions make sense only

Table 9.1
Internal versus External Network

Managerial Dimensions	Internal Network	External Network
Shared vision	Yes	No
Animating mind-set	Cooperation	Cooperation and competition
Organizational mandates	Clear	Ambiguous
Organizational objective	Global optimization	Develop win-win approaches
Emphasis on systems	More	Less
Emphasis on people	Less	More
Lines of authority	Clear	Ambiguous at best

in the context of options, it is best to define the parameters of the problem and review the relevance of the global network corporation and other organizational choices for their resolution.

Fundamentally, the problem facing firms in most global industries is how to vie against rivals from many nations that bring to the competitive arena different bundles of competitive advantages. Firms have essentially two options: go it alone (the internal network solution) or forge a network of external alliances (in addition to the internal network). We contend that, in the context of limited resources and rapidity of competitive moves and technological advances (particularly the confluence of technologies), external networks make eminent sense.

Consider General Motors and IBM, ranked among the five largest corporations in the world for the past two decades. Neither lacks an extensive multinational network of subsidiaries or ample resources. Either could have chosen to compete globally on its own, relying solely on internal capabilities, yet each has chosen to develop extensive networks of alliances to further its competitive strategies.[26] If the likes of GM and IBM consider it inevitable, what more need be said about the rise of the global network corporation?[27]

It is inappropriate to pose alliances, as some have, as a substitute for internal networks.[28] We have emphasized repeatedly that arrival of a GNC does not entirely erase the boundaries of a corporation. To the contrary, strategic alliances are meant to further the interests of individual companies. Alliances permit firms to redirect resources and concentrate their efforts on building core competencies within, which clearly includes internal networks of subsidiaries.[29] Indeed, alliances enable firms to use their subsidiaries more effectively by freeing resources to support more focused efforts.

The alleged instability of alliances is a red herring. Even unsteady collaborations may be necessary if all of a firm's rivals are employing them to compete against it. Partners' interests do diverge over time, which may lead some alliances in a network to break up, but such associations are not marriages meant to last forever. The artistry in managing networks of alliances lies, at least partly, in accommodating such developments. When AT&T's alliance with Olivetti ended, for example, both firms were able to find new partners for the same strategic purposes.[30]

Another argument advanced against alliances holds that commitments in a context of environmental turbulence may prove unreliable and pose a major business risk. Environmental disorder is, if anything, a reason to enter into alliances; alliances as a source of strategic flexibility are certainly to be preferred to massive irreversible investments that may come to naught.[31]

Nothing better illustrates both the link between environmental uncertainty and alliances as well as the network-based future of global competition as the emerging multimedia industry. Five traditional industries—computing, communications, consumer electronics, entertainment, and publishing—are converging as technology to convey cheaply large chunks of video, sound, graphics, and text in digital form becomes available. As a vast new field goes through its birth pangs, alliances within and across national borders, between large and small firms, have proliferated.[32] Figure 9.2 depicts some of the industry alliances.

A major reason for the proliferation of alliances, according to industry participants, is the uncertainty, technological and market-related, as to what combinations of content, delivery, and manipulation of information would be successful. "In an uncertain industrial atmosphere, alliances can help to establish technical standards and spread costs and risks."[33] Many firms have hedged their bets by joining several alliance groups.

Inevitably, the different consortia bring together firms that are fierce competitors elsewhere. For example, the General Magic consortium (see Figure 9.2) includes AT&T and Motorola (rivals in wireless networks and devices) as well as Sony, Matsushita, and Philips (foes in consumer electronics). It is said that the General Magic company, in which six companies (the above five and Apple) hold equity shares, struggles to keep the partners happy by constantly striving to keep its work with each partner compartmentalized from the work of the others. "When backers visit General Magic's premises in Mountain View, California, they cannot enter a locked design wing where future products from all the alliance members lie in plain view on workbenches."[34] Still, even as partners bicker, no one wants to leave the alliance. Such is the pull of competitive associations.

Clearly, therefore, multiple alliances, and the resultant networks of mixed-motive relationships spanning the globe, are going to be a permanent feature of the competitive landscape of the future. The role of alliances in corporations is changing profoundly. They used to be seen as a way of filling well-defined competence gaps through learning and restructuring. Not anymore. They are becoming a basic, permanent building block of

Figure 9.2

Making the Connection: Multimedia's Equity Alliances

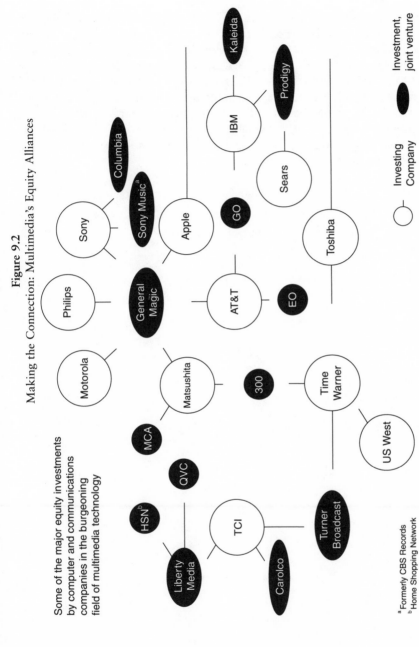

Some of the major equity investments by computer and communications companies in the burgeoning field of multimedia technology

○ Investing Company

● Investment, joint venture

[a] Formerly CBS Records
[b] Home Shopping Network

Source: Reprinted by permission of the *Wall Street Journal,* © 1993 Dow Jones & Company, Inc. All rights reserved worldwide.

"global network" companies. Such a network corporation comes about only through an imaginative reconceptualization of businesses, and in more and more industries such entrepreneurial globalization is becoming the norm.

The inevitable rise of the global network corporation is yet another milestone—perhaps the last—in the long march to develop organizational capabilities that meet the strategic needs of the environment.[35] It is not a panacea for all of a global corporation's problems, but this much is certain: the ability to build, develop, manage, and sustain a global network will be the critical dimension that separates winners from also-rans in the evolving global environment of the future.

Notes

CHAPTER 1

1. In the parlance of the former, industries are either global or multidomestic (M. E. Porter, ed., *Competition in Global Industries* [Boston: Harvard Business School Press, 1986]). But as almost any industry can be contested on a global basis, it seems more appropriate to think in terms of global competition, which, by recognizing the primacy of firms' competitive strategies, fits with the purpose and management of alliances—the topics of this book.
2. K. Ohmae, in *Triad Power: The Coming Shape of Global Competition* (New York: Free Press, 1985), introduced the terms "triad" and "triadization." Since then they have gained considerable popular currency.
3. Communicated to M. Y. Yoshino in a personal interview, August 10, 1989.
4. Many writers on strategic alliances do not define what they are, giving writers the flexibility to talk about any kind of interfirm links, be they mergers, acquisitions, majority-owned ventures, minority equity participation, equal or co-owned joint ventures, or licensing. The approach makes it difficult to provide general guidelines to the readers.
5. M. Hergert and D. Morris, in "Trends in International Collaborative Agreements," in F. J. Contractor and P. Lorange, eds., *Cooperative Strategies in International Business* (Lexington, Mass.: Lexington Books, D. C. Heath, 1988), have used a similar definition for what they call collaborative agreements.
6. ASEA remains involved in other businesses while holding a 50% stake in Asea Brown Boveri. Brown Boveri Corporation is now a shell company that exists almost exclusively for the purpose of holding a 50% stake in Asea Brown Boveri. Brown Boveri Corporation shareholders could as well have settled for shares in Asea Brown Boveri, in which case there would not be even two independent firms! Perhaps the best way to view this interfirm link, recognizing the existence of the two firms, is to treat it, as we do in Chapter 8, as a rationalizing corporate-level, as opposed to a business-level, alliance.
7. The work of J. M. Stopford and L. T. Wells, *Managing the Multinational*

Enterprise: Organization of the Firm and Ownership of the Subsidiaries (New York: Basic Books, 1972), remains the landmark study of international joint ventures of multinational corporations. J. W. Tomlinson, *The Joint Venture Process in International Business: India and Pakistan* (Cambridge, Mass.: MIT Press, 1970), is a good study of international joint ventures in developing countries. R. D. Hall, *International Joint Ventures* (New York: Praeger, 1984), is a practitioner-oriented work on international joint ventures.

8. See D. J. Encarnation and S. Vachani, "Foreign Ownership: When Hosts Change the Rules," *Harvard Business Review,* September–October 1985, pp. 152–160, for some of the innovative approaches MNCs have used to maintain control over joint ventures even in the face of hostile local government laws.

9. Multinationals in India managed not only to regain majority control, but also to do it cheaply by having new equity issued at big discounts, much to the chagrin of Indian shareholders and the government of India. See S. Wagstyl and R. C. Murphy, "Foreign Buying Triggers Concern in India," *Financial Times,* (November 4, 1993). p. 30.

10. Indeed, early research on overseas subsidiaries of multinational corporations and their participation in international trade dealt with aspects of such integrated corporate systems. See G. K. Helleiner, "Manufactured Exports from Less Developed Countries," *Economic Journal* 83 (March 1973): 21–47; J. P. Jarrett, "Offshore Assembly and Production and the Internalization of International Trade within the Multinational Corporation," Ph.D. diss., Harvard University, 1979; G. L. Reuber, *Private Foreign Investment in Development* (Oxford: Clarendon Press for the OECD, 1973); and C. V. Vaitsos, *Intercountry Income Distribution and Transnational Enterprises* (Oxford: Clarendon Press, 1974).

11. The joint venture is actually between Rank Xerox of Great Britain, a 51%-owned subsidiary of Xerox, and Fuji of Japan. This structure of the joint venture is merely a historical accident and has no relevance for our discussion.

12. For more details, see Ben Gomes-Cassares, "Xerox and Fuji-Xerox," Case No. 9-391-156 (Boston: Harvard Business School, 1991).

13. The joint venture Fuji-Xerox was structured so as to eliminate any flow of technology from the joint venture to Fuji Photo Film. The latter, in turn, did not contribute any technology to the joint venture, which, as such, is largely dependent on continuing flows of technology from only one parent, Xerox.

14. The relationship between Xerox and Fuji-Xerox cannot be an alliance mainly because the latter is not an independent company in any meaningful sense of the term. For one thing, Fuji-Xerox needs parent-company Xerox's concurrence in every major business area: capital expenditures, business and operating plans, relations with third parties, and sales outside the licensed territory. Whatever autonomy it has is largely a historical accident because of the way it was structured as a joint venture between Rank Xerox and Fuji Photo Film. The autonomy is being maintained because, among other things, Xerox does not want to offend its partner, Fuji Photo Film. Second, Xerox has unfettered access to all the technology developed by the joint venture but Fuji Photo Film does not. One way to recognize the dominance of Xerox in the relationship is to pose a counterfactual question: What will happen if Xerox and Fuji Photo Film decide to dissolve the joint venture? Xerox can then simply and easily reestablish

itself in Japan through a wholly owned subsidiary. On the other hand, with no access to the technology developed in Fuji-Xerox, Fuji Photo Film cannot enter the xerography business that easily. Indeed, it is quite likely, therefore, that Xerox will be able to buy out Fuji Photo Film and retain much of the joint venture's personnel to maintain managerial continuity.

15. Many studies on strategic alliances have included licensing in their definition of alliances. Some examples include R. N. Osborn and C. C. Baughn, "Forms of Interorganizational Governance for Multinational Alliances," *Academy of Management Journal* 33, no. 3 (September 1990): 503–519, and B. Gomes-Casseres, "Computers: Alliances and Industry Evolution," in D. B. Yoffie, ed., *Beyond Free Trade: Firms, Governments, and Global Competition* (Boston: Harvard Business School Press, 1993), pp. 79–128.

16. For several decades, Pilkington, the U.K. glassmaker, has used licensing as its preferred strategy to penetrate overseas markets (George Graham, "Washington's new anti-trust vigour," *Financial Times,* May 27, 1994, page 6). On the use of licensing as part of international strategy, see F. J. Contractor, *Licensing in International Strategy* (Westport, Conn.: Quorum Books, 1985).

17. See Ben Gomes-Cassares "Mips Computer Systems (A)," Case No. 9-792-055 (Boston: Harvard Business School, 1992), p. 8.

18. On the other hand, because they involve independent firms, shared control, and continuing contributions, especially of technological expertise, consortia formed to set technological standards do qualify as strategic alliances.

19. G. B. Richardson, an academic economist, was perhaps one of the earliest observers of the phenomenon of interfirm alliances ("The Organisation of Industry," *Economic Journal,* September 1972, pp. 883–896).

20. See General Motors Corporation, "General Motors' Position on United Control of Foreign Operations," February 1, 1966, p. 3.

21. On IBM's traditional policy stance on joint ventures and its experience in India, see J. M. Grieco, "Between Dependence and Autonomy: India's Experience with the International Computer Industry," *International Organization,* Summer 1982, pp. 609–632.

22. See "Unable to Beat Them, IBM Joins Them," *New York Times,* July 6, 1992, sec. D, p. 1.

23. The IBM-Ricoh deal, entered into in September 1987, was made public in the *Japan Economic Journal,* March 19, 1988.

24. For Japanese automakers' use of close links with suppliers, see M. Cusumano, *The Japanese Automobile Industry* (Cambridge, Mass.: Harvard University Press, 1985). On how Matsushita made its VHS standard prevail over Sony's rival Betamax, see the cover story on Sony, Amy Borrus, "Sony's Challenge," *Business Week,* June 1, 1987, pp. 64–69. For an insightful review of the working of the Japanese consortium approach to research, see D. I. Okimoto, *Between MITI and the Market: Japanese Industrial Policy for High Technology* (Stanford: Stanford University Press, 1989).

25. See G. Hamel, C. K. Prahalad, and Y. Doz, "Collaborate with Your Competitors—and Win," *Harvard Business Review,* January–February 1989, pp. 133–139.

26. See H. W. Perlmutter and D. A. Heenan, "Cooperate to Compete Globally," *Harvard Business Review,* March–April 1986, pp. 136–142.

27. See K. Ohmae, "The Global Logic of Strategic Alliances," *Harvard Business Review,* March–April 1989, pp. 143–154.
28. See Hamel, Prahalad, and Doz, "Collaborate with Your Competitors."
29. See R. D. Reich and E. Mankin, "Joint Ventures with Japan Give Away Our Future," *Harvard Business Review,* March–April 1986, pp. 78–86.
30. See H. Itami, *Mobilizing Invisible Assets* (Cambridge, Mass.: Harvard University Press, 1987), regarding how a number of Japanese and some highly successful American firms, e.g., Boeing, have used learning from customers, suppliers, and even competitors to enhance their competitive position.
31. We use the phrases "core competencies" and "strategic advantages" rather broadly, along the lines of G. Dosi, D. J. Teece, and S. G. Winter, "Towards a Theory of Corporate Coherence," in G. Dosi, R. Giamatti, and P. A. Toninelli, eds., *Technology and the Enterprise in a Historical Perspective* (Oxford: Oxford University Press, 1991), to refer to "a set of differentiated skills, complementary assets, and the organizational routines and capacities that provide the basis for a firm's competitive capacities in a particular business."
32. See F. M. Scherer, *Industrial Market Structure and Economic Performance* (Boston: Houghton Mifflin, 1980), and J. Pennings, "Strategically Interdependent Organizations," in P. C. Nystrom and W. H. Starbuck, eds., *Handbook of Organization Design,* vol. 1 (New York: Oxford University Press, 1981), for arguments on how uncontrolled disclosure of information can cause much damage to firms, especially in oligopolistic markets.
33. The chapter by P. J. Killing in Contractor and Lorange, *Cooperative Strategies in International Business,* considers only the frequency and routine or nonroutine nature of interaction. R. W. Moxon, T. W. Roehl, and J. F. Truitt, "International Cooperative Ventures in the Commercial Aircraft Industry: Gains, Sure, but What's My Share?" in the same volume, is mainly concerned with long-term conflict potential. Our framework goes beyond these elements.
34. Clearly, there are intermediate stages of conflict and cooperation, which we ignore for expository reasons.
35. The notion of value-adding partnerships between companies that perform different steps along the value-added chain was introduced by R. Johnston and P. R. Lawrence, "Beyond Vertical Integration: The Rise of the Value-Adding Partnership," *Harvard Business Review,* July–August 1988, pp. 94–101, HBR Reprint No. 88407.
36. Again, we are concerned with more than frequency of interaction; clearly, partner firms' managers often meet and exchange information in supplier relationships.
37. In such alliances, partners tend to come from different "strategic groups." For an exposition of strategic groups, see M. E. Porter, *Competitive Strategy: Techniques for Analyzing Industries and Competitors* (New York: Free Press, 1980).
38. For an interesting description of how erstwhile allies IBM and Microsoft turned into rather bitter rivals, see P. Carroll, *Big Blues: The Unmaking of IBM* (New York: Crown Press, 1993). As for the relationship between IBM and Intel, see *The Wall Street Journal,* August 24, 1993, sec. A., p. 4.
39. It can be seen that our typology of alliances avoids proliferation of alliance types based on such things as the identity of the partner (e.g., universities versus other firms, large versus small firms) or the value activity involved (marketing, manufacturing, or research and development). Such narrow alliance definitions,

while helpful (D. Dimancescu and J. Botkin, *The New Alliance: America's R&D Consortia* [Cambridge, Mass.: Ballinger, 1986]), ignore the broad commonalities in the forging and management of strategic alliances of all kinds.

40. In examining interfirm links ranging from arm's-length contracts to joint ventures, we have moved away from the dichotomy commonly presented in the literature between equity and nonequity alliances. We believe equity participation or nonparticipation to be an implicit part of the forging and managing of strategic alliances and distinctions based solely on equity to be immaterial.

41. U.S. antitrust laws generally do not permit close links between domestic firms in the same industry. Witness the controversy that surrounded even a casual meeting in the early 1980s of senior managers of the Big Three auto firms to discuss the implications of the federal government's Clean Air Act proposals. Recent legislation relating to research and development collaboration (National Cooperative Research Act of 1984) by domestic firms and the relaxed view of the Clinton administration toward domestic alliances, especially when the federal government is a member of the alliance, as in the case of developing an energy-efficient car, may alter this situation and render much of the present discussion relevant to such links.

CHAPTER 2

1. While most commentators consider the automobile industry to be mature, some writers dispute such a characterization, suggesting that there is considerable evidence of "dematuring" in the automobile industry (W. J. Abernathy and D. Ginsburg, eds., *Government, Technology, and the Future of the Automobile* [New York: McGraw-Hill, 1980]).

2. Although the arrival in the 1980s of Yugoslav (Yugo) and Korean (Hyundai) automobile manufacturers may seem to contradict this assertion, both are small companies largely confined to geographic and product niches; neither is, or is soon expected to become, a global player.

3. Between 1916 and 1924, for example, the price of a Model T dropped in current (not constant) dollars from $400 to $290 (*Automotive Industries,* February 1978, p. 81).

4. The in-house long-range planning groups of many firms, notably General Motors, had by the early 1970s begun to foresee the prospect of a sharp rise in oil prices and resultant need to redesign their cars. But these efforts were largely in the discussion stage when the crisis occurred. In this they were in good company; even oil companies, which had an even more urgent need to anticipate the coming and timing of price increases, were caught unawares when oil prices rose steeply owing to the 1973 Arab-Israeli war (P. Wack, "Scenarios: Uncharted Waters Ahead," *Harvard Business Review,* September–October 1985, pp. 73–89, and "Scenarios: Shooting the Rapids," *Harvard Business Review,* November–December 1985, pp. 139–150, and D. Yergin, *The Prize: The Epic Quest for Oil, Money, and Power* [New York: Simon and Schuster, 1990]).

5. The notion that past investments that might well have provided the entry barriers needed for higher profitability (P. Ghemawat, *Commitment* [New York: Free

Press, 1991]) could also become difficult exit barriers by denying flexibility is well understood by academics (M. E. Porter, *Competitive Strategy: Techniques for Analyzing Industries and Competitors* [New York: Free Press, 1980]) and managers. In this context, strategic alliances can be seen as enhancing the flexibility of a corporation in an era of increasing global competition and rising technological uncertainty.

6. Bennett Bidwell, vice president, Ford Motor Company, quoted in *Business Week,* February 2, 1981, p. 63.

7. A. Altshuler, *The Future of the Automobile* (Cambridge, Mass.: MIT Press, 1984), p. 139.

8. This is yet another instance of the impact of globalization of competition on the firms' strategies. We will have more to say about it in Chapter 3. Suffice it to say here that under global competition, simple generic strategies are being replaced by complex global strategies that combine the elements of cost leadership and differentiation.

9. In 1980, a Ford general manager remarked that he was afraid to raise prices on the company's Escort models enough to make a profit because "right now, cars on the low end can least stand a price increase." To make up for the lack of profit on Escort, Ford jacked up prices on already slow-moving larger models (*Business Week,* February 2, 1981).

10. In the strategic management literature, this approach to strategy making is referred to as the resource-based view of the firm. See, for example, J. B. Barney, "Strategic Factor Markets: Expectation, Luck, and Business Strategy," *Management Science* 32, no. 10 (October 1986): 1231–1241; "Types of Competition and the Theory of Strategy: Toward an Integrative Perspective," *Academy of Management Review* 11 (1986): 79–80; and "Firm Resources and Sustained Competitive Advantage," *Journal of Management* 17, no. 1 (March 1991), and D. J. Collis, "A Resource-based Analysis of Global Competition: The Case of the Bearings Industry," *Strategic Management Journal* 12 (1991): 49–68.

11. Chrysler emerged from its financial problems perhaps earlier than Ford, but in choosing this route, it may have mortgaged its future. Industry observers have begun to posit its replacement as one of the Big Three by Honda or Toyota. See *Fortune,* June 22, 1990, for a related story.

12. Interestingly enough, academic writing in the area of strategic management has put much less stress on such an entrepreneurial approach. In the economics literature, especially of the Austrian school, this approach is related to the risk-taking behavior of entrepreneurs, who, it is said, think of new opportunities and then think up new ways to take advantage of them. See, for example, M. Casson, ed., *Entrepreneurship* (London: E. Elgar, 1990), and I. M. Kirzner, *The Economic Point of View* (Kansas City, Kans.: Sheed and Ward, subsidiary of Universal Press Syndicate, 1976). This approach has been used to contrast administrative (or trustee) behavior and entrepreneurial management behavior (H. H. Stevenson, "A Perspective on Entrepreneurial Management," Working Paper, Harvard Business School, 1983, and "Entrepreneurship: A Process, Not a Person," Working Paper, Harvard Business School, June 1987).

13. *Business Week,* February 2, 1981, p. 62.

14. On the notion of "emerging" strategy, see H. Mintzberg, "Of Strategies, Deliberate and Emergent," *Strategic Management Journal,* 1985, pp. 257–272, and

"Crafting Strategy," *Harvard Business Review,* July–August 1987, pp. 66–75. J. B. Quinn, *Strategies for Change* (Homewood, Ill.: Richard D. Irwin, 1980), calls it logical incrementalism.

15. That firms tend to become more focused as market expands, leaving value activities formerly done in-house to specialist firms, is an old and accepted axiom in economics (G. Stigler, "The Division of Labor Is Limited by the Extent of the Market," *Journal of Political Economy* 59 [June 1951]: 185–193). Ford's innovation was to force such "deintegration" earlier and to forge novel organizational links and ways to manage them, as we shall see later.

16. Not coincidentally, it was at about this time that Japanese firms such as Toyo Kogyo (Mazda) were in the process of evaluating such new production methods as Toyota's just-in-time (kanban) system. This factor, too, weighed in Ford's selection of Mazda as a potential partner. On Mazda's transforming itself into a modern manufacturing firm in just five short years, 1975 to 1980, see G. Stalk and J. C. Abegglen, *Kaisha: The Japanese Corporation* (New York: Basic Books, 1985).

17. One reason Ford opted for a joint venture (in which it held a 50% equity stake) was that it called for transfer of sensitive, proprietary, patented technology from Ford to the venture. Ownership stake at that level permitted Ford to ensure that the technology did not leak out of the venture. The joint-venture arrangement also permitted Ford access to any process-technology improvements that the venture might yield.

18. The automatic transmission was itself the product of a collaborative design effort among Ford, General Motors, and Borg-Warner.

19. Japan's Ministry of International Trade and Industry relaxed its policy of not permitting foreign investment in Japanese automakers in 1970; in 1971, General Motors bought a 35% stake in Isuzu, and Chrysler acquired a 15% interest in Mitsubishi.

20. "The Partners," *Business Week,* February 10, 1992, p. 104.

21. See "Ford Explores New High Tech Field," *Automotive News,* April 15, 1985, p. 22.

22. Ibid, p. 58.

23. See *The New York Times,* September 22, 1988, sec. D, p. 2.

24. On how investments in R&D, new ventures, and production platforms could be analyzed using an options theory framework, see C. Baldwin and K. Clark, "Capabilities and Capital Investment: New Perspectives on Capital Budgeting," Working Paper No. 92-004, Harvard Business School, 1992, and B. Kogut, "Designing Global Strategies: Comparative and Competitive Value Added Chains," *Sloan Management Review,* Summer 1985, pp. 27–38.

25. A 1992 study by a Detroit auto industry consulting firm attested to the effectiveness of Ford's learning from its Japanese allies. The report concluded that Ford was the most productive among North American carmakers, using only three workers per car produced, which was just a shade more than the Japanese firms did. Ford's Kansas City plant was even more efficient, using just 2.3 workers per car. GM and Chrysler were far behind Ford on this measure of productivity.

26. The rise of Japanese global competitors in consumer electronics in general, and the television industry in particular, has been traced in several case studies. See, for example, M. E. Porter, "U.S. Television Set Market, Prewar to 1970," Case

No. 9-380-180 (Boston: Harvard Business School, 1980), and M. E. Porter, "U.S. Television Set Market, 1970–79," Case No. 9-380-181 (Boston: Harvard Business School, 1980). An effort by General Electric to reenter the TV set industry is described in D. J. Collis, R. Phelps, and N. Donohue, "General Electric: Consumer Electronics Group," Case No. 9-389-048 (Boston: Harvard Business School, 1989).

27. *Business Week,* March 29, 1982, p. 129.

28. J. O'Toole, *Vanguard Management: Redesigning the Corporate Future* (New York: Doubleday, 1985), p. 91.

29. Others in the semiconductor business have followed similar reasoning. Extending the usefulness of their libraries was precisely the motivation for another early 1980s semiconductor design-related three-way alliance among General Electric, Toshiba, and Siemens.

30. For a more detailed look at the global semiconductor industry in the early 1980s, see D. I. Okimoto, T. Sugano, and F. B. Weinstein, eds., *Competitive Edge: The Semiconductor Industry in the U.S. and Japan* (Stanford: Stanford University Press, 1984).

31. It has been suggested that the useful half-life of a graduate engineer in areas such as semiconductors and computers is just five years. Thus, unless continuous human capital investment through training, learning by doing, and skills upgrading occurs, even a world-class semiconductor company can quickly lose its competitive edge ("The Great Educational Gap," *Far Eastern Economic Review,* October–November, 1983, pp. 71–74; Richard Kazis, "Education and Training in the United States: Developing the Human Resources We Need for Technological Advance and Competitiveness," *Working Papers of the MIT Commission on Industrial Productivity 2* [Cambridge, Mass.: MIT Press, 1989]).

32. Only Texas Instruments set up a semiconductor manufacturing facility in Japan before Motorola.

33. National Semiconductors was among U.S. semiconductor manufacturers that, faced with a similar situation, adopted defensive strategic postures. Its competitive position gradually eroded, and by the end of the decade the firm was part of a Japanese company.

34. Recalling Motorola's second-sourcing arrangement with Hitachi, one senior manager remarked, "We were burned by that deal. We learned from that how wary we should be when dealing with potential competitors. We are trying to put those lessons to good use in our more recent efforts at alliance making [with Toshiba]." Indeed, the Motorola-Hitachi arrangement had been the subject of a long-running court battle. See, for example, *Wall Street Journal,* January 26, 27, 1989; March 30, April 2, 11, May 9, June 19, 20, 26, 28, and October 9, 1990.

35. In January 1990, when it introduced its 68040 microprocessor chip, Motorola also presented a list of 36 computer manufacturers that it said planned to build machines with the chip (*Wall Street Journal,* January 19, 1990), thus gaining instant credibility for the chip among software vendors. Part of that strategic savvy came from the experience Motorola had gained in forging and managing alliances.

36. One can conjecture that Toshiba's own strategic use of alliances may have had some impact on the thinking of Motorola executives. To bolster its semiconduc-

tor business, Toshiba had, by 1986, entered into cooperative arrangements with Olivetti of Italy (1984), AT&T (1985), LSI Logic (1985), Siemens of Germany (1985), Hewlett-Packard (1985), and Siemens and General Electric (1986). It is doubtful that this lesson was lost on Motorola's shrewd business leaders.

37. For more details on the Motorola-Toshiba alliance, see Press Release, Motorola Inc., November 25, 1986; *Austin Statesman,* November 26, 1986; and *Arizona Republic,* December 1, 1986. For Toshiba's point of view, see *Wall Street Journal,* December 5, 1986.

38. See subsequent chapters on structuring and managing alliances for elaboration of the various ways by which many firms have sought to protect their strategic interests.

39. *Dataquest,* research newsletter, December 1986.

40. Ibid.

41. Again, we draw the reader's attention to our arguments in the following chapter on global competition and how it pushes firms to adopt complex global strategies that combine low cost and differentiation.

42. The following paragraphs on lessons learned uses the Ford experience as the main vehicle for discussion, as we did not consider it appropriate to jump back and forth between Ford and Motorola. A similar narrative would follow had we decided to use the Motorola example.

43. H. Mintzberg, "Strategy Formation: Ten Schools of Thought," in J. Fredricksen, ed., *Perspectives on Strategic Management* (Cambridge, Mass.: Ballinger, 1990), suggests that strategy is often the cumulative effect of a series of small decisions made over time.

44. The two sets of feedback loops and the organizational learning they imply roughly correspond to what C. Argyris, "Single-Loop and Double-Loop Models in Research on Decision-Making," *Administrative Science Quarterly* 21, no. 3, 1976, and Argyris and D. Schon, *Organizational Learning: A Theory-in-Action Perspective* (Reading, Mass.: Addison-Wesley, 1978), called single-loop learning and double-loop learning. In the former, behavior (or action) is adjusted to fixed goals, norms, and assumptions. In the latter, goals, norms, and assumptions are also changeable. If a firm (or organization) desires to evolve into a long-lasting institution (P. Selznick, *Leadership in Administration* [New York: Harper and Row, 1957]), such adaptive learning (B. Hedberg, "How Organizations Learn and Unlearn," in *Handbook of Organizational Design,* vol. 1 [London: Oxford University Press, 1981], pp. 3–27, and C. M. Fiol and M. A. Lyles, "Organizational Learning," *Academy of Management Review* 10, no. 4 [1985]: 803–813) is a must.

45. Ford and Nissan were, in the mid-1970s, roughly the same size in terms of sales, assets, and employees. Mazda, on the other hand, was about one-eighth in dollar sales, one-sixth in unit sales, one-fifth in assets, and one-seventh in number of employees the size of Ford. Right up to the early 1990s, Nissan maintained its parity with Ford and Mazda remained much smaller than Ford. Ford and Nissan have been, and continue to be, mass marketers of cars that compete in every product segment; Mazda, on the other hand, has always been, and continues to be, a niche player in the global automobile industry.

46. See, for example, J. L. Badaracco, Jr., "General Motors' Asian Alliances," Case No. 9-388-094 (Boston: Harvard Business School, 1988).

47. We address more specifically, in a later chapter, top management's role in shaping the behavior of middle managers through such signals as effective articulation of the strategy-alliance nexus.

48. Among these are R. B. Reich and E. D. Mankin, "Joint Ventures with Japan Give Away Our Future," *Harvard Business Review,* March–April 1986, pp. 78–86, and G. Hamel, C. K. Prahalad, and Y. Doz, "Collaborate with Your Competitors—and Win," *Harvard Business Review,* January–February 1989, pp. 133–139.

49. For a sample of writings offering largely unstinted praise for strategic alliances and anodyne prescriptions for managing them, see H. W. Perlmutter and D. A. Heenan, "Cooperate to Compete Globally," *Harvard Business Review,* March–April 1986, pp. 136–142, and K. Ohmae, "The Global Logic of Strategic Alliances," *Harvard Business Review,* March–April 1989, pp. 143–154.

CHAPTER 3

1. In 1989, when two of the world's largest accounting firms—Arthur Andersen and Price Waterhouse—entered into discussions to explore a possible merger, the chief executives of the two firms said, in a joint statement, that they were undertaking discussions to "benefit from the continuing rapid globalization of world economies, the accelerating pace of technological change, and broad-based need for new services and investments" (*New York Times,* July 7, 1989, sec. A, p. 1). Also see cases on the globalization of advertising; (David Collis, "Saatchi and Saatchi Co. PLC: Corporate Strategy," Case No. 9-792-056 [Boston: Harvard Business School, 1992]); banking (Thomas Malnight, "Citibank (A): European Strategy," Case No. 9-392-021 [Boston: Harvard Business School, 1992]); and management consulting (Charles Ormiston, "Bain & Co., Inc.: Growing the Business," Case No. 9-391-069 [Boston: Harvard Business School, 1991]).

2. We refer to a network of subsidiaries owned by a firm, multinational or otherwise, as an internal network, a network of links with independent companies outside the firm as an external network. This distinction is desirable inasmuch as these two types of networks have to be managed differently, a point often missed by network theorists.

3. There is an irony to the current integration of the world. An integrated world has long been the dream of philosophers. That it should emerge through the efforts of entrepreneurs and business managers rather than those of idealistic one-world visionaries is worthy of note. With the liberation of Eastern Europe and the former Soviet Union, this phenomenon is likely to gather speed. Indeed, there are already indications that former Eastern bloc countries will become part of the global alliances we refer to in this book. In 1992, an imaginative U.S. semiconductor firm, Sun Microsystems, formed an alliance with a prestigious research institute in the former USSR, which would work on a contractual basis on some of the technological problems faced by Sun (*Wall Street Journal,* September 1, 1992, sec. B, p. 2). Similarly, AT&T and Corning Inc. have entered into contractual agreements with Russian research institutes to work on glass-

material technology related to fiber optics (*New York Times,* June 4, 1992, sec. D, p. 1).

4. According to International Civil Aviation Organization statistics, more than 70% of all international flights originate or end in one of the triad regions (*ICAO Statistical Yearbook,* Civil Aviation Statistics of the World, 17th ed., 1992).

5. Levitt was the first to bring the issue of globalization to the forefront of academic discussion. See T. Levitt, "The Globalization of Markets," *Harvard Business Review,* May–June 1983, pp. 92–102.

6. Ibid. This view of global integration, like any view of a complex phenomenon, is partial. It ignores impediments to global standardization and scale, whether peculiarities of national taste, government-imposed barriers, or simply different ways of doing business. The need to balance the demands of global economics and local political and consumer requirements has been a subject of researchers going back at least to R. Vernon, *Sovereignty at Bay* (New York: Basic Books, 1971). We come to this issue in the context of external networks later in the chapter.

7. Much of the following analysis of globalization of supply follows M. Casson, ed., *Multinationals and World Trade* (London: Macmillan, 1986).

8. On the rise of a liberal trading regime and the U.S. contribution to it, see R. Vernon, "Exploring the Global Economy," Center for International Affairs, Harvard University (Cambridge, Mass.: University Press of America, 1985). In this work Vernon also describes the trade problems of the United States in recent years in the face of moves for illiberal trade practices by some countries. As for the role played by the liberal international trading order in international prosperity, see C. P. Kindleberger, *America in the World Economy* (New York: Foreign Policy Association, Headline Series, No. 237, 1977), and *Government and International Trade* (Princeton: International Finance Section, Department of Economics, Princeton University, Essays in International Finance, No. 129, 1978).

9. On the development of international shipping, see Casson, *Multinationals and World Trade.* The improvements in transport logistics and lowering of transport costs are best appreciated when one compares the ease with which heavy equipment was moved across the oceans during the 1991 Persian Gulf war with the difficulties of doing the same in the 1951 Korean War.

10. As A. D. Chandler, *Strategy and Structure* (New York: Doubleday, Anchor Books, 1966), indicated, organizational innovations for improving administrative coordination are as entrepreneurial as other types of innovation.

11. Computing cost per transaction, according to one estimate, has fallen a thousandfold in the last decade alone (*Wall Street Journal,* January 27, 1993, sec. A, p. 4). The real cost of a transatlantic call has also fallen steeply in the past two decades.

12. One should not forget the role played by business schools in this context. This peculiarly American institution has contributed to the ease of coordination by educating the business elite in developed and developing countries, speeding the use of almost identical management techniques and concepts, including Anglo-Saxon legal traditions and, most important, by fostering English as the lingua franca of international commerce. See K. P. Sauvant and F. G. Lavipour, eds.,

Controlling Multinational Enterprises (London: Wilton House Publications, 1976) for elaboration of the argument on how the English language and Anglo-Saxon tradition have come to dominate management education and international commerce.

13. A firm is a bundle of discrete activities that need to be performed in business in a particular industry. These "value activities" are technologically separable and physically distinct. The operation of a firm is characterized by a chain of activities from raw materials through technology development and manufacturing to sales and distribution.

14. See *New York Times,* December 6, 1986, sec. D, p. 6, for an illustration of this point in the context of South Korea, recent political developments notwithstanding.

15. In this context see M. Olson, *The Rise and Decline of Nations* (New Haven: Yale University Press, 1982), for an analysis of the role of institutional rigidities in the decline of nations. With respect to productivity differentials between developed and less-developed nations, at least in the case of newly industrializing countries (NICs), they seem to be diminishing fast as skill levels in NICs rise, owing to large and sustained investments in human capital by NICs (World Bank, *The East Asian Miracle* [Oxford: Oxford University Press, 1993]).

16. R. Vernon, who is credited as the originator of the idea that American multinationals owe their market success to their innovations based on technological prowess ("International Investment and International Trade in the Product Cycle," *Quarterly Journal of Economics* 80 [May 1966]: 190–207, and *Sovereignty at Bay*), wrote a decade later that U.S. firms no longer had a technological edge over firms in other developed nations and that innovations were as likely to come from abroad as from the United States ("The Product Cycle Hypothesis in a New International Environment," *Oxford Bulletin of Economics and Statistics* 41 [November 1979]: 255–267).

17. In the late 1980s, Bosch, the West German computer manufacturer, located some key component manufacturing facilities at Singapore in preference to Germany.

18. Some writers have distinguished between knowledge that is more fungible (U. S. Rangan, "Sourcing Relationships: An Exploratory Study," DBA diss., Harvard Business School, 1988), and hence more migratory (J. L. Badaracco, Jr., *Knowledge Link* [Boston: Harvard Business School Press, 1991]), and knowledge that is less fungible and thus organizationally bound (Rangan, "Sourcing Relationships"). These have implications for external strategic networks, as we argue in later chapters of this book.

19. In recent years, the largest numbers of U.S. patents have been awarded to Japanese rather than U.S. firms. In 1989, for instance, the top four recipients of U.S. patents were Japanese corporations: Hitachi, Toshiba, Canon, and Fuji. Just six years earlier, the top four were American: GE, IBM, AT&T, and RCA (*Los Angeles Times,* June 10, 1990, p. 1). Indeed, by 1989, Japanese inventors owned more patents in the United States than those from Britain, Germany, and France combined (*The Economist,* May 20, 1989, p. 143). These trends are believed to have continued since then.

20. As Casson *(Multinationals and World Trade)* pointed out, ever since the Industrial Revolution, two processes have been at work in the area of organization

of production. The first, which predominated in the first two centuries of the Industrial Revolution, emphasized finding better ways to produce a given design of a product. Scientific management is an example. This is not to suggest that there were no smart entrepreneurs who adapted product designs to suit the requirements of mass production, but this second process was much less used and came into its own only much later.

21. Even in traditionally closed and highly protected markets, the advantages of global plant efficiencies are now recognized. See, for example, the interview of a leading Indian industrialist on this notion and on how the notoriously protectionist Indian government is coming around to recognize its importance in today's world (*Financial Times*, June 19, 1989).

22. The rise in the cross-hauling of parts and components across nations is evidence of this trend toward spatial specialization. The growth in intrafirm trade in components and finished goods is another piece of evidence. See Casson, *Multinationals and World Trade*.

23. The three ways of using the new international division of labor (NIDL)—to achieve global scale for individual plants based on existing value-chain configuration; to specialize value activities in various parts of the globe without changing the value configuration; to deliberately and creatively reconstruct value activities to take advantage of opportunities for NIDL—apply differently to different groups of industries. To the first belongs such industries as telecommunications and aerospace, to the second, industries such as automobiles, and to the third the soft drink and packaged consumer goods industries. In general, the managerial effort needed to take advantage of opportunities for NIDL becomes more important as we move down the list, leading one observer (U.S. Rangan, "Global Competitive Strategy and Multinational Enterprises," doctoral subfield paper, Harvard Business School, November 1984) to classify global industries into three categories: those that are "born global" (aerospace and telecommunications); those that "achieve globalness" (automobiles); and those that have "globalness thrust upon them" (soft drinks).

24. In the early 1980s, Procter & Gamble was successful in creating a European brand in a consumer item—laundry powder—by using this approach of disaggregating the value chain and concentrating each part of it in different nations. See Christopher Bartlett "Procter & Gamble Europe: Vizir Launch," Case No. 9-384-139 (Boston: Harvard Business School, 1984).

25. R. J. Barnet and R. E. Muller, *Global Reach: The Power of the International Corporations* (New York: Simon and Schuster, 1974), popularized this term, albeit with a somewhat negative connotation.

26. As indicated earlier, T. M. Hout, M. E. Porter, and E. Rudden, "How Global Companies Win Out," *Harvard Business Review*, September–October 1982, pp. 98–108, were the first to draw a distinction between global and multidomestic industries.

27. C. K. Prahalad and Y. L. Doz, in *The Multinational Mission* (New York: Free Press, 1987), preferred this term.

28. Hout, Porter, and Rudden, "How Global Companies Win Out," divide the universe of industries in which MNCs compete into two categories: multidomestic and global. Multidomestic industries are those in which "competition in each country is essentially independent of competition in other countries," global

industries those "in which firms' competitive policies are strongly influenced by their competitive position in other countries." This dichotomous view, though useful, is too confining. In any industry, a firm always does well to take a global view of competition. General Foods in the branded foods industry (multidomestic for Hout et al.) would do better if it considered the implications of, say, Nestlé's entry into Canada for its U.S. operations than ignore it, thinking it of no consequence because the firm has traditionally treated the industry as multidomestic. The household products industry is similarly multidomestic, again according to Hout et al. Managers of P&G and Unilever who face each other all over the world, however, are more apt to say that they are in a global industry.

29. Vernon (*Sovereignty at Bay*), F. T. Knickerbocker, *Oligopolistic Reaction and Multinational Enterprise* (Boston: Division of Research, Harvard Business School, 1973), and E. M. Graham, "Oligopolistic Imitation and European Direct Investment in the United States," DBA diss., Harvard Business School, 1974, and "Transatlantic Investment by Multinational Firms: A Rivalistic Phenomenon," *Journal of Post-Keynesian Economics* 1 (Fall 1978): 82–99, are some of the earliest writers who recognized this notion of competitive interdependence.

30. Many writers fail to distinguish between "strategies" and "industries." MNCs can have multidomestic strategies or global strategies in the same industry. The degree to which various activities in different locations have to be coordinated may well differ depending on a firm's choice of strategic approach. In some industries, it may happen, although one doubts it, that all the players have adopted a multidomestic strategic approach. It still does not make it a multidomestic industry. Indeed, as many observers of multinationals have argued, MNCs exist only in oligopolistic industries (see R. E. Caves, *Multinational Enterprise and Economic Analysis* [Cambridge: Cambridge University Press, 1982]). Oligopolistic industries, by definition, are those in which competitive interdependence is recognized by firms. A multidomestic industry, by definition, is one in which such interdependence is not recognized. So a multinational enterprise in a multidomestic industry is a contradiction in terms (Rangan, "Global Competitive Strategy"). All industries in which MNCs compete are at least potentially global, as we previously asserted.

31. This strategic view may, among other things, call for a *threat* to cross-subsidize between operations in various markets. However, it is unnecessary to actually cross-subsidize, as is implied by G. Hamel and C. K. Prahalad, "Do You Really Have a Global Strategy?" *Harvard Business Review,* July–August 1985, pp. 133–139, for global competition to exist. See M. Casson, *The Firm and the Market* (Cambridge, Mass.: MIT Press, 1987), for an elucidation of this subtle argument.

32. The view that global competition is feasible with self-contained subsidiaries has a long intellectual pedigree (S. H. Hymer, "The International Operations of National Firms: A Study of Direct Foreign Investment" [Cambridge, Mass.: MIT Press, 1976]; Vernon, *Sovereignty at Bay;* R. E. Caves, "International Corporations: The Industrial Economics of Foreign Investment," *Economics* 38 [February 1971]: 1–27; Knickerbocker, *Oligopolistic Reaction;* and Graham, "Transatlantic Investment by Multinational Firms").

33. Much of the recent writing on global competition and global strategies has paid some attention to the notion of interdependencies we list below. What is lacking is a sense of how such strategies have followed a sequential evolution over time. Indeed, it is the absence of a sense of historical perspective that has led to the current fashion for admiring everything Japanese and decrying everything American, implying that the Japanese have been better global players. Both American and Japanese firms have pursued global strategies, albeit of different kinds. The challenge for both now is to move to the next rung in complex global strategies, the one involving the use of alliances, as we argue in the last chapter.

34. Economy-of-scale benefits were identified long ago by Hymer, "International Operations of National Firms," followed by Vernon, *Sovereignty at Bay,* and Caves, "International Corporations."

35. Almost every book on international management has devoted some attention to this aspect of international competition. See, for example, the various editions of R. Vernon and L. T. Wells's familiarly known textbook on international management, *Manager in the International Economy,* 6th ed. (New York: Prentice Hall, 1991).

36. W. Baumol, J. Panzer, and R. Willig, *Contestable Markets and the Theory of Industry Structure* (New York: Harcourt Brace Jovanovich, 1982), brought economies of scope to the attention of researchers in the context of contestability of markets. D. J. Teece, "Economies of Scope and Scope of an Enterprise," *Journal of Economic Behavior and Organization,* September 1980, pp. 223–247, and "Capturing Value from Technological Innovation," in B. R. Guile and H. Brooks, eds., *Technology and Global Industry* (Washington, D.C.: National Academy Press, 1987), suggests that learning from different geographic markets might be a competitive advantage enjoyed by multinationals over their nonmultinational rivals. M. E. Porter, *Competitive Advantage: Creating and Sustaining Superior Performance* (New York: Free Press, 1985), further generalized the analysis to include competitive scope across segments and industries.

37. J. M. Stopford and L. T. Wells, *Managing the Multinational Enterprise: Organization of the Firm and Ownership of the Subsidiaries* (New York: Basic Books, 1972), in the context of management of overseas subsidiaries, referred to this issue of learning through subsidiaries and using the knowledge elsewhere. R. Vernon, "The Product Cycle Hypothesis in a New International Environment," *Oxford Bulletin of Economics and Statistics* 41 (November 1979): 255–267, discusses explicitly the cross-learning capabilities of multinational networks. B. Kogut, "A Note on Global Strategies," *Strategic Management Journal* 10, no. 4 (July–August 1989): 383–389, draws attention to the long tradition in international business research that recognizes the notion of multinationals' transferring acquired capabilities across national borders.

38. Since many readers are likely to be familiar with developments in the United States, Europe, and to some extent Japan, the following narrative relies heavily on illustrations from these areas. The arguments, however, are more general and applicable to other countries, mutatis mutandis.

39. See S. B. Linder, *An Essay on Trade and Transformation* (New York: Wiley, 1967), for an elaboration of export-as-vent-for-surplus theory.

40. The product cycle theories of Vernon, "International Investment and International Trade in the Product Cycle," and L. T. Wells, *The Product Cycle and International Trade* (Boston: Division of Research, Harvard Business School, 1972), also fit this sequence of events.

41. Knickerbocker, *Oligopolistic Reaction.*

42. Graham, "Transatlantic Investment."

43. J. H. Dunning, in *Economic Analysis and the Multinational Enterprise* (London: George Allen and Unwin, 1974), calls them locational advantages. International economists tend to refer to them as comparative advantages. Low-cost labor and access to raw materials are two such advantages.

44. M. E. Porter, *Competition in Global Industries* (Boston: Harvard Business School Press, 1986), would call this the multidomestic strategy.

45. We wish to stress the fact that this is only a stylized version of global competitive development. Some firms may have recognized all three of the interdependencies right from the time they went abroad, either through exports or through the establishment of overseas affiliates. What has perhaps been lacking on the part of many such firms is the ability to develop and sustain organizational capabilities needed to manage such interdependencies.

46. As we pointed out earlier, it must be borne in mind that we are not here contrasting country-centered (multidomestic in the parlance of Porter) and global strategies. Global strategies exist as long as firms recognize competitive interdependence, irrespective of whether they compete through exports, foreign affiliates, or both. We distinguish among three kinds of global strategies: export-based, cross-hauling-based, and network-based. The management complexity of these global strategies increases from the first to the last.

47. Japanese firms have not always been the first to adopt complex global strategies. Electrolux in Europe and U.S. firms in such industries as aerospace have also been pioneers in opting for global strategies.

48. As structural factors like transport costs began to favor globalization, the actions of managers transformed motorcycles and automobiles into global industries. Indeed, some firms—Renault in France, for example—are still competing with "national champion" strategies, albeit with shrinking chances of continued success or even existence.

49. In the past decade or so, Ford has moved aggressively to foster a more global approach to strategy. Its announced plan to develop a world car, named Mondeo, is but an extension of this approach. GM, too, seems to be making some headway in this direction.

50. Hamel and Prahalad, "Do You Really Have a Global Strategy?" stress this aspect of exploiting first-mover advantage.

51. P. Ghemawat, *Commitment* (New York: Free Press, 1991), seeks to explain persistence of success and associated strategies through organizational commitment to certain courses of action.

52. See, for example, H. Mintzberg, "Strategy Formation: Ten Schools of Thought," in J. Fredricksen, ed., *Perspectives on Strategic Management* (Cambridge, Mass.: Ballinger, 1990), D. Miller and P. H. Friesen, *Organizations: A Quantum View* (Englewood Cliffs, N.J.: Prentice Hall, 1984), and Miller, *The Icarus Paradox* (New York: Harper Collins, 1990).

53. The following discussion draws from Porter, *Competitive Advantage,* which refers to the various business-related activities a firm engages in as value activities and to a complete string of such activities, sometimes ranging from product design through operations to service, as a value chain.

54. Ibid., p. 36.

55. P. Ghemawat, "Sustainable Advantage," *Harvard Business Review,* September–October 1986, pp. 53–58, traces the different bases of sustainable advantages and how they come into being.

56. The difference between a temporary advantage and a sustainable one lies in ease of duplicability. If a source of advantage can be copied by a rival at low or no cost, any advantage is likely to be fleeting. If, on the other hand, the advantage can be defended against reproduction by rivals, it is by definition sustainable.

57. D. J. Collis, "The Value Added Structure and Competition within Industries," Ph.D. diss., Harvard University, 1986, links irreversible asset deployments and strategic groups. J. S. Bain, *Industrial Organization* (New York: Wiley, 1968), identified the role of entry barriers in oligopolistic markets. Later researchers have suggested that irreversible asset investments tend to deter potential entrants into an industry (A. K. Dixit, "The Role of Investment in Entry Deterrence," *Economic Journal,* March 1980, pp. 95–106).

58. S. M. Oster, *Modern Competitive Analysis* (Oxford: Oxford University Press, 1990), stresses this asset disposition aspect.

59. On the notion of strategic groups, see Porter, *Competitive Advantage;* K. J. Hatten and D. Schendel, "Heterogeneity within an Industry: Firm Conduct in the United States Brewing Industry, 1952–1971," *Journal of Industrial Economics,* December 1977; Hatten, Schendel, and A. C. Cooper, "A Strategic Model of the United States Brewing Industry, 1952–1971," *Academy of Management Journal* 21, no. 4 (1978): 529–610, and Hatten and M. L. Hatten, "Strategic Groups, Asymmetrical Mobility Barriers, and Contestability," *Strategic Management Journal* 8, no. 4 (1987): 329–342.

60. Alternatively, competitive strategy can be construed as a plan of action chosen by a firm to gain a higher rate of profitability than its rivals. However, the outcome of the plan depends on the actions of the competitors. Therefore, firms resort to strategies that avoid destructive price competition and direct confrontation against as many rivals as possible with a view to "create a defendable position in the long run" in order to "outperform competitors" (Porter, *Competitive Advantage).* Such a notion of avoiding some rivals relates to the notion of strategic groups referred to earlier.

61. See R. E. Caves and M. E. Porter, "From Entry Barriers to Mobility Barriers," *Quarterly Journal of Economics* 91 (May 1977): 241–261, for the relationship between strategic groups and mobility barriers.

62. Porter, *Competitive Advantage,* p. 35.

63. A sequenced-entry approach is an attempt to penetrate entry barriers through a series of small, reversible, or multiple-use investments. A firm that establishes a beachhead in an industry and then expands its base through investments in other assets may be able, through sequenced investments in various value activities that bestow sustainable competitive advantage, to penetrate different strate-

gic groups. By broadening and combining different sources of differentiation and cost leadership, the entrant might be able to unscramble completely the existing strategic groups, making it difficult for the current competitors to preserve their cozy coexistence.

64. Vernon, in "International Investment" and "Product Cycle Hypothesis," argued that product and process innovations of firms are a function of their home-country characteristics. U.S. firms, for example, have traditionally pioneered high-technology products and labor-saving machinery. Japanese firms, on the other hand, tend to put a premium on material-saving innovations.

65. X. Gilbert and P. Strebel, "Strategies to Outpace the Competition," *Journal of Business Strategy,* Summer 1987, pp. 28–37, suggest that firms tend to alternate between cost reduction and value enhancement in order to outpace the competition. Such outpacing efforts are a subset of our argument regarding the efforts of global competitors to strive constantly to create new strategic groups.

66. Major home appliances are "white goods" such as freezers, refrigerators, air conditioners, microwave ovens, dishwashers, washing machines, and dryers; power systems refers to products that help in the generation, transmission, and utilization of power such as turbines, controls, instrumentation panels, transformers, circuit breakers, switchgears, cables, drive systems, and motors.

67. Our arguments thus far regarding global competition as a dynamic process are not meant to imply that globalization negates strategy notions such as sustainability, strategic groups, and generic strategies. Far from it. These concepts retain their analytical appeal to academics and managers alike. We simply argue that, in the more turbulent global competitive environment, dynamic aspects of strategic management need to receive equal attention from managers.

68. On the issue of organizational problems involved in the coordination of international operations, see Y. L. Doz, *Government Control and Multinational Strategic Management: Power Systems and Telecommunication Equipment* (New York: Praeger Press, 1979), and C. A. Bartlett, "Building and Managing the Transnational: The New Organizational Challenge," in M. E. Porter, ed., *Competition in Global Industries* (Boston: Harvard Business School Press, 1986).

69. The notion of using time as a competitive weapon was raised explicitly by the Boston Consulting Group. For a few early elaborations of the concept, see G. Stalk, "Time—The Next Source of Competitive Advantage," *Harvard Business Review,* July–August 1988, pp. 41–51, J. L. Bower and T. M. Hout, "Fast-Cycle Capability for Competitive Power," *Harvard Business Review,* November–December 1988, pp. 110–118, and Stalk and Hout, *Competing Against Time* (New York: Free Press, 1990).

70. On how convergence of technologies has come to play a major role in the formation of interfirm alliances, especially among European multinationals, in a range of industries such as biotechnology, semiconductors, software, and robotics, see R. van Tulder and G. Junne, *European Multinationals in Core Technologies* (New York: Wiley, 1988).

71. On how the production-system innovations of Japanese corporations had their origin in the managerial system of Japanese corporations, see Japan Management Association, *Canon Production System* (Stamford, Conn.: Productivity Press, 1987), and *Kanban: Just-in-Time at Toyota* (Stamford, Conn.: Productivity

Press, 1989), and T. Ohno, *Toyota Production System: Beyond Large-Scale Production* (Cambridge, Mass.: Productivity Press, 1988).

72. On Japan's managerial system, see M. Y. Yoshino, *Japanese Management System: Tradition and Innovation* (Cambridge, Mass.: MIT Press, 1968). M. Gerlach, *Alliance Capitalism* (Los Angeles: University of California Press, 1992), is a good exposition of Japanese *keiretsu*, and S. K. Kim, "Business Concentration and Government Policy: A Study of Business Groups in Korea," DBA diss., Harvard Business School, 1987, explores the evolution of Korean *chaebols*. On the rising role of family and ethnic ties in international business, see J. Kotkin, *Tribes: How Race, Religion, and Identity Determine Success in the New Global Economy* (New York: Random House, 1993).

73. Porter, *Competitive Advantage*, p. 53.

74. For a distinction between comparative advantage and competitive advantage in the context of global competition, see B. Kogut, "Designing Global Strategies: Comparative and Competitive Value Added Chains," *Sloan Management Review,* Summer 1985, pp. 27–38.

75. Porter, *Competitive Advantage*, p. 57.

76. Needless to add, the coalition (alliance) option is available to a multinational firm as well.

77. On Xerox's transformation through strategic refocusing, see "Back in Focus," *Forbes,* June 6, 1994, pp. 72–76.

78. On how U.S.automobile manufacturers have absorbed many lessons in supplier management from Japanese firms but still have some distance to go, see James Bennet, "Detroit Struggles to Learn Another Lesson from Japan," *New York Times,* June 19, 1994, sec. 3, p. 5.

79. In the celebration of the birth of Apple Computer, for instance, what is often overlooked is the fact that its early success is attributable largely to its skillful use of alliances relying on suppliers of various services and components (see Steven C. Wheelwright, "Apple Computer, Inc.—Macintosh (A)," Case No. S-BP-234 (Stanford: Stanford University, 1984) and D. B. Yoffie, "Apple Computer—1992," Case No. 9-792-081 [Boston: Harvard Business School, 1992]). As we pointed out in Chapter 1, IBM's quick response was also based on the skillful use of alliances.

CHAPTER 4

1. We use a pseudonym to protect the firm's identity.

2. While we consider such "deintegration" of a value chain the starting point for entrepreneurial recasting of the business, others have been more critical (J. Thackaray, "America's Vertical Cutback," *McKinsey Quarterly,* Summer 1986, pp. 41–52).

3. See, for example, K. R. Harrigan, *Strategies for Joint Ventures* (Lexington, Mass.: Lexington Books, 1985), *Strategic Flexibility* (New York: Free Press, 1985), and *Managing for Joint Venture Success* (New York: Free Press, 1986); various chapters in F. J. Contractor and P. Lorange, eds., *Cooperative Strategies*

in International Business (New York: Free Press, 1987); and J. D. Lewis, *Partnerships for Profit* (New York: Free Press, 1990).

4. On the impact of differing time horizons of partner firms and their influence on alliances, see J. Ganitsky, U. S. Rangan, and G. E. Watzke, "Time Perspectives in International Joint Ventures," *Journal of Global Marketing* 5, no. 1 (1991): 13–33. Similarities in corporate cultures ease the task of communication and coordination by lowering transaction costs. Swissair's alliance with Delta is believed to have foundered on cultural differences, whereas its Singapore Airlines alliance thrives because of similar corporate views on such issues as service and efficiency. For more details on Swissair's alliance strategy, see D. B. Yoffie and E. J. Vayle, "Swissair," Case No. 9-391-111 (Boston: Harvard Business School, 1991).

5. This line of argument has been advanced by such authors as R. B. Reich and E. D. Mankin, "Joint Ventures with Japan Give Away Our Future," *Harvard Business Review*, March–April 1986, pp. 78–86, in the context of American firms' alliances with Japanese firms.

6. On how strong design capabilities may bestow a sustainable competitive advantage, see P. Kotler and G. A. Rath, "Design: A Powerful but Neglected Strategic Tool," *Journal of Business Strategy* 5, no. 2 (1984): 16–21.

7. AMC's alliance contracts—whether fifty-fifty joint ventures, minority-stake deals, or arm's-length relationships—carried different provisions that permitted AMC access to manufacturing-related information. The role of alliance structures in information flows, inward and outward, is touched on later in this and in subsequent chapters.

8. The issue of managing the information flow between strategic alliance partners is elaborated in a subsequent chapter.

9. In many of the alliances we examined, managers in partner firms gradually tended to recognize the need to create strategic options for the future through investments in related areas. It is managers' failure to recognize this need that results in the so-called hollowing of the corporation, a point often missed by critics of alliances.

10. For a large data-based study confirming this conclusion on lack of correspondence between alliance structure and alliance activity, see P. Ghemawat, M. E. Porter, and R. A. Rawlinson, "Patterns of International Coalition Activity," in M. E. Porter, ed., *Competition in Global Industries* (Boston: Harvard Business School Press, 1986).

11. Recall our definition of an alliance from the first chapter: independent firms, shared control, and continuing contributions. Interfirm links in which one partner has more than 50% of the equity in a joint venture or partner firm are more properly called subsidiaries of the majority shareholder, there being no shared control, a sine qua non of our definition.

12. See "AT&T Is Trying Hard to Get a Major Role in Multimedia Future," *Wall Street Journal*, April 23, 1993.

13. G. Hamel, C. K. Prahalad, and Y. L. Doz, "Collaborate with Your Competitors—and Win," *Harvard Business Review*, January–February 1989, p. 139.

14. K. Ohmae, "The Global Logic of Strategic Alliances," *Harvard Business Review*, March–April 1989, p. 147.

15. A more benign interpretation of the ideas of Hamel and his collaborators and Ohmae is to say that their views indicate their frustration with what they perceive as the "obsession" of American managers with legal niceties of ownership. Even here, we beg to disagree. Acknowledging that obsession of any kind can be faulted, we argue that managers, American or Japanese, are not ignorant of business needs when they seek optimal structures for interfirm relationships.

16. We invoke here a fundamental principle that guided our research: we believe that, on the whole, managers are rational and competent at adapting their behavior to suit the situation at hand. Even if they err at first, they are quick to learn from their mistakes. That so many of them spend so much time thinking about the most efficacious structure for alliances should, therefore, say something about the importance of structure for the success of alliances.

17. The alliance structure shown in Figure 4.2 omits some details for reasons of confidentiality. Also for reasons of confidentiality, we have not given the full details of the entire set of complex side agreements between the two alliance firms.

18. Isuzu was perhaps the weakest Japanese automaker at that time. Still, MITI blocked acquisition of even one-third of its shares by GM until it could satisfy itself that the remaining two-thirds of Isuzu shareholders had sufficient financial backing to prevent GM from eventually, should the company's losses continue, gaining complete control.

19. *Ward's Automotive Reports,* August 12, 1981, p. 241. In the late 1970s, GM increased its shareholdings in Isuzu to 41% through subscription to convertible debentures.

20. Nor are these examples isolated incidents. GE's Medical Systems Group strove to gain strategic control, initially with a minority stake and eventually with a majority equity stake, in ventures with Yokagawa Electric Company of Japan and Samsung Group of Korea. Press reports indicate that Hewlett-Packard similarly worked hard to acquire a 51% stake in its joint venture with Yokagawa Electric. British Airways' original effort in 1992 to forge an alliance with USAir was structured in a complex way to provide British Airways control over key decisions without violating U.S. laws that deny foreign airlines majority stakes in U.S. carriers, but it was abandoned in the face of opposition from an alert American administration ("U.S. Approves British Air Stake in USAir Group," *Wall Street Journal,* March 16, 1993).

21. Among the writers who have emphasized these dichotomies are O. E. Williamson, *Markets and Hierarchies: Analysis and Antitrust Implications* (New York: Free Press, 1975); P. J. Buckley and M. Casson, *The Future of the Multinational Enterprise* (New York: Holmes and Meier, 1976); and J. C. McManus, "The Theory of the International Firm," in G. Paquet, ed., *The Multinational Firm and the Nation State* (Toronto: Collier Macmillan, 1972).

22. Among others who have used this term is U. S. Rangan, in "Sourcing Relationships: An Exploratory Study," DBA diss., Harvard Business School, 1988.

23. M. Casson, ed., *Multinationals and World Trade* (London: Macmillan, 1986).

24. See, for example, D. J. Teece and T. M. Jorde, "Competition and Cooperation—Striking the Right Balance," *California Management Review* 31, no. 3 (Spring 1989): 25–37, and W. Shan, "An Empirical Analysis of Organizational Strategies

of Entrepreneurial High Technology Firms," *Strategic Management Journal* 11 (February 1990): 129–139.

25. See, for example, Lewis, *Partnerships for Profit*, and Harrigan, *Managing for Joint Venture Success*.

26. Although widespread use of alliances by firms may be a recent phenomenon, interfirm links have received some attention from academics since the late 1950s. Much of the past research has focused on joint ventures (JVs) and licensing. In the domestic arena, the main concerns have been with the anticompetitive effects of horizontal joint ventures (D. R. Fusfeld, "Joint Subsidiaries in the Iron and Steel Industry," *American Economic Review* 48 [1958]: 578–587, and P. R. Dixon, "Joint Ventures: What Is Their Impact on Competition?" *Antitrust Bulletin* 7 [1962]: 397–410). Others have looked at factors favoring interfirm links such as diversification, capital constraints, and pooling of know-how (M. W. West, "The Jointly Owned Subsidiary," *Harvard Business Review,* July–August 1959, pp. 31–34, 165–172; P. S. Friedman, S. V. Berg, and J. Duncan, "External versus Internal Knowledge Acquisition: Joint Venture Activity and R&D Intensity," *Journal of Economics and Business* 32 [1979]: 103–110; K. J. Murphy, *Macroproject Development in the Third World: An Analysis of Transnational Partnerships* (Boulder, Colo.: Westview Press, 1983); and W. J. Murphy, "Cooperative Action to Achieve Competitive Strategic Objectives," DBA diss., Harvard Business School, 1987). In the international arena, the primary focus has been on JVs between multinational enterprises and local firms (J. W. Tomlinson, *The Joint Venture Process in International Business: India and Pakistan* [Cambridge, Mass.: MIT Press, 1970]; J. M. Stopford and L. T. Wells, *Managing the Multinational Enterprise: Organization of the Firm and Ownership of the Subsidiaries* [New York: Basic Books, 1972]; P. J. Killing, *Strategies for Joint Venture Success* [New York: Praeger, 1983]; and B. Gomes-Casseres, "Multinational Ownership Strategies," DBA diss., Harvard Business School, 1985). Interfirm links between companies in developed countries have also received some attention (S. Gullander, "Joint Ventures in Europe: Determinants of Entry," *International Studies of Management and Organizations* 16 [1976]: 85–111; P. Mariti and R. H. Smiley, "Co-operative Agreements and the Organization of the Industry," *Journal of Industrial Economics* 31 [1983]: 437–451; and J. A. Stuckey, *Vertical Integration and Joint Ventures in the Aluminum Industry* [Cambridge, Mass.: Harvard University Press, 1983]). Most of the studies, however, do not explicitly deal with "quasi-hierarchies" of the kind we see in the context of strategic alliances.

27. A. D. Chandler, *Strategy and Structure* (New York: Doubleday, Anchor Books, 1966).

28. Ibid., p. 13.

29. For instance, when it developed tetraethyl lead in the 1920s, GM entered into a joint venture with Standard Oil, which was already in the gasoline business and had distribution expertise. It seems that GM's strategy was to be a technology developer, not a distributor of automotive fuels (A. Thompson, *Economics of the Firm* [Englewood Cliffs, N.J.: Prentice Hall, 1977], pp. 52–53. As one executive we interviewed put it, "Where you stand depends on where you sit. We don't enter into a sourcing relationship or, for that matter, any relationship, without a strategic purpose. It is that *purpose* which *largely determines* the kind of [contractual] structure we get into." (Emphasis supplied.)

30. See Reich and Mankin, "Joint Ventures with Japan," for instances in which OEM suppliers used a sourcing opportunity to enter a final product market.

31. For a detailed theoretical analysis of the issue of strategic determinants of alliance structures, see Rangan, "Sourcing Relationships."

32. Recall that, for purposes of this chapter, hierarchies imply equity holdings of 50% or more, market relationships no equity holdings. Our arguments are thus framed in terms of the two extremes—markets and hierarchies. Quasi-hierarchies, to which we referred earlier, often arise because of the inability of would-be partners to agree on a clean—market or hierarchical—solution.

33. The IBM example is instructive in other ways. One, it would appear that IBM was far less worried about Microsoft's than Intel's becoming a competitor. To some extent, it would seem that IBM was more concerned about rapid developments in chip hardware than in software, a reflection perhaps of a mind-set born of mainframe dominance. Two, IBM was able to structure the alliances the way it wanted, suggesting its considerable bargaining power. Three, if IBM is to be faulted in hindsight, it should not be for lacking negotiating ability, but for not assessing better the scenarios for technology development in the personal computer business. IBM seems to have vastly underestimated the software side of the nascent industry. Incidentally, critics of IBM's alliances with Intel and Microsoft fault IBM for not choosing more involved, hierarchical links that would have helped it better control the evolution of the personal computer industry (see, for example, "New World Order: How IBM's Heirs Plan to Expand Empires in Computer Industry," *Wall Street Journal,* December 21, 1992). The decisions of IBM managers make more sense, a priori, if one recognizes that they were preserving their strategic options through the alliance structures they chose. If the industry had evolved somewhat differently, say, in a direction favoring IBM, the same critics would be singing the praises of IBM managers' foresight! Of course, one can still criticize IBM for not anticipating correctly the development path the personal computer industry would take. That is a different issue from the choice of alliance structures. As for faulty scenario planning at IBM with respect to the personal computer industry, one can only invoke H. Simon's notions of bounded rationality and limited search, in *Administrative Behavior* (New York: Free Press, 1945, rev. ed., 1978). There is some indirect evidence that IBM's internal strategic planning approach might have been too focused on the short term and on the hardware rather than on the software. William Lowe, formerly with IBM for 26 years and currently CEO of Gulf Stream, said recently that IBM's successful strategy in the personal computer (PC) industry went awry after 1985 because it was "not able to forecast changing market trends and respond to them quickly." Although originally the release of IBM's second generation of PCs was scheduled for 1985, the success of the first model blinded management to the potential failure of future models. Indeed, R&D for IBM's second line was initiated in the same year as its scheduled release, leading to rapid decline in IBM's market share from over 80% in 1985 to 28% in 1987 (*Babson Free Press,* October 28, 1993, p. 1).

34. See H. Itami, *Mobilizing Invisible Assets* (Cambridge, Mass.: Harvard University Press, 1987).

35. See S. V. Berg, J. Duncan, and P. Friedman, *Joint Venture Strategies and Corporate Innovation* (Cambridge, Mass.: Oelgeschlager, Gunn, and Hain, 1982).

36. As "appropriability" of valuable information is important for most companies (S. P. Magee, "Information and Multinational Corporations: An Appropriability Theory of Direct Foreign Investment," in J. Bhagwati, ed., *The New International Economic Order* [Cambridge, Mass.: MIT Press, 1977]), the more valuable the information generated in the context of the alliance, the more involved the interfirm arrangement is likely to be. The structure and side agreements in the case of AMC's Far Eastern alliances appear to make sense in this light.

37. Academics will recognize that many of the issues addressed below fall under the rubric of transaction costs (O. E. Williamson, *Markets and Hierarchies*, "Transaction Cost Economics: The Governance of Contractual Relations," *Journal of Law and Economics* 22 [October 1979]: 3–61, "Credible Commitments: Using Hostages to Support Exchange," *American Economic Review* 73 [September 1983]: 519–540, and *Economic Organization: Firms, Markets and Policy Control* [New York: New York University Press, 1986]; Buckley and Casson, *The Future of the Multinational Enterprise;* M. Casson, *Multinationals and World Trade,* and *The Firm and the Market* [Cambridge, Mass.: MIT Press, 1987]). See also Rangan, "Sourcing Relationships," on the impact of transaction costs on interfirm arrangement structures.

38. K. J. Arrow, *Essays in the Theory of Risk Bearing* (Chicago: Markham, 1971).

39. M. C. Jensen and W. H. Meckling, "Theory of the Firm: Managerial Behavior, Agency Costs, and Ownership Structure," *Journal of Financial Economics* 3 (October 1976): 305–360, and Jensen, "Organization Theory and Methodology," *Accounting Review* 50 (April 1983): 319–339.

40. In the literature, these costs are considered agency costs. How do principals ensure that agents act in their interest? Part of the problem is monitoring, which is costly, and part is changing the incentive structure. In the context of interfirm relationships, the agency problem can be subsumed under transaction costs. See O. E. Williamson, "Transaction Cost Economics," and *The Economic Institutions of Capitalism* (New York: Free Press, 1985).

41. The distinction between transition costs and strategic costs (considered earlier) is a fine, but essential one. If transaction-cost theory is to have any operational and scientific meaning, it must be seen as related to the immediate environs of a transaction and thus concerned with "efficient" performance of the transaction. Strategic factors, on the other hand, are concerned with the long-run implications of interfirm relationships. See Rangan, "Sourcing Relationships," for elaboration of this distinction.

42. To suggest that an "efficient" alliance arrangement is likely to be chosen is to imply that managers' approach to the question of choice of contractual arrangements is a rational one. The assumption of rationality on the part of decision makers has been questioned in the management literature (Simon, *Administrative Behavior*). However, if managers choose alliance arrangements without rational analysis, it is likely that as problems—strategic or transaction— crop up, they will seek to change the arrangement. To that extent, we are apt to see mostly rational arrangements that have survived revision. Thus, the assumption of rationality on the part of managers seems to be defensible.

43. See T. C. Schelling, *The Strategy of Conflict* (Cambridge, Mass.: Harvard University Press, 1960); H. Raiffa, *The Art and Science of Negotiation* (Cambridge, Mass.: Harvard University Press, 1982); and D. A. Lax and J. K. Sebenius, *The*

Manager as Negotiator: Bargaining for Cooperation and Competitive Gain (New York: Free Press, 1986).

44. The story of Nike draws considerably from C. R. Christensen and D. C. Rikert, "Nike (A)," Case No. 9-385-025, "Nike (B)," Case No. 9-385-027, "Nike (C)," Case No. 9-385-029, "Nike (D)," Case No. 9-385-031 (Boston: Harvard Business School, 1985), and J. E. Austin and F. J. Aguilar, "Nike in China," Case No. 9-386-065 (Boston: Harvard Business School, 1986).

45. See M. Y. Yoshino and T. B. Lifson, *The Invisible Link* (Cambridge, Mass.: MIT Press, 1986), for a good description of how Japanese trading companies, the *sogashosha,* excel in these areas.

46. The following discussion draws on U. Srinivasa Rangan, "Caterpillar," Case No. 9-385-276 (Boston: Harvard Business School, 1985), Christopher Bartlett, "Caterpillar," Case No. 9-390-036 (Boston: Harvard Business School, 1990), and U. Srinivasa Rangan, "Komatsu," Case No. 9-385-277 (Boston: Harvard Business School, 1985).

47. For example, Caterpillar moved into Japan because, as one of its managers put it, management believed that "wherever a market existed in an industrially advanced country, a local competitor would eventually emerge and later move abroad."

48. As one can notice, Caterpillar carefully managed many of the international dependencies—scale, competitive, and scope. Only in operational flexibility did Caterpillar lag, as much of the value addition took place in the United States.

49. Indeed, Komatsu's in-house slogan was "Maru-C," which translates roughly to "encircle Caterpillar."

50. This is another example of a quasi-hierarchical structure preferred by the alliance partners over simple market or purely hierarchical structures.

CHAPTER 5

1. George Taucher, "Beyond Alliances," *Perspectives for Managers* (Lausanne: IMEDE, no. 1), 1988.

2. M. E. Porter, *Competitive Advantage of Nations* (New York: Free Press, 1990), pp 612–613.

3. Ibid. Porter is not the only academic with such a pessimistic view of alliances. Given his stature among academics and practitioners alike, we felt that his views were worth considering in detail.

4. That the longevity of an interfirm relationship did not provide a criterion for success of an alliance was also the conclusion of a longitudinal study of several interorganizational links forged by one company over several decades (R. G. Bertodo, "The Strategic Alliance: Automotive Paradigm for the 1990s," *International Journal of Technology* 5, no. 4 [1990]: 375–388).

5. C. A. Bartlett and S. Ghoshal, in *Managing Across Borders* (Boston: Harvard Business School Press, 1991), raise this argument of managerial complexity against alliances.

6. See D. Lei and J. W. Slocum, "Global Strategy, Competence Building, and Strategic Alliances," *California Management Review* 35, no. 1 (Fall 1992): 81–97, for some of the difficulties involved in managing alliances.

7. There is a striking parallel here between a firm and a country. Trade theorists argue that autarky at the level of a nation could be expected to lead to progressive loss of international competitiveness. Similarly, firm-level autarky leads to progressive loss of competitiveness as resources are misdirected, key investments fail to be made, and core competitive advantages compromised. In an era of global competition, superior competitive performance is achieved when firms combine country-based, government-based, and firm-based advantages (D. B. Yoffie, ed., *Beyond Free Trade: Firms, Governments, and Global Competition* (Boston: Harvard Business School Press, 1993). It is difficult for a firm to acquire such a diverse set of advantages by itself. As global competition intensifies, no firm can hope to function as an island of self-sufficiency or attain strategic autarky.

8. It is easy to see how illegitimate it is to throw up one's hands in despair at the obvious difficulties involved in managing alliances when we look at another interesting development in international business. Imagine what would have been the fate of many of today's multinational companies if, in the past, they had given up on foreign markets based simply on the many great difficulties involved in managing overseas subsidiaries!

9. Structuring alliances, part of managing alliances as structures, can help or hinder the management process. As we argued in the previous chapter, structures are influenced by transaction costs (linked closely to the cost of managing alliances) and strategic factors (linked largely to forging alliances). As we shall see in this chapter, even within similar structures the process of managing can differ and may lead to different results.

10. One of the American managers experienced in dealing with alliance partners in the Far East compared the firm's Japanese allies and its Korean partners. "[The Koreans] are not like the Japanese. Japanese come to any meeting with an analysis of the problem, available options, and their preferred solution. Koreans rarely do." Such perceptions of cultural differences play a subtle but powerful role in alliance management.

11. Some observers of alliances have criticized American managers and engineers as being too willing to play "teachers" to wily and observant "students" from Asia and thus share knowledge too freely. The smart Asians then turn around and beat the American companies in the marketplace with the knowledge they have gained. While this may be true, especially in the early alliances of a company, it may not be appropriate to generalize. In the case described, for instance, the service engineers and managers were smart enough to recognize, very early on, the importance of not sharing service-related information too freely with the suppliers. In fact, after the new alliance manager took over, the American company drew up strict guidelines as to what information could and what could not be shared with the vendors. We pick up this notion of information management in greater detail in the next chapter.

12. On achieving credible commitments in transactions through a series of small steps, see A. K. Dixit and B. Nalebuff, *Thinking Strategically* (New York: W. W. Norton, 1991), pp. 157–158.

13. It is possible that the Taiwanese managers had all along treated the alliance as more competitive than did the U.S. managers. Alternatively, they might have decided to seize the opportunity to move to a more competitive mode as they

gained access to the U.S. firm's technology. Either way, the ambiguous nature of the relationship cannot be ignored.

14. As we indicated in Chapter 1, there are different types of alliances, only one of which is of the competitive variety, in which partners are direct competitors. This being the most complex to forge and manage, we have tended to focus on it. Managers who become familiar and comfortable with managing competitive alliances should have little trouble dealing with other types of alliances.

15. "The Partners," *Business Week,* February 10, 1992, p. 107.

16. Indeed, this is why checklists that suggest one or the other—trust your partner implicitly or watch out for partners who plan to stab you in the back—are too facile to be of much help to managers. The key is to hew a path between the Scylla of naive trust and the Charybdis of excessive distrust.

17. General Motors Corporation, *General Motors' Position on United Control of Foreign Operations,* February 1, 1966, p. 3.

18. A. G. Athos and R. T. Pascale, *The Art of Japanese Management: Applications for American Executives* (New York: Simon and Schuster, 1981), in work foreshadowed by C. I. Barnard (*The Functions of the Executive* [Cambridge, Mass.: Harvard University Press, 1938], and H. Simon, *Administrative Behavior* [New York: Free Press, 1945], provide an illuminating narrative on how the "7-S's" of management fit together.

19. Research and development alliances are especially difficult to manage. On some interesting issues relating to managing R&D in general, see M. B. W. Graham, *The Business of Research: RCA and the Video Disc* (Cambridge: Cambridge University Press, 1986).

20. On corporate culture and its implications, see V. Sathe, "Demystifying Corporate Culture," Working Paper, Division of Research, Harvard Business School, September 15, 1982, and *Culture and Related Corporate Realities* (Homewood, Ill.: R. D. Irwin, 1985). That corporations differ in their cultures and that such differences may affect the competency or efficiency of those organizations is widely recognized. When organizations of vastly differing corporate cultures come together to form an alliance, management can be difficult. Indeed, in one of the major auto companies we studied, a senior manager recounted how he and some of his colleagues successfully resisted the formation of an alliance with a Japanese auto company owing to what they perceived to be major differences in the two corporate cultures. G. Hofstede, in *Culture's Consequences: International Differences in Work-related Values* (Beverly Hills: Sage, 1980), suggests that even multinational firms are not immune to national cultural differences. Subsidiaries of the same multinational company differ along such key managerial dimensions as power distance and respect for authority. A major joint venture between Corning and the Mexican company Vitro fell apart because of incompatible corporate and, to some extent, national business cultures (Anthony DePalma, "It Takes More Than a Visa to do Business in Mexico," *New York Times,* June 26, 1994, sec. 3, p. 5).

21. We are not suggesting that such information leakage from IBM to its partners did occur or that the partner firms did benefit strategically. What we are illustrating is such a possibility and its managerial implications.

22. Arm's-length links are becoming fewer as firms establish closer links with suppliers and others in the value chain (R. Johnston and P. R. Lawrence, "Beyond

Vertical Integration: The Rise of the Value-Adding Partnership," *Harvard Business Review*, July–August 1988, pp. 94–101, HBR Reprint No. 88407). Such arm's-length relationships as remain are largely confined to commodity-type raw material purchases. These developments put a premium on firms that master alliance management skills.

23. On the traditional model of adversarial relationships between manufacturers of final goods and their parts suppliers, see M. E. Porter, *Competitive Strategy: Techniques for Analyzing Industries and Competitors* (New York: Free Press, 1980). A good example of such relationships is the one that used to exist in the United States between automakers and automobile component makers. See M. E. Porter, "Note on Supplying the Automobile Industry, Case No. 9-378-219 (Boston: Harvard Business School, 1978). Automobile manufacturers traditionally relied on the "exit" option rather than the "voice" option (A. O. Hirschman, *Exit, Voice, and Loyalty* [Cambridge, Mass.: Harvard University Press, 1970]) in their dealings with suppliers. In recent years, more and more automakers seem to be discovering the need to pay attention to cooperation (voice) as well as to competition (exit), a point stressed by R. D. Shapiro, "Towards Effective Supplier Management: International Comparisons," Working Paper No. 9-785-062, Division of Research, Harvard Business School, 1985, and S. R. Helper, "Supplier Relations and Technical Change: Theory and Application to the U.S. Automobile Industry," Ph.D. diss., Harvard University, 1987. A study by the Boston Consulting Group of the challenge posed by the Japanese automobile firms to the European auto industry concluded that for the European industry to survive, it would have to move away from confrontation and "towards . . . partnership [between the vehicle makers and their suppliers] where profit is shared among the different players in the value chain" (*Financial Times*, October 18, 1993, p. 4).

24. Political scientists have long recognized the need to manage the cooperation-competition tension, especially in international relations (Z. Brzezinski, *Power and Principle* [New York: Farrar, Straus and Giroux, 1983).

25. Again, it is not our intention to imply that the Japanese firm was engaged in some sort of industrial espionage. Indeed, the U.S. firm's managers suspected that the information was leaked as a consequence of their firm's inadvertence and negligence rather than by design on the part of the Japanese firm.

26. It does little good to blame the perfidy of the Japanese or, for that matter, of the Asians or Europeans, for loss of information. Knowledge exists in all firms and managers and is constantly being leaked in all kinds of ways, ranging from casual conversations to well-orchestrated "digging" by the other side. It is up to managers to safeguard information, not up to the other side to close its eyes and ears.

27. Caterpillar's experience is not an isolated one. On how managing supplier relationships calls for much internal realignment of organizations, see J. A. Carlisle and R. C. Parker, *Beyond Negotiation* (New York: Wiley, 1989).

CHAPTER 6

1. Digital, Hewlett-Packard, Ford, Motorola, Lotus, Intel, Olivetti, Siemens, Toshiba, Mazda, and Isuzu are among the firms that have created such a separate

alliance interface office. In some companies the general manager is helped by a small group of staff.

2. In general, the alliance manager's position is a full-time job. Also, there is a dedicated alliance manager for each alliance. In some firms, there is an overall alliance office within which there are separate managers for each significant alliance.

3. In many R&D links, firms exchange résumés of researchers apt to be assigned to alliance work. Firms often present a list of candidates. Each firm is free to reject anyone it does not want to accept from the other's list.

4. Indeed, some GM managers indicated that Toyota brought (to NUMMI) the latest "software" for its vaunted production system, but not the latest "hardware" (e.g., robotics and so forth).

5. An American business magazine suggested that knowledge workers are the key to the future ability of U.S. firms to compete in the global marketplace (John Huey, "Finding New Heroes for a New Era," *Fortune,* January 25, 1993, pp. 62–69). This is only a partial view of the issue of knowledge and its importance for firms. Knowledge, especially of the embedded variety, is critical for a firm's survival (J. Badaracco, *Knowledge Link* [Boston: Harvard Business School Press, 1991]). Writings on the resource-based view of the firm in the strategic management literature also stress the need to view each firm as a learning organization that constantly adds to its repertoire of capabilities through its experience in applying its existing base of knowledge (R. Nelson and S. G. Winter, *An Evolutionary Theory of Economic Change* [Cambridge, Mass.: Harvard University Press, 1982]; C. K. Prahalad and G. Hamel, "The Core Competence of the Corporation," *Harvard Business Review,* May–June 1990, pp. 79–91; I. Nonaka, "The Knowledge Creating Company," *Harvard Business Review,* November–December 1991, pp. 96–105.).

6. H. Itami, *Mobilizing Invisible Assets* (Cambridge, Mass.: Harvard University Press, 1987), and Nonaka, "The Knowledge Creating Company," stress knowledge creation and information-processing capabilities of firms as key determinants of competitive advantage. See also W. G. Egelhoff, "Strategy and Structure in Multinational Corporations: An Information Processing Approach," *Administrative Science Quarterly* 27, no. 3 (September 1982): 435–458; A. K. Gupta and V. Govindarajan, "Knowledge Flow and the Structure of Control within Multinational Corporations," *Academy of Management Review* 16, no. 4 (October 1991): 768–792; and D. Leonard-Barton, "Core Capabilities and Core Rigidities: A Paradox on Managing New Product Development," Working Paper No. 92-005, Harvard Business School, 1992.

7. On how American and Japanese firms use marketing research differently, see R. Deshpande, "The Organizational Context of Market Research Use," *Journal of Marketing Research* 46 (Fall 1982): 91–101.

8. Much of the writing on alliances implies that firms which employ them, particularly U.S. firms, are not good at managing information flows. Although this may have been true in the early days of alliances, it is not true today. Nor is it correct to assert that firms in other nations, Asia in particular, are better at this task. Among the alliances we studied, the ability to manage information flows consciously does not seem to be a virtue possessed only by non-U.S. firms.

9. In the late 1980s, General Electric's consumer electronics division ended its sourcing alliance with Matsushita of Japan for color television sets when the

two firms could not agree on a new basis for dealing with the steep rise in the value of the Japanese yen, clearly an unforeseen event for both. See "Japanese Firm to Stop Selling TVs to GE in Price Dispute Over Higher Yen Value," *Wall Street Journal,* January 7, 1987, p. 10 and "GE Will Resume Some U.S. Output of Color TV Sets," *Wall Street Journal,* February 13, 1987, p. 15.

10. A partner firm's perception of an alliance manager's rank and effectiveness has implications for the role of top management vis-à-vis alliances. Suffice it to say here that the "signaling" effect of who is chosen to lead an alliance can have important consequences for its success.

11. Often, therefore, alliance managers have to exert "influence without authority" (A. R. Cohen and D. L. Bradford, *Influence without Authority* [New York: Wiley, 1991]).

12. See articles on product development and related topics in the 1990 special issue of the *California Management Review.* See also U. S. Rangan, G. E. Watzke, and J. Ganitsky, "Time Perspectives in International Alliances: Implications for Product Development," Draft Working Paper, 1992.

13. See H. Uyterhoeven, "General Managers in the Middle," *Harvard Business Review,* March–April 1972, pp. 75–85; reproduced in *Harvard Business Review,* September–October 1989, pp. 136–145, for an early appraisal of the tough job of middle managers.

14. That researchers can get carried away by their own enthusiasm for particular projects is well known. But it is not something to be dismissed derisively. Not too long ago, an AT&T researcher was reported to have done a major service to his firm by persisting with a fiber optics project that the head of Bell Labs had told him to abandon. See "R&D Hardball: Defying Boss's Orders Pays Off for Physicist and His Firm, AT&T," *Wall Street Journal,* June 25, 1991, sec. A, p. 1).

15. See R. M. Kanter, *The Change Masters: Innovation for Productivity in the American Corporation* (New York: Simon and Schuster, 1983), on the role of "champions" in fostering innovations.

16. See G. Hamel, C. K. Prahalad, and Y. L. Doz, "Collaborate with Your Competitors—and Win," *Harvard Business Review,* January–February 1989, pp. 113–119, for a line of argument which, unwittingly perhaps, perpetuates such a stereotyping of alliances as Trojan horses.

17. The manager referred to such visits [and pre- and postvisit discussions] as major opportunities to sensitize members of the firm to issues relating to information flow.

18. This illustrates again how the alliance manager's job is very much a general management position. J. Kotter, *The General Managers* (New York: Free Press, 1982) found that general managers tend to be characterized by an ability to move with ease across organizational levels and a proclivity to acquire information from various levels of an organization.

CHAPTER 7

1. Some of the material in this section comes from an article on the Ford-Mazda alliance. See *Business Week,* February 10, 1992, pp. 102–107.

2. Ibid.

3. General Electric's CEO Jack Welch and Alain Gomez, chairman of state-owned Thomson, France's leading electronics manufacturer, in the course of a meeting at the French Open in June 1987, concluded·that GE and Thomson could swap their respective assets in consumer electronics and medical systems with mutually beneficial results. A few months later, GE became the largest medical systems player in Europe, having exchanged its consumer electronics business in the United States for Thomson's European assets in medical systems (*Business Week,* August 10, 1987, p. 36). See also "G.E., a Pioneer in Radio and TV, Is Abandoning Production of Sets," *New York Times,* July 23, 1987, sec. A, p. 1.

4. This can be construed as a special application of what H. Simon, *Administrative Behavior* (New York: Free Press, 1945, rev. ed., 1976), termed "constrained" or "domain limited" search when people confront new problems.

5. O. E. Williamson, *The Economic Institutions of Capitalism* (New York: Free Press, 1985), would say that the transaction costs of dealing with known partners are lower than those of dealing with new partners.

6. As we pointed out in Chapter 1, ideas such as better resource utilization and maintaining independence are true, by definition, in the case of strategic alliances.

7. On the importance of strategic intent, see G. Hamel and C. K. Prahalad, "Strategic Intent," *Harvard Business Review,* May–June 1989, pp. 63–76.

8. The need to foster better understanding of an alliance in general and the cooperation-competition tension in particular is especially important in American firms because their human resource practices tend to foster too much specialization. Japanese firms, by contrast, tend to inculcate a more generalist perspective in its employees. At Sanyo, for example, all newly hired engineers must spend some time in sales and in rotations between research and manufacturing (MIT Commission on Industrial Productivity, *Made in America* (Cambridge, Mass.: MIT Press, 1989).

9. The notion of being aware of both the cooperative and competitive nature of an alliance and being prepared to protect one's interest in the context of the alliance is quite different from the notion of entering into an alliance with the intention of extracting as much as possible from the other firm, then abandoning the alliance. The former constitutes prudent alliance management, the latter Machiavellian practice that leads to the dissolution of the alliance and makes it difficult for the firm to find future partners.

10. On some instructive examples of how perverse incentive schemes prevent companies from benefiting from alliances, see A. N. Link and L. L. Bauer, *Cooperative Research in U.S. Manufacturing* (Lexington, Mass.: Lexington Books, D.C. Heath, 1989).

11. On the issue of differences between American and Japanese approaches to product development, see K. B. Clark and T. Fujimoto, *Product Development Performance* (Boston: Harvard Business School Press, 1991).

12. For a detailed look at organizational learning in the context of international alliances, see G. Hamel, "Competition for Competence and Inter-Partner Learning within International Strategic Alliances," *Strategic Management Journal* 12, special issue (Summer 1991): 83–104.

13. See, for example, G. Hamel, C. K. Prahalad, and Y. L. Doz, "Collaborate with Your Competitors—and Win," *Harvard Business Review,* January–February 1989, pp. 133–139.

14. Organizational learning involves both assimilating new knowledge and adapting work approaches to reflect new knowledge. As such it is clearly in the domain of top management. How firms as diverse as Xerox and Corning have institutionalized effective learning is described in D. A. Garvin, "Building a Learning Organization," *Harvard Business Review,* July–August 1993, pp. 78–91.

CHAPTER 8

1. See M. E. Porter, *Competitive Strategy: Techniques for Analyzing Industries and Competitors* (New York: Free Press, 1980), for arguments on treating industry as the locus of attention for strategists. Questioning of such industry determinism (J. B. Barney, "Strategic Factor Markets: Expectation, Luck, and Business Strategy," *Management Science* 32, no. 10 (October 1986): 1231–1241; D. J. Teece, G. P. Pisano, and A. Shuen, "Firm Capabilities, Resources, and the Concept of Strategy," Consortium on Competitiveness and Cooperation, Working Paper No. 90-8, Center for Research in Management, University of California at Berkeley, 1990) has not refuted the fundamental need to define the competitive field and to rely on industry as the natural definition thereof. On the question of how an industry should be defined, see D. F. Abell, *Defining the Business* (Englewood Cliffs, N.J.: Prentice Hall, 1980), and T. Levitt, "Marketing Myopia," *Harvard Business Review,* September–October 1975, pp. 26–44.
2. Some authors have tried to draw further distinctions. A. A. Thompson and A. J. Strickland, in *Strategic Management: Text and Cases,* 5th ed. (Homewood, Ill.: R. D. Irwin, 1990), for example, distinguish between business strategy and competitive strategy. Such fine distinctions are not germane to our discussion.
3. Researchers have advanced the notion of multipoint competition between firms that vie in the same and in other industries (A. Brandenburger, "Multimarket Entry," Case No. 9-793-098 (Boston: Harvard Business School, 1993). This is a key distinguishing feature of diversified firms.
4. Y. L. Doz and C. K. Prahalad, in "Managing DMNCs: A Search for a New Paradigm," *Strategic Management Journal* 12 (Winter 1991): 145–164, suggest that a key feature of the globalization of international business has been the emergence of diversified multi-industry, multimarket firms and their dominance over smaller rivals. M. Beer and S. M. Davis, in "Creating a Global Organization, Failures Along the Way," *Columbia Journal of World Business,* Summer 1976, pp. 72–84, and Davis and P. R. Lawrence, in *Matrix* (Reading, Mass.: Addison-Wesley, 1977), are among the early researchers to identify some of the problems inherent in organizing and managing such diversified multinational corporations (Prahalad and Doz, "Strategic Management of Diversified Multinational Companies, in A. Negandhi, ed., *Functioning of the Multinational Corporation* (Oxford: Pergamon Press, 1980).
5. The diversified firm counterpart of the CEO of a nondiversified firm is the head of an SBU, not its CEO.
6. In recent years, even General Motors' preoccupation with the auto industry has waned; witness its investments in Hughes Aerospace and EDS subsidiaries. These businesses are small, but as GM's non–auto businesses grow in importance,

Smith's job description is apt to begin to approximate that of a CEO of a diversified firm.

7. These roles in practice are, of course, highly interrelated.
8. Noel Tichy and Ram Charan, "Speed, Simplicity, and Self-Confidence: An Interview with Jack Welch," *Harvard Business Review,* September–October 1989, p. 115.
9. R.A. Bettis and William Hall, "Strategic Management in the Multibusiness Firm," *California Management Review,* Fall 1981, pp. 23–38; Bettis, "The Business Portfolio Approach—Where It Falls Down in Practice," *Long Range Planning,* April 1983, pp. 95–104; P. Haspeslagh, "Portfolio Planning: Uses and Limits," *Harvard Business Review,* January–February 1982, pp. 58–73.
10. GE, with help from the consulting firm McKinsey and Company, pioneered a widely used portfolio technique it called the Industry Attractiveness/Business Strength Matrix.
11. Michael Porter, *Competitive Advantage: Creating and Sustaining Superior Performance* (New York: Free Press, 1985), p. 309.
12. See ibid., p. 321.
13. "Speed, Simplicity, and Self-Confidence," p. 116.
14. See "The Enemy of My Enemy," *Forbes,* November 1988.
15. The following draws from C. A. Bartlett and A. Nanda, "Corning Inc.: A Network of Alliances," Case No. 9-391-102 (Boston: Harvard Business School, 1991).
16. This is another instance of transferring resources to gain competitive leverage through new investments made in the context of strategic alliances.
17. GEC is unrelated to the U.S. company of the same name.
18. Procter & Gamble and Kimberly-Clark are among other prominent companies that have made access to distribution channels the core of their business expansion strategies.
19. Emphasis supplied.
20. *Financial Times,* November 29, 1988, p. 33.
21. Of course, not all the blame can be laid at management's door. Simple pressure to improve the bottom line in a difficult industry beset with foreign competition, combined with the probable disinclination of division managers to deal with the problems of managing a network of alliances, perhaps contributed as much to the exit decision. Imaginative leadership must, nevertheless, be seen as a critical difference between the fate of GE's motor business and that of Westinghouse.
22. The list of alliances would have been longer if GEC's efforts to arrange a fifty-fifty venture for its subsidiary Picker in medical electronics with Philips had been successful. See reports on the failure of GEC's efforts to form a joint venture with Philips in *The Wall Street Journal,* April 17, 1987, and February 2, 1988, and in the *Financial Times,* February 2, 1988. Interestingly enough, both reports indicated that GEC might be on the lookout for another partner after the Philips efforts collapsed.
23. This diminishing of managerial influence will be even more rapid as new managers are brought in by the joint venture and as more and more managers from the dominant firm are brought in for short tours of duty, ostensibly to oversee such mundane things as the transfer and adaptation of technology and management systems.

24. The notion of "center of gravity" of organizations and its implications for strategy, organization, planning, and management were first articulated by J. R. Galbraith, in "Strategy and Organization Planning," *Human Resources Management* 22, no. 1/2 (Spring–Summer 1983): 64–77.
25. See *Financial Times,* January 24, 1990.
26. That a firm's changing center of gravity has serious implications for corporate management is true even of firms that seek to discard old businesses in favor of new ones through acquisitions or internal growth. Westinghouse Electric Corporation, for instance, has made a transition from a technology-based manufacturing firm in many related industries to a diversified firm with dozens of unrelated businesses, ranging from broadcasting and financial services to community development, truck refrigeration, and waste disposal, with no clear focus for future growth. As in the case of GEC of Britain, Westinghouse top management does not appear to have thought through the implications of such a corporate metamorphosis. As an analyst put it, "[Westinghouse has] good numbers but *no focal point.*" (Emphasis supplied) See "Corporate Focus: Westinghouse Relies on Ruthless Pruning," *Wall Street Journal,* January 24, 1990, sec. A, p. 4.

CHAPTER 9

1. This is not to deny that national responsiveness in product offering (a supply-side factor) plays a crucial role in international strategy. Nevertheless, evidence suggests that increasing convergence of consumer preferences (a demand-side factor) among critical markets, such as the Triad of North America, Europe, and Japan, plays an even more crucial role.
2. C. A. Bartlett and A. Nanda, "Corning Inc.: A Network of Alliances," Case No. 9-391-102 (Boston: Harvard Business School, 1991), p. 19.
3. The need to internalize, and thus meld into corporate culture, the best practices of the managerial systems of various countries is exemplified by Honda and Chrysler. Often hailed as a quintessentially Japanese firm in its managerial culture, Honda has adopted a number of American management practices in order "to compete more effectively in the global arena" (*Wall Street Journal,* April 11, 1991). At the same time, a key rival, Chrysler, was moving in the opposite direction, adopting many of Honda's managerial practices after a thorough internal study! Chrysler's successes in the areas of product development and market orientation are attributed by observers to its willingness to learn from Honda (*Wall Street Journal,* March 3, 1992). This notion of mutual learning is not unique. Ford and Mazda, Toyota and GM, Motorola and Toshiba, are all examples of successful cross-cultural flow of best practice.
4. Academic researchers on alliances (see, for example, F. J. Contractor and P. Lorange, eds., *Cooperative Strategies in International Business* [Lexington, Mass.: D. C. Heath, Lexington Books, 1988]) have suggested that managers need to consider other ways of acquiring needed competitive capabilities, such as mergers, acquisitions, and licensing contracts. We believe these options are not always available or viable. Firms stand to lose their identities through

mergers and acquisitions. Moreover, acquisitions are not selective. Firms are bundles of capabilities, and a firm needing only a few may not want to buy an entire company to get them. Finally, many of the capabilities an alliance-seeking firm might look for are not readily available, off the shelf, for licensing.

5. The earliest proponents of "anationalization" (E. P. Lions, "The Anational Corporation," doctoral diss. in political science, Thesis No. 233, Graduate School of International Studies, University of Geneva, Switzerland) or "transnationalization" of the corporation, particularly of the multinational firms from the West, were at the UN Center for Transnational Corporations (see UNCTC, *Transnational Corporations in the International Auto Industry* [New York: United Nations, 1983]). Much of their analysis stemmed from a political premise that multinationals had grown too powerful and thus posed a challenge to the sovereignty of nation-states (R. Vernon, *Sovereignty at Bay* [New York: Basic Books, 1971]). A more benign view of transnationalization has emerged more recently among writers who have taken an economically deterministic view of corporations' not having to bother about nation-states as world integration grows (C. A. Bartlett and S. Ghoshal, *Managing Across Borders* [Boston: Harvard University Press, 1991]). Other writers on globalization of firms also tend to underemphasize the importance of national borders (G. S. Yip, "Global Strategy . . . in a World of Nations?" *Sloan Management Review* 31, no. 1 [Fall 1989]). pp. 29–41.

6. That nations determine the "competitiveness" of firms has been the underlying assumption of writers, past and present, who have addressed the question of national competitiveness (J. Zysman and L. Tyson, eds., *American Industry in International Competition: Government Policies and Corporate Strategies* [Ithaca: Cornell University Press, 1983]; S. S. Cohen and Zysman, *Manufacturing Matters: The Myth of Post-industrial Economy* [New York: Basic Books, 1987]; G. C. Lodge and B. R. Scott, eds., *U.S. Competitiveness in the World Economy* [Boston: Harvard Business School Press, 1985]; Lodge and E. F. Fogel, eds., *Ideology and National Competitiveness* [Boston: Harvard Business School Press, 1987]). M. E. Porter, in *The Competitive Advantage of Nations* (New York: Free Press, 1990), has made this assumption explicit, arguing that the notion that corporations could divorce themselves from the parent nation is fanciful. Such nation-centered views tend to cast the growth of alliances as a temporary relaxation of competitive pressures.

7. Bartlett and Ghoshal *(Managing Across Borders),* who also distrust alliances as part of firms' strategic armory, imply that firms should rely largely on building competitive strength through "internal" networks of overseas subsidiaries.

8. W. J. Murphy, *R&D Cooperation among Marketplace Competitors* (New York: Quorum Books, 1991), for example, deals with alliances in the context of technological consortia within one nation. J. A. Welch and P. R. Nayak, "Strategic Sourcing: A Progressive Approach to the Make-or-Buy Decision," *Academy of Management Executive* 6, no. 1 (February 1992), p. 399, for example, argue that make-or-buy decisions should take into account such factors as the technology involved, marketing needs, and so forth. R. B. Reich and E. D. Mankin, in "Joint Ventures with Japan Give Away Our Future," *Harvard Business Review,* March–April 1986, pp. 78–86, argue that Japanese firms use alliances with U.S. firms largely to gain as much as they can from the latter in terms of technologies,

market knowledge, and so forth. G. Hamel, C. K. Prahalad, and Y. L. Doz, in "Collaborate with Your Competitors—and Win," *Harvard Business Review,* January–February 1989, pp. 133–139, go one step further, arguing that to sap rivals' strength and win against competitors through the ruse of alliances is the main reason to collaborate in the first place. Hamel ("Competition for Competence and Inter-Partner Learning within International Strategic Alliances," *Strategic Management Journal* 12, special issue [Summer 1991]: 83–104), taking a "skill-based view" of the firm, considers an alliance largely a route to acquire another firm's skills. K. Ohmae (*Triad Power: The Coming Shape of Global Competition* [New York: Free Press, 1985]) is the leading proponent of the idea that strategic alliances are critical for entering new markets, especially in Japan. A. N. Link and G. Tassey (*Strategies for Technology-based Competition* [Lexington, Mass.: Lexington Books, D. C. Heath, 1987]) favor technology alliances in the context of global competition.

9. Defining a business in terms of markets, products, and technologies was first suggested by D. F. Abell (*Defining the Business* [Englewood Cliffs, N.J.: Prentice Hall, 1980]). J. M. Stopford and C. Baden-Fuller (*Rejuvenating the Mature Business: The Competitive Challenge* [Boston: Harvard Business School Press, 1994]) used a similar approach to describe the managerial problems faced by global firms.

10. This phenomenon relates directly to what we term the "globalization of strategies." Industries as diverse as computers and communications are converging, and their need to master such converging technologies is overwhelming. Similarly, most global firms now seek to serve more than one or two narrowly defined product niches.

Kodak, for example, serves both high-volume and low-volume copiers whereas not long ago it served only the former; GM, Ford, and Toyota sell an entire range of vehicles, from subcompacts to luxury models; Caterpillar and Komatsu compete in every conceivable segment of the construction-equipment market, and so forth. Firms cannot hope to thrive behind national barriers. The underlying message in much of the literature on globalization is that being a simple multidomestic competitor may no longer be a viable strategy in many industries. M. E. Porter, in *Competition in Global Industries* (Boston: Harvard Business School Press, 1986), and *The Competitive Advantage of Nations,* and K. Ohmae, in *Triad Power* and "The Global Logic of Strategic Alliances," *Harvard Business Review,* May–June 1989, pp. 143–154, among others, elucidate this line of reasoning.

11. Usually, successful firms do either of two things to stay abreast of competition. They may keep shifting the portfolio of competitive advantages on which they rely for success. Dr. Edwin Land, the legendary founder of Polaroid, is credited with saying, "Either you obsolete your own competitive position and move on to other things, or your rivals will do it for you." Alternatively, a company can commit substantial resources to erect an impregnable barrier to entry (or mobility) against its rivals. P. Ghemawat, in *Commitment* [New York: Free Press, 1991] refers to such efforts as making "irreversible" commitments. Innovative companies that hope to sustain their competitive success tend to do both. Clearly, in an age of technological cost and complexity and global integration, the

resource demands of such a strategic approach are very high. Firms that hope to be both flexible and make substantial irreversible commitments must free up resources. Alliances are one way to do this.

12. If, as the Austrian school of economists argues, the essence of entrepreneurship lies in seeing "new combinations" (J. A. Schumpeter, *Capitalism, Socialism and Democracy* [New York: Harper and Row, 1950]; I. M. Kirzner, *The Economic Point of View* [Kansas City, Kans.: Sheed and Ward, subsidiary of Universal Press Syndicate, 1976]), a global network of alliances provides a range of experiences that cannot help but trigger ideas for new combinations in managers involved in alliances.

13. C. A. Bartlett and A. Nanda, "Corning Inc.: A Network of Alliances," Case No. 9-391-102 (Boston: Harvard Business School, 1991).

14. See "Jack Welch Reinvents General Electric—Again," *The Economist*, March 30, 1991, pp. 59–60.

15. Porter (*The Competitive Advantage of Nations*) argues cogently and convincingly that firms cannot divest themselves of a core nation, which in most cases is the parent firm's location, where key competitive-strategy-related decisions are made.

16. While "boundaryless" ownership of global corporations with shareholdings spread among citizens of several nations may well come to pass in an era of integrated capital markets, corporate boundaries between firms are unlikely to be erased. *The Economist* article on GE cited above also chronicles how some GE suppliers (clearly assumed to benefit from being part of the boundaryless General Electric) tell "horror stories" and "grumble" about GE's efforts to profit at their expense. Not all members are equal in terms of their ability to influence a network, its partners, and the apportionment of benefits.

17. See Vernon, *Sovereignty at Bay;* P. J. Buckley and M. Casson, *The Future of the Multinational Enterprise* (New York: Holmes and Meier, 1976), and *The Economic Theory of the Multinational Enterprise* (London: Macmillan, 1985); S. H. Hymer, *The International Operations of National Firms: A Study of Direct Foreign Investment* (Cambridge, Mass.: MIT Press, 1976); and M. Wilkins, *The Maturing of Multinational Enterprise: American Business Abroad from 1914 to 1970* (Cambridge, Mass.: Harvard University Press, 1974), for the reasons, economic and organizational, for this development.

18. See A. D. Chandler, *Scale and Scope: The Dynamics of Industrial Capitalism* (Cambridge, Mass.: Harvard University Press, 1990), for a historical analysis of organizational innovation by U.S. firms. So feared were the organizational innovations pioneered by U.S. multinational enterprises (MNEs) that they provoked the famous diatribe against their coming domination of the world (see J. J. Servan-Schreiber, *The American Challenge* [New York: Atheneum, 1968]). The dispersal of value activities among many countries led to a backlash from the nation-state. See S. Lall and P. Streeten, *Foreign Investment, Transnationals, and Developing Countries* (London: Macmillan, 1977); Lall, *The Multinational Corporation: Nine Essays* (London: Macmillan, 1980); and R. J. Barnet and R. E. Muller, *Global Reach: The Power of the International Corporations* (New York: Simon and Schuster, 1974), for the reasons many countries sought to obtain part of the value-added. In recent years, debate over where most of the

value-added for products sold by MNEs belongs has been revived in the guise of decrying Japanese firms' European investments as putting up "screwdriver" plants.

19. See J. M. Stopford and L. T. Wells, *Managing the Multinational Enterprise: Organization of the Firm and Ownership of the Subsidiaries* (New York: Basic Books, 1972), for an early elucidation of U.S. MNEs' organizational strategies, one being controlling equity stakes in overseas affiliates (B. Gomes-Casseres, "Multinational Ownership Strategies," DBA diss., Harvard Business School, 1985). See D. J. Encarnation and S. Vachani, "Foreign Ownership: When Hosts Change the Rules," *Harvard Business Review,* September–October 1985, pp. 152–160, for some of the ingenious ways U.S. and European MNEs have retained control of their overseas affiliates even in the face of host-government regulations that would force them to relinquish such control.

20. M. Gerlach, *Alliance Capitalism* (Los Angeles: University of California Press, 1992), is an excellent exposition of how the *keiretsu* form of business organization works. Clearly, being adept at using and managing such an organization bestows a not so easily replicable organizational capability, thus a sustainable competitive advantage, on Japanese multinationals.

21. Korea and Germany, as well as Japan, may also bring to the international arena some familiarity with ambiguous interfirm relationships. Korean *chaebols* and German conglomerates operate through cross-holdings of equity and interlocking boards of directors.

22. Japanese managers' difficulty managing relationships with firms from other nations could partially explain their tendency to encourage their *keiretsu* partners, which supply components and parts, to invest abroad or why Japanese firms invest proportionately more in Asian countries such as Taiwan and Thailand, cultures with which Japan shares some commonalities.

23. Generally, network theorists tend to ignore the distinction between internal and external networks (H. B. Thorelli, "Networks: Between Markets and Hierarchies," *Strategic Management Journal* 7 (1986): 37–51.

24. Much of the material on ABB comes from "Asea Brown Boveri," Case No. 9-192-139, and "Asea Brown Boveri: The ABACUS System," Case No. 9-192-140 (Boston: Harvard Business School, 1992).

25. See "Xerox and Fuji-Xerox," Case No. 9-391-156 (Boston: Harvard Business School, 1991), for details of major agreements governing the role of Fuji-Xerox from 1960 to 1986.

26. See J. Badaracco, *Knowledge Link* (Boston: Harvard Business School Press, 1991), for more details on GM's and IBM's alliances. While GM and IBM have been endeavoring to build a network of alliances for some years, most observers believe that they had not been very successful in managing them to their best advantage.

27. A number of articles published in the popular business press in the early 1990s suggest that IBM may be involved in as many as 20,000 alliances and GM in a few hundred.

28. As described earlier, by "internal network" we mean the network of national subsidiaries of especially multinational corporations as opposed to the "external network" of alliances. Neither is to be confused with a "network of managers" within a firm (multinational or otherwise) "assembled by the CEO and the senior

executive team" (R. Charan, "How Networks Reshape Organizations—For Results," *Harvard Business Review,* September–October 1991, p. 105), to make the organization work faster and smoother.

29. For additional examples of how firms have used internal and external networks to leverage their competitive position, see P. Strebel, *Breakpoints: How Managers Exploit Radical Business Change* (Boston: Harvard Business School Press, 1992).

30. For a detailed look at the origins, evolution, and ending of the AT&T-Olivetti alliance, see the IMD and London Business School case series: "Building Alliances (A): AT&T," IMD Case No. GM 351; "Building Alliances (B): Olivetti," IMD Case No. GM 352; and "Building Alliances: AT&T and Olivetti (C), (D), and (E)," London Business School, 1991.

31. Ghemawat, *Commitment,* argues that "irreversible" commitments and investments are the cornerstone of strategic success. One must contend, however, with the need to maintain flexibility in the face of uncertainty. Alliances, by providing some flexibility while allowing a firm to commit irreversibly, and perhaps massively, in other areas, afford greater strategic flexibility.

32. Alliances have been used to cope with environmental uncertainty even in traditional industries. As the computer industry goes through "tremendous transformation" (A. S. Grove, "The Future of the Computer Industry," *California Management Review,* Fall 1990, pp. 148–160), alliances have become the norm in that industry.

33. "Digital Media Business Takes Form as a Battle of Complex Alliances," *Wall Street Journal,* July 14, 1993.

34. Ibid., sec. A, p. 4.

35. Our discussion of alliances has focused mainly on large firms. Smaller firms also engage in alliances, and many of the issues we raise apply to them as well. It is possible, given their size, that smaller firms have difficulty managing such relationships for lack of managerial resources. On the other hand, their size makes it easier for one or two senior managers to deal with all alliances nimbly and flexibly, sans a large bureaucracy. Walden Paddlers, a Massachusetts-based kayak-building company, is a good example. The business is largely a collection of alliances with designing, manufacturing, and distribution in the hands of alliance partners, with Walden focusing efforts and investments only on marketing (*Inc.,* August 1993, pp. 50–58). Moreover, small firms are in a better position to experiment with new interfirm links and with learning from and about alliances. In other words, small firms are not necessarily worse off in the coming world of global network corporations. If anything, as specialization spreads through the creation of such networks, the competitive environment becomes more, not less hospitable to small firms.

Index

About the Authors

Michael Y. Yoshino is the Herman C. Krannert Professor of Business Administration at the Harvard Business School. His primary fields of specialization are competitive strategy, global strategy, and management. He is a member of the Executive Committee of the Reischauer Institute at Harvard University and also serves on the board of directors of the National Bureau of Economic Research, the leading economic research organization in the United States. He has been a consultant to a number of major corporations in North America, Europe, Asia, and Latin America and has extensive experience in designing and implementing management development programs for senior executives in leading firms internationally. He has published five books, most recently *The Invisible Link: Japan's Sogo Shosha and the Organization of Trade*. Dr. Yoshino received a Ph.D. in management from Stanford University.

U. Srinivasa Rangan is the Kingsbury Term Chair Assistant Professor of Management and International Business at Babson College. Professor Rangan previously taught at A.B. Freeman School of Business at Tulane University, where in 1992 he received the Howard Wissner Outstanding Teacher of the Year Award. He has also served on the faculty of the International Management Development Institute (IMD) at Lausanne, Switzerland. Professor Rangan's research focuses on competitive strategy, joint ventures, strategic alliances, and national competitiveness. He is currently engaged in a comprehensive research project on India's economic development approach and its impact on India's global competitiveness that takes an in-depth look at a number of industries ranging from bicycles to software. Professor Rangan is the author of several case studies on global competition and strategic management, published by both Harvard Business School and IMD. He received a doctorate in international business from Harvard University.